Football: From England to the World

This book of scholarly articles documents the popularization of Association Football, charts the diverse and changing nature of the modern British game, and then examines the spread of the game from England and its global appropriation, and domestication in new homes, across the planet. The book also investigates the exchanges which are increasingly taking place between these new homes and in the concluding part, football's global expansion is compared with attempts at globalizing baseball drawing out the larger patterns that characterise football's international dissemination.

This book was published as a special issue in *Soccer and Society*.

Dolores P. Martinez is a Senior Lecturer in Anthropology and Associate Dean of Research at the School of Oriental and African Studies, London.

Projit Bihari Mukharji is a Lecturer in Modern History at Newcastle University and an avid fan of Bengali football.

Football: From England to the World

Edited by Dolores P. Martinez and Projit B. Mukharji

Routledge
Taylor & Francis Group
LONDON AND NEW YORK

First published 2009 by Routledge

Published 2016 by Routledge
2 Park Square, Milton Park, Abingdon, Oxon OX14 4RN

Simultaneously published in the USA and Canada
by Routledge
711 Third Avenue, New York, NY 10017, USA

Routledge is an imprint of the Taylor & Francis Group, an informa business

First issued in paperback 2015

Typeset in Times New Roman by Value Chain, India

British Library Cataloguing in Publication Data
A catalogue record for this book is available from the British Library

ISBN 978-0-415-48061-1 (hbk)
ISBN 978-1-138-88353-6 (pbk)

CONTENTS

Series Editors' Foreword

SPORT IN THE GLOBAL SOCIETY was launched in the late nineties. It now has over one hundred volumes. Until recently an odd myopia characterised academia with regard to sport. The global *groves of academe* remained essentially Cartesian in inclination. They favoured a mind/body dichotomy: thus the study of ideas was acceptable; the study of sport was not. All that has now changed. Sport is now incorporated, intelligently, within debate about *inter alia* ideologies, power, stratification, mobility and inequality. The reason is simple. In the modern world sport is everywhere: it is as ubiquitous as war. E.J. Hobsbawm, the Marxist historian, once called it the one of the most significant of the new manifestations of late nineteenth century Europe. Today it is one of the most significant manifestations of the twenty-first century world. Such is its power, politically, culturally, economically, spiritually and aesthetically, that sport beckons the academic more persuasively than ever – to borrow, and refocus, an expression of the radical historian Peter Gay – 'to explore its familiar terrain and to wrest new interpretations from its inexhaustible materials'. As a subject for inquiry, it is replete, as he remarked of history, with profound 'questions unanswered and for that matter questions unasked'.

Sport seduces the teeming 'global village'; it is the new opiate of the masses; it is one of the great modern experiences; its attraction astonishes only the recluse; its appeal spans the globe. Without exaggeration, sport is a mirror in which nations, communities, men and women now see themselves. That reflection is sometimes bright, sometimes dark, sometimes distorted, sometimes magnified. This metaphorical mirror is a source of mass exhilaration and depression, security and insecurity, pride and humiliation, bonding and alienation. Sport, for many, has replaced religion as a source of emotional catharsis and spiritual passion, and for many, since it is among the earliest of memorable childhood experiences, it infiltrates memory, shapes enthusiasms, serves fantasies. To co-opt Gay again: it blends memory and desire.

Sport, in addition, can be a lens through which to scrutinise major themes in the political and social sciences: democracy and despotism and the great associated movements of socialism, fascism, communism and capitalism as well as political cohesion and confrontation, social reform and social stability.

The story of modern sport is the story of the modern world – in microcosm; a modern global tapestry permanently being woven. Furthermore, nationalist and imperialist, philosopher and politician, radical and conservative have all sought in sport a manifestation of national identity, status and superiority.

Finally, for countless millions sport is the personal pursuit of ambition, assertion, well-being and enjoyment.

For all the above reasons, sport demands the attention of the academic. *Sport in the Global Society* is a response.

J.A.Mangan, Boria Majumdar
and Mark Dyreson – Series Editors

Sport in the Global Society

Sport in the Global Society

Series Editors: J.A. Mangan, Boria Majumdar and Mark Dyreson

Football: From England to the World

Sport in the Global Society

Series Editors: J.A. Mangan, Boria Majumdar and Mark Dyreson

As Robert Hands in *The Times* recently observed the growth of sports studies in recent years has been considerable. This unique series with over one hundred volumes in the last decade has played its part. Politically, culturally, emotionally and aesthetically, sport is a major force in the modern world. Its impact will grow as the world embraces ever more tightly the contemporary secular trinity: the English language, technology and sport. *Sport in the Global Society* will continue to record sport's phenomenal progress across the world stage.

Other Titles in the Series

Africa, Football and FIFA
Politics, Colonialism and Resistance
Paul Darby

Amateurism in British Sport
'It Matters Not Who Won or Lost'
Edited by Dilwyn Porter and Stephen Wagg

Amateurism in Sport
An Analysis and Defence
Lincoln Allison

America's Game(s)
A Critical Anthropology of Sport
Edited by Benjamin Eastman, Sean Brown and Michael Ralph

American Sports
An Evolutionary Approach
Edited by Alan Klein

A Social History of Indian Football
Striving to Score
Kausik Bandyopadhya and Boria Majumdar

A Social History of Swimming in England, 1800–1918
Splashing in the Serpentine
Christopher Love

A Sport-Loving Society
Victorian and Edwardian Middle-Class England at Play
Edited by J.A. Mangan

Athleticism in the Victorian and Edwardian Public School
The Emergence and Consolidation of an Educational Ideology, New Edition
J.A. Mangan

Australian Beach Cultures
The History of Sun, Sand and Surf
Douglas Booth

Australian Sport
Antipodean waves of change
Edited by Kristine Toohey and Tracy Taylor

Barbarians, Gentlemen and Players
A Sociological Study of the Development of Rugby Football, Second Edition
Eric Dunning and Kenneth Sheard

Baseball and Moral Authority in Contemporary Cuba
Edited by Benjamin Eastman

Beijing 2008: Preparing for Glory
Chinese Challenge in the 'Chinese Century'
Edited by J.A. Mangan and Dong Jinxia

'Blooding' the Martial Male
The Imperial Officer, Field Sports and Big Game Hunting
J.A. Mangan and Callum MacKenzie

Body and Mind
Sport in Europe from the Roman Empire to the Renaissance
John McClelland

British Football and Social Exclusion
Edited by Stephen Wagg

Capoeira
The History of an Afro-Brazilian Martial Art
Matthias Röhrig Assunção

Crafting Patriotism for Global Dominance
America at the Olympics
Mark Dyreson

Cricket and England
A Cultural and Social History of Cricket in England between the Wars
Jack Williams

Cricket in Colonial India, 1780–1947
Boria Majumdar

Cricketing Cultures in Conflict
Cricketing World Cup 2003
Edited by Boria Majumdar and J.A. Mangan

Cricket, Race and the 2007 World Cup
Edited by Boria Majumdar and Jon Gemmell

Critical Events in Baseball History
Class, Race and Politics
Edited by Benjamin Eastman and John D. Kelly

Disciplining Bodies in the Gymnasium
Memory, Monument, Modernity
Sherry McKay and Patricia Vertinsky

Disreputable Pleasures
Less Virtuous Victorians at Play
Edited by Mike Huggins and J.A. Mangan

Diversity and Division – Race, Ethnicity and Sport in Australia
Edited by Christopher J. Hallinan

Doping in Sport
Global Ethical Issues
Edited by Angela Schneider and Fan Hong

Emigrant Players
Sport and the Irish Diaspora
Edited by Paul Darby and David Hassan

Ethnicity, Sport, Identity
Struggles for Status
Edited by J.A. Mangan and Andrew Ritchie

European Heroes
Myth, Identity, Sport
Edited by Richard Holt, J.A. Mangan and Pierre Lanfranchi

Europe, Sport, World
Shaping Global Societies
Edited by J.A. Mangan

Flat Racing and British Society, 1790–1914
A Social and Economic History
Mike Huggins

Football and Community in the Global Context
Studies in Theory and Practice
Edited by Adam Brown, Tim Crabbe and Gavin Mellor

Football: From England to the World
Edited by Dolores P. Martinez and Projit B. Mukharji

Football, Europe and the Press
Liz Crolley and David Hand

Football Fans Around the World
From Supporters to Fanatics
Edited by Sean Brown

Football: The First Hundred Years
The Untold Story
Adrian Harvey

Footbinding, Feminism and Freedom
The Liberation of Women's Bodies in Modern China
Fan Hong

France and the 1998 World Cup
The National Impact of a World Sporting Event
Edited by Hugh Dauncey and Geoff Hare

Freeing the Female Body
Inspirational Icons
Edited by J.A. Mangan and Fan Hong

Fringe Nations in Soccer
Edited by Kausik Bandyopadhyay, Martha Saavedra and Sabyasachi Malick

From Fair Sex to Feminism
Sport and the Socialization of Women in the Industrial and Post-Industrial Eras
Edited by J.A. Mangan and Roberta J. Park

Gender, Sport, Science
Selected Writings of Roberta J. Park
Edited by J.A. Mangan and Patricia Vertinsky

Global and Local Football
Politics and Europeanization on the Fringes of the EU
Gary Armstrong and Jon P. Mitchell

Globalised Football
Nations and Migration, the City and the Dream
Edited by Nina Clara Tiesler and João Nuno Coelho

Heritage, Sport and Tourism
Sporting Pasts – Tourist Futures
Edited by Sean Gammon and Gregory Ramshaw

Human Rights in Youth Sport
A Critical Review of Children's Rights in Competitive Sports
Paulo David

Italian Fascism and the Female Body
Sport, Submissive Women and Strong Mothers
Gigliola Gori

Japan, Sport and Society
Tradition and Change in a Globalizing World
Edited by Joseph Maguire and Masayoshi Nakayama

Law and Sport in Contemporary Society
Edited by Steven Greenfield and Guy Osborn

Leisure and Recreation in a Victorian Mining Community
The Social Economy of Leisure in North-East England, 1820–1914
Alan Metcalfe

Lost Histories of Indian Cricket
Battles Off the Pitch
Boria Majumdar

Making European Masculinities
Sport, Europe, Gender
Edited by J.A. Mangan

Making Men
Rugby and Masculine Identity
Edited by John Nauright and Timothy J.L. Chandler

Making the Rugby World
Race, Gender, Commerce
Edited by Timothy J.L. Chandler and John Nauright

Militarism, Sport, Europe
War Without Weapons
Edited by J.A. Mangan

Modern Sport: The Global Obsession
Essays in Honour of J.A.Mangan
Edited by Boria Majumdar and Fan Hong

Muscular Christianity and the Colonial and Post-Colonial World
Edited by John J. MacAloon

Native Americans and Sport in North America
Other Peoples' Games
Edited by C. Richard King

Playing on the Periphery
Sport, Identity and Memory
Tara Brabazon

Pleasure, Profit, Proselytism
British Culture and Sport at Home and Abroad 1700–1914
Edited by J.A. Mangan

Rain Stops Play
Cricketing Climates
Andrew Hignell

Reformers, Sport, Modernizers
Middle-Class Revolutionaries
Edited by J.A. Mangan

Representing the Nation
Sport and Spectacle in Post-Revolutionary Mexico
Edited by Claire and Keith Brewster

Rugby's Great Split
Class, Culture and the Origins of Rugby League Football
Tony Collins

Running Cultures
Racing in Time and Space
John Bale

Scoring for Britain
International Football and International Politics, 1900–1939
Peter J. Beck

Serious Sport
J.A. Mangan's Contribution to the History of Sport
Edited by Scott Crawford

Shaping the Superman
Fascist Body as Political Icon – Aryan Fascism
Edited by J.A. Mangan

Sites of Sport
Space, Place and Experience
Edited by John Bale and Patricia Vertinksy

Soccer and Disaster
International Perspectives
Edited by Paul Darby, Martin Jones and Gavin Mellor

Soccer in South Asia
Empire, Nation, Diaspora
Edited by Paul Dimeo and James Mills

Soccer's Missing Men
Schoolteachers and the Spread of Association Football
J.A. Mangan and Colm Hickey

Soccer, Women, Sexual Liberation
Kicking off a New Era
Edited by Fan Hong and J.A. Mangan

Sport: Race, Ethnicity and Indigenity
Building Global Understanding
Edited by Daryl Adair

Sport and American Society
Exceptionalism, Insularity, 'Imperialism'
Edited by Mark Dyreson and J.A. Mangan

Sport and Foreign Policy in a Globalizing World
Edited by Steven J. Jackson and Stephen Haigh

Sport and International Relations
An Emerging Relationship
Edited by Roger Levermore and Adrian Budd

Sport and Memory in North America
Edited by Steven Wieting

Sport, Civil Liberties and Human Rights
Edited by Richard Giulianotti and David McArdle

Sport, Culture and History
Region, Nation and Globe
Edited by Brian Stoddart

Sport in Asian Society
Past and Present
Edited by Fan Hong and J.A. Mangan

Sport in Australasian Society
Past and Present
Edited by J.A. Mangan and John Nauright

Sport in Europe
Politics, Class, Gender
Edited by J.A. Mangan

Sport in Films
Edited by Emma Poulton and Martin Roderick

Sport in Latin American Society
Past and Present
Edited by Lamartine DaCosta and J.A. Mangan

Sport in South Asian Society
Past and Present
Edited by Boria Majumdar and J.A. Mangan

Sport, Media, Culture
Global and Local Dimensions
Edited by Alina Bernstein and Neil Blain

Sport, Nationalism and Orientalism
The Asian Games
Edited by Fan Hong

Sporting Cultures
Hispanic Perspectives on Sport, Text and the Body
Edited by David Wood and P. Louise Johnson

Sporting Nationalisms
Identity, Ethnicity, Immigration and Assimilation
Edited by Mike Cronin and David Mayall

Sport Tourism
Edited by Heather J. Gibson

Superman Supreme
Fascist Body as Political Icon – Global Fascism
Edited by J.A. Mangan

Terrace Heroes
The Life and Times of the 1930s Professional Footballer
Graham Kelly

The Changing Face of the Football Business
Supporters Direct
Edited by Sean Hamil, Jonathan Michie, Christine Oughton and Steven Warby

The Commercialisation of Sport
Edited by Trevor Slack

The Cultural Bond
Sport, Empire, Society
Edited by J.A. Mangan

The First Black Footballer
Arthur Wharton 1865–1930: An Absence of Memory
Phil Vasili

The Flame Relay and the Olympic Movement
John J. MacAloon

The Football Manager
A History
Neil Carter

The Future of Football
Challenges for the Twenty-First Century
Edited by Jon Garland, Dominic Malcolm and Mike Rowe

The Games Ethic and Imperialism
Aspects of the Diffusion of an Ideal
J.A. Mangan

The Global Politics of Sport
The Role of Global Institutions in Sport
Edited by Lincoln Allison

The Lady Footballers
Struggling to Play in Victorian Britain
James F. Lee

The Magic of Indian Cricket
Cricket and Society in India, Revised Edition
Mihir Bose

The Making of New Zealand Cricket
1832–1914
Greg Ryan

The 1940 Tokyo Games: The Missing Olympics
Japan, the Asian Olympics and the Olympic Movement
Sandra Collins

The Nordic World: Sport in Society
Edited by Henrik Meinander and J.A. Mangan

The Politics of South African Cricket
Jon Gemmell

The Race Game
Sport and Politics in South Africa
Douglas Booth

The Tour De France, 1903–2003
A Century of Sporting Structures, Meanings and Values
Edited by Hugh Dauncey and Geoff Hare

This Great Symbol
Pierre de Coubertin and the Origins of the Modern Olympic Games
John J. MacAloon

Tribal Identities
Nationalism, Europe, Sport
Edited by J.A. Mangan

Who Owns Football?
The Governance and Management of the Club Game Worldwide
Edited by David Hassan and Sean Hamil

Women, Sport and Society in Modern China
Holding up More than Half the Sky
Dong Jinxia

Prologue

Projit Bihari Mukharji

One of my first memories is that of being surprised on seeing a photograph of a group of men in half-pants on the family altar, next to other sundry gods at an uncle's house. As an average Hindu Bengali boy in Calcutta, I was used to the icons, idols and photographs of a variety of gods and saints on family altars (*thakur-ghor*), but I had never, before that day, seen one who wore shorts! I was taken by the sight and over the years it has become one of those quirky childhood memories that somehow retain its vibrancy and surprise, whilst all else from the time is largely forgotten.

It was only later that I got to know that the group of men in the fading photograph were the Mohun Bagan team that had been the first Indian team to have lifted the IFA Shield (India's premiere footballing trophy), beating the white teams in 1911. Better still, they had played bare-feet. Stories of their perseverance, talent and, above all, valour have regaled many a Bengali youth. Even Bengali grandmothers, a social group usually averse to most sport, used to revel in telling the story.

Much has changed since. Worshipping sporting heroes has become much more commonplace in India and grandmothers have become much more knowledgeable about sport. Most importantly cricket has largely overshadowed football in the life of the middle-class Bengali youth. Moreover if 20 years ago one asked a Bengali youth which team he supported, the answer would be 'Amra Mohun Bagan' or 'Amra East Bengal' (literally 'We are Mohun Bagan/East Bengal'). The 'we' stood for one's family. It was like saying 'we are Brahmins' or 'we are Bengalis'; it designated an identity you were born into and did not or could not choose. As Majumdar points out in this volume, today's youth are more likely to say, 'I support X or Y'.

Yet, I would perhaps have never noted any of these changes had I not been forced to live half way across the globe and find out to my somewhat naive surprise that arguably the nation craziest about the game and the bearer of the first spark that ignited the flaming passion that influences so much of modern Bengali culture was almost unaware that South Asians still played football. I had always assumed that everyone would know what a big deal football was to us, how people died, killed and much more importantly lived for the game. It was the rude shock of British pub jokes about South Asian disinterest and incompetence at the 'beautiful game' that made me see our footballing cultures afresh. As my friends at the Northumberland Arms, the-pub-down-the-road, told of how Asians did not play football as they were busier opening a corner shop than taking a corner kick, the madness of Calcutta football no longer seemed as natural as it had all my life.

I realized that there was a very specific, curious and local history to our love affair with football. I wondered how local the global game had become. I wondered also how many more such local stories there were. Everyone seemed to have a different reason for their fascination with the game, everyone seemed to express that fascination differently, everyone seemed to play and enjoy the game differently. Yet, it was the same game. I am no philosopher and would not like to make any grandiloquent comparisons between this interplay of the local and the global, but it does seem to somehow capture so much that we associate with the contemporary predicament.

I mentioned it to my good friend and the leading Indian historian of sport, Boria Majumdar. Our friendship had indeed matured on the terraces of the sports grounds of Calcutta and our repertoire of the 'good story at the game' often overlapped. But I also knew him to be a mine of information on all matters sporting. Boria immediately suggested that it might be a good thing to compare all these stories. To see how the game was adopted and adapted in different parts of the world. To see how the variety of local stories, styles, fan-cultures could still fit into a single game. It was Boria who encouraged me to think of a conference to bring together stories of adaptation and evolution of the game from across the world.

But Sports Studies was a relatively specialized field and I wondered if anyone at SOAS would be interested in the idea at all. The initial response was disappointing. Academics I mentioned it to laughed at the idea and said if we must have a conference it ought to be about something 'serious'. Something that mattered. 'Why not do something on Islamophobia or Race in the twenty-first century?' one helpfully suggested.

It was at this time that I mentioned this to Lola (Dolores P.) Martinez, without the slightest inkling of her own passion for the game. It turned out that not only was Lola an enthusiast, but indeed she had been a talented player and pioneer of women's football in Chicago! Serendipity now looked increasingly like destiny and we started to think of the conference in all earnest.

Jonathan Manley at Taylor and Francis, on hearing of the plans, immediately agreed most graciously to sponsor the event and became one of its staunchest supporters.

Tom Tomlinson, who had apparently long since given up watching Scottish games amidst English fans in the SOAS Staff Common Room, told us of the interesting story of how Newcastle and Juventus came to share similar jerseys through the employment of Newcastle workers to build Italian railways. His support and enthusiasm added much to our team and colleagues at SOAS now took us seriously.

Next break: we managed to convince Tony Mangan, the grand old man of Sports History, to set the ball rolling with his characteristically brilliant new work on the roots of the popularity of the British game among school teachers.

A host of other internationally renowned scholars also agreed to contribute their recent works. Papers ranged from the role of new forms of masculinity in the rise of the J-League to the new British football venue at the local pub; from the beginnings of American women's football to the national drug cultures in European football; from South Africa's search for a united football culture to the role of African footballers in Bengali club football.

The conference eventually coincided with the 2006 World Cup.

The focus was firmly on resurrecting the local aspects of the global game. The outcome was enriched not only by the global spread, but also by the wide variety of disciplinary and methodological backgrounds that contributors brought to it. Moreover some of the contributors were not historians of sport. This allowed them to bring a fresh new perspective to the discussions on sport and sporting cultures which were informed by their own specializations.

While dwelling on the local aspects of the game, the conference yet succeeded in pre-empting any sense of rigid spatial essences. The historical dimension allowed contributions to stress the crossovers as well as the evolutions. It broke down simple binarisms of East and West, without wallowing in the romance of a sporting universalism. It dwelt on oppositions and conflicts, but did so historically and in context, hastening to show how changed contexts resolved old conflicts and raised new ones.

Interestingly, despite the historic scope of most of the contributions, few dealt with a past so remote that we could no longer relate to it. Instead they brought the stories they told up to date, conveying the sense and the promise that despite the stunting uniformity of contemporary global cultural forms, vernacularization and localization were thriving. Identities were not drowned in a sea of global sameness, but rather, as Stuart Hall has suggested, continually re-worked and refashioned. It conveyed the hope that despite the corrosive effects of globalization, the local-identities survive, evolve and appropriate the global to its own ends. Alan Klein's paper, which wrapped up the conference, sought to tackle this plethora of global forms and give us a theoretical rubric within which to conceptualize them without either a wholesale opposition to a process that is undoubtedly here to stay or a complete surrender to the forces of capital.

As the beautiful game today becomes the vehicle of glitzy commercialization and ruthless globalization, the ethics of spectatorship becomes an issue that many are forced to think about. It is a dilemma in many ways comparable to the one C.L.R. James had faced many decades ago. James, a staunch Caribbean Marxist, felt he had to justify his all-consuming love for cricket – a game associated with much that he opposed. The result of his personal quest for justification was *Beyond a Boundary*, a classic by all accounts. While none of us can match James' literary talents perhaps, our quest remains the same.

Football may have come to most parts of the world as a conqueror's pastime, it may today more than ever be seen as being run by big-businesses and oppressive global capitalism, yet, it is a game we love!

O football, football! Wherefore art thou football?
Deny thy father and refuse thy name!
Or, if thou wilt not, be but sworn my love,
And I'll no longer be an Anti-Globalist!

Missing men: schoolmasters and the early years of Association Football

J.A. Mangan

On Christmas Eve 2006, just four days after the Chief Executive of Charlton Athletic had declared that the position of the club's newly appointed, but beleaguered manager Les Reed, to be secure, his contract was terminated. He had lasted 41 days! His apparent faults: he had failed to inspire the players, had been too cerebral in his approach, had never played professionally and had become a professional coach after a career as a physical education teacher.[1]

In this latter regard, in today's professional game, he was a rarity. This has not always been the case. In fact, Les Reed was part of a long, and largely forgotten, association between schoolteachers and professional football. These men, and more particularly, those who were elementary schoolteachers in the early years of the game, are the concern of the forthcoming *Soccer's Missing Men*. It will concentrate on merely a small fraction of English elementary schoolteachers and their not insignificant part in the growth of what is now a global game. There is more than enough evidence to do this; there is insufficient space to do more. No doubt others in time will have the satisfaction of rescuing other schoolteachers from past neglect.

The uncovering of these English roots should not end simply with the exposure of a past conceit too dependent on the too prevalent assertion that modern football had its origins on the expensive and extensive playing fields of nineteenth century public schools along with a narrowly atomistic perspective. There is an exigent need for historians to probe the cliché and to dig for other roots of the game at home and abroad.[2] It is a journey with lost landscapes, unfrequented places and forgotten terrain: a modest ingression into the unknown involving a topologically unique tour contributing to an eventual empirical map complete, it is hoped, in due course with both highways and byways. If the origins of modern Association Football were global, the earliest origins were substantially English.

A quarter of a century ago or more, James Walvin argued, with regard to the history of sport, that greater emphasis should be given to local themes in the pursuit of national themes. He argued that generalizations, of course, had their place but needed to be built on specificities.[3] The forthcoming *Soccer's Missing Men*, marries both approaches. In doing so it will strongly assert a new point of view concerning the origins of modern English Association Football. New points of view, of course, need time to be absorbed: the startled must be given time to recover and academic apple carts given time to be righted. Rather further back in time than James Walvin, John Locke stated sententiously that new opinions tended to be suspect for no reason other than the fact that they are not already commonplace.[4] Since the new evidence presented here is incontrovertible, it is a danger that must be accepted.

The web, warp and weave of the early evolution of English Association Football are thought to be reasonably well-known. There have been innumerable books and articles chronicling its emergence and evolution from a multitude of perspectives.[5] Yet it remains a valuable but still elusive prize in any race for completeness in the historiography of sport and social change in England.

Broadly speaking there are two competing schools of thought regarding this evolution. The first, and for many years the prevailing view, was that the modern game of football was 'invented' or at the very least codified, nurtured and promoted by a number of former public schoolboys subsequent to the formation of the Football Association in a meeting at the Freemason's Tavern in London in 1863.[6] This view, which recognized that there had always been a tradition of unruly 'mob' football, sees the events of 1863 as pivotal in the widespread acceptance of the game among all social classes. Take, for example, the early claim of Geoffrey Green, Cambridge 'Blue', talented amateur soccer player and doyen of football writers, who was for many years the chief football correspondent for *The Times*, who believed that

> it is true to say that while 'the manly game of football' has flourished for centuries in these islands, it was the public schools who took it from the streets and the fields, civilized it, brought law and order and system to it ... until finally it was shaped and polished and unified under one set of rules drawn up for national acceptance by the Football Association in 1863. Nor can we forget the Universities of Cambridge, and later Oxford, who were to take their place in this developing process of creating one set of laws so that all could play and enjoy the same game.
>
> So as a last thought, the development of football, though stretched across the centuries, none the less has a shape and a pattern to it. From the streets and the fields and the 'mob' games of the people, it found its way to the public schools. Then it moved to the universities, finally to be co-ordinated in one game, with one set of laws by the Football Association. From being a game of the people, it became the pastime of the leisured upper classes. But by the end of the nineteenth century the people had taken it back again to be shared by all those who wanted it.[7]

This secular hymnody in praise of the creation of Association Football while confidently fortissimo, was, in fact, a little off key!

Green's fabular analysis fits neatly into the 'heroic great men' school of historical studies; in his case as social class innovators. Whilst acknowledging other class antecedents of the game, he believed that the popularity of the game owed most to the formation of the Football Association and its middle-class inspirationalists:

> Football itself spread from the city streets to the public schools; from the schools to the Universities of Cambridge and Oxford, and thence to London with the formation of the F.A. From London it spread to the north of England, to Scotland, Ireland and Wales, and finally overseas. In all this spread from London the influence of the F.A. has been incalculable across the years and in watching the general development and control of the game, the part it has played must never be forgotten.[8]

For generations, Green, with others such as C.W. Alcock,[9] exercised architectonic control over Association Football's historical edifice. Nevertheless both Green and Alcock were selective in their use of building materials. Green, for example, among other things, paid scant attention to the fact that Association Football, apparently, was more rapidly adopted by the working-classes in the midlands and the north than in the south. Sir Montague Shearman[10] provides period support for this assertion:

> Until about 1875 there was practically no Association football in the provinces except at Sheffield. About 1875 the provincial movement began, and the game was taken up in Lancashire, Staffordshire, and the whole of the Midlands by all classes of players, but chiefly by the mechanics and the artisans. The rapidity with which the movement spread was little short of marvellous. In 1874, only one club

> played Association football in Birmingham. In 1876, an association of over twenty clubs was formed in the district. The rapidity with which the new players acquired their skill was equally remarkable.[11]

What Green, Alcock and Sherman all applauded, however, was the rapid growth of the game and the Football Association. After the formation of the Football Association the number of affiliated clubs grew rapidly. By 1888, as is well known, the Football League was established as a result of the efforts of William McGregor[12] of Aston Villa. The 12 founding clubs of 1888 grew to 14 in 1891, 28 in 1892, 31 in 1893, 32 in 1894 and 36 in 1898. By 1905 it had risen to 40 and after the First World War to 44. There were, however, a number of famous football clubs that had not joined the League. Most southern teams played in the Southern League that had been set up in 1894. A meeting was held in Anderson's Hotel in London's Fleet Street to see if there was enough support for the formation of a Southern League to rival the Football League. 'Woolwich Arsenal put their case so well that the meeting enthusiastically approved the proposition and proceeded to elect 12 clubs.'[13] However,

> The enthusiasm generated in Fleet Street seems to have rapidly gone off the boil when the delegates returned to their own committees. Playing with professionals, even if retaining their amateur status, would incur the displeasure of the London Football Association. They only had to look at Woolwich Arsenal to see what this would mean. The Clubs refused to ratify the decisions which their delegates had overwhelmingly agreed at the meeting – and so the idea was quietly allowed to die.[14]

Between then and 1920, when 22 clubs from the Southern League were admitted to the Football League, six southern clubs joined the league. Eventually, by 1950 the number of clubs in the League had risen to 92 while across the country there were now thousands of clubs large and small.

The view of football as a game owing its massive twentieth century appeal to the earlier codifying work of a number of upper and middle-class enthusiastic 'missionaries' has steadily undergone revision. The main thrust of the revisionists is that past reconstruction did not deal in sufficient detail with what can be broadly termed history of breadth and depth. It failed to take sufficient account of the backgrounds, aspirations, motives and activities of other crucial enthusiasts, advocates and missionaries. This response is understandable. Green and Alcock were not the only early commentators predisposed to class selectivity. The early popular books on the game such as *Association Football and the People who Made It*,[15] and *League Football and the Men who Made It*[16] offer clear signals about the class preferences of the authors. Furthermore, unhappily, these works were inadequate also because of their analytical pauperism and glib superficiality; concentrating on 'the great and the good', focussing on the glamorous, giving special attention to the public school and 'varsity innovators and later the 'big clubs' and 'star' players, thus distorted the historical image due to a lack of sufficient breadth and depth of perspective. Only a consideration of that nature will ensure the filling of vacuities and a comprehensive understanding of the early evolution of Association Football in England.

Adrian Harvey has had much to say regarding a reconstruction of the orthodox narrative. In his essay 'Football's Missing Link: The Real Story of the Evolution of Modern Football', he argued that

> Conventional accounts of the development of modern football stress the roles of the public schools, a view derived in large measure from the most influential of the game's early historians, the Old Harrovian C.W. Alcock. For him, history was progress. This was expressed in the spread of 'rationalised' football of the public schools throughout the population. Alternative varieties of the game were of no interest to him.[17]

The road to redemption for historians, in Harvey's view, therefore, was to take an interest in these alternative varieties.

Sensibly, Harvey did not underestimate the importance of the public schools. He accepted that 'after 1850 sport generally, and football specifically, became far more organised within the public schools'. However, he maintained, 'the importance given to the role of the public schools in the diffusion and codification of Association Football is exaggerated and based on a failure to appreciate both the extent and sophistication of the football played in the wider community in the years preceding 1863'.[18] Harvey believed that, contrary to received wisdom, Association Football was codified before 1863 and that the influence of the public schools system has been exaggerated. Moreover, 'an organised football culture would have emerged in the latter half of the nineteenth century even if there had been no public school model'.[19] Be that as it may, nevertheless, it remains a fact that there was this model and it had an influence! Judicious recognition of this fact ensures historical accuracy by way of balance.

Harvey's position, set out more fully in *Football: The First Hundred Years. The Untold Story*,[20] is that football was played in an organized fashion before 1863, and he refutes the theory that the football played before that date was essentially of the 'mob' type with few if any rules and played between villages on high days and holidays and most commonly on Shrove Tuesday. He writes that 'football is a much older game than the Shrove-variety, and for at least 300 years matches have been occurring between teams made up of equal numbers of players, often consisting of fewer than ten people on each side'.[21]

With regard to his confident title, incidentally, it should not be overlooked that there are many football stories still to be told.[22] One will be told in the pages that follow. It is also as well to recall that untold stories of the first hundred years of Association Football embrace a global network not just simply the English matrix: 'For a good part of its first one hundred years and certainly well back into the nineteenth century, football especially Association Football, was much more than just a British game.'[23]

The polarized arguments of Green and Harvey present the historian with a conundrum. Which of the two hypotheses is more convincing? Indeed, could there be something missing? While Harvey is certainly correct in his view that the playing of football was more widely organized than Green and others argued, and while he recognizes that, 'in the period after 1850 sport generally, and football specifically, became far more organised within the public schools',[24] he underplays (as does Colm Kerrigan incidentally, in his *Teachers and Football; Schoolboy Association Football in England, 1885–1915*) both the ideological impact of athleticism and the ways in which its values were absorbed into the fabric of regional, national and global football. Kerrigan, for his part, in his study of school football associations, regrettably was throttled by a self-applied analytical stranglehold: a dubitative inclination due to a limited understanding of forces at work in training colleges and elementary schools and a too narrow and too trusting reliance upon school logbooks – seldom the repositories of philosophical reflection, but the records of mundane matters.[25]

Tom Stoppard, in his play *The Coast of Utopia*, had the nineteenth-century liberal Alexander Herzen remark of the English: 'They invented personal liberty without any theories at all.' In some circles, however, Association Football was, and is, pregnant with moralistic intention, injection and assertion. To provide merely one illustration: note the lasting ubiquity of the concept of 'fair play' so stressed on nineteenth-century public school playing fields and note the publicity given to it in the recent FIFA World Cup. Equally, the hagiographical analysis provided by Green, an early 'Norbert Elias' of football replete with simplistic patrician views of the moral benefits of football brought to it by men who '*civilised*' the game, who brought '*law and order*' to it under rules that were '*shaped, polished and unified for national acceptance*', leaves something to be desired. Both the mirror and the reflection are flawed.

The truth of the matter is that evolutionary reality was complex and embraces the arguments of Green, Harvey, Kerrigan and indeed others. For one thing, Association Football's growth was affected by economic developments in society such as the reduction in the working week for the average industrial worker. Working men gradually won their Saturday half holiday. Initially, between 1857–62 in Liverpool, it tended to be the privilege of skilled workers such as stonemasons, coach makers, building workers and cabinet-makers, 'but it was the late 1880s or early 1890s before most of the unskilled labour force, dockers and carters for example, had a similar privilege… the shorter working week and the weekly half day off were a unique experience in nineteenth-century Europe and go far to explain Britain's dominant influence in the development of new forms of recreation'.[26] One recreation, football, was well suited to the new increased leisure time available to industrial workers.

> The process of the industrialisation of Britain and her transformation into the workshop of the world had brought two major results. Work or the prospect of work had brought employees into large urban environments … when successive factory acts allowed for some leisure time from the machine and bench there was a great demand … for something to bring to a Saturday afternoon. Football for players, and even more for spectators, came to fill this gap as if it had been invented for the purpose.[27]

And it was football rather than any other game that especially gripped the attention of the working-class man.

And then there was also the undoubted effect of athleticism,[28] an educational ideology that had both an ulterior and altruistic impact in the universities, public and grammar schools of the middle-classes *and*, less well publicized, on the teacher-training colleges and elementary schools of the working-class.[29] It is important not to overlook, but equally not to overstate the emergence and consolidation of athleticism in the schools for the privileged and its assimilation in an adapted form, in the schools of the less privileged. It must be added to the analytical 'melting pot'[30] It had an insufficiently appreciated influence. Its significance in elementary education has only recently begun to be revealed.[31]

Athleticism was formulated by the bourgeoisie and adapted by the proletariat. Of importance to its proletarian adoption was the role of teacher training colleges. These colleges were *de facto* in part working-class universities, as they were the only institutions of higher education generally accessible to the impecunious but talented, elementary-trained pupil teacher. After the Cross Commission of 1888, athleticism was utilized by the training colleges as a means of moral training, and staff at all levels were recruited directly from 'Oxbridge' where athleticism was rampant,[32] which ensured that the ideology was embedded in this training. It was in these colleges that the students could now indulge a sanctioned enthusiasm for games, especially football, which were introduced to them in a systematic way for the first time as part of their professional training. However, the teacher training colleges proved to be important to the growth of Association Football; not only in the narrow context of the elementary school and associated club and missions, but also in the wider community context in the formation of professional clubs, in the production of professional club players and managers; in the contribution of administrators at every level, and in the provision of referees at every level.

The last 30 years of the nineteenth century saw a rapid proliferation of English football clubs, and elementary schoolteachers were involved in the formation of a number of them. One area that witnessed a close relationship between teachers and clubs was the Midlands, where at least four league clubs were formed as a direct or indirect result of their efforts. Yet the Midlands are merely the tip of an English 'iceberg'. As Marples Morris commented almost 50 years ago: 'Thousands of clubs must have been started at one time or another by schoolmasters.'[33] His observation offered an exploratory route for other historians to take. Yet it remains one down which few have ventured even a little way. The part that elementary schoolteachers played in the early development of modern English football remains puzzlingly untold.

The time has come to tell their story.

The extraordinary fact is that although occasional brief and random accounts of elementary schoolteachers can be found in the histories of individual clubs, until now there has been no systematic attempt to record and analyse the quite substantial contribution that these teachers made to the early evolution of what became the national game. They have been filtered out of history. Green fails to mention them; Holt ignores them; Hardy fails to give them adequate consideration; others such as Walvin and Mason are almost as remiss. It is time to rectify this state of affairs. There is a vacuum to be filled. While too much should not be claimed for these men in the present, too little has been claimed in the past.

The part played in the spread of modern football by the teacher training college has already been stressed. Only Walvin in his *The People's Game*, however, has come close to a general reality, but not very close: 'One factor which encouraged the growth of school-based teams was the role of training colleges and the teachers they educated.'[34] Walvin records an indisputable reality; he falls well short of an adequate consideration of the contribution of these men to football. He is correct in his analysis as far as it goes. It does not go very far! There are wide 'pavement cracks' in it. There is a need to record the efforts of these pedagogic pioneers more adequately. The Midlands offers one opportunity. There the importance of the local teacher training college, St Peter's Saltley, was considerable.

Perhaps the most significant evidence of the part played by elementary schoolteachers in the creation of a major professional football club is provided by Wolverhampton Wanderers. In the 1870s the headmaster of St Luke's National School there was W.H. Barcroft. In 1876 he gave a football to two of his pupil teachers, Jack Brodie and John Baynton, who later went to St Peter's. They established St Luke's Junior F.C. In 1879 with two other clubs, one formed by Barcroft himself, St Luke's became Wolverhampton Wanderers. The *Book of Football* published in 1906 reported: 'Like many another club which has risen to an important place in the football world, Wolverhampton Wanderers owe their inception to the enthusiasm of a band of scholars and choristers.'[35]

Three of the leading figures in the early years of the club were Jack Brodie, John Baynton and John Addenbrooke. All three attended St Luke's and St Peter's. All three became elementary schoolteachers. Brodie was an outstanding footballer. He scored 44 goals in 65 league and cup appearances for Wolves and in addition, won three England 'caps'. He eventually became a member of the Board of Directors of Wolverhampton Wanderers. Baynton played for the club for 12 years in eight positions including goalkeeper in the FA Cup Final of 1889. Addenbrooke was the weakest player of the three. He only made the Second Eleven. Over time, however, he was probably the most influential of the three in the history of the club. He was Secretary Manager for 37 years from 1885 to 1922. These years saw Wolves help found the Football League and play in five FA Cup Finals. In his obituary, he was attractively described as 'a very keen and scrupulous sportsman, and therefore, in the best sense of the word a gentleman … and as a gentleman liked and respected by his colleagues'.[36] It could be said, therefore, that he personified the ideals of athleticism inculcated in his training college.

In the early twentieth century, the club saw elementary schoolteachers on the pitch, in the 'dug out' and in the boardroom. In short, Wolverhampton Wanderers owed much of its early playing and administrative survival and success to elementary schoolteachers. They helped the club to early and sustained success and retained a strong influence and interest in the club until well after the First World War.

The evidence for schoolteachers making similar contributions to clubs, both amateur and professional, the length and breadth of England, is extensive if ignored. The Midland Wanderers, even in the Midlands, is simply a 'splinter' of a large 'slab' of evidence!

In short, English elementary schoolteachers, with a commitment to the game, fostered, in part, in their colleges and imbued, in many instances, with the ideals of athleticism, an enthusiasm for football and a desire to experience, share and pass on one or both, took the game to schools, clubs and communities and helped lay the foundations of a global game.

Elementary schoolteachers became involved in Association Football for a variety of reasons, in a range of roles and at various levels. Involvement in professional clubs, largely unrecorded as it has been, was by no means, of course, their only contribution to the early years of the game. They contributed in a remarkable number of ways. Collectively, they made an important contribution: individually, they made varied contributions. The best way to appreciate this is to present for inspection some significant early schoolteacher pioneers; a mere handful in the space available.

Teachers played at the highest club levels and with major professional clubs, but some of these club players remained resolutely amateur for pragmatic and principled reasons. One teacher, who throughout his playing career remained an amateur footballer, was Joseph Holmes Gettins. He was born in Middlesborough in November 1874, and attended Denmark Road Board School before training as a teacher at Borough Road College in 1893. There, Gettins, good at games, was popular and successful – one of 12 'Poets' who were the leaders of the student community.[37] On completion of his college course, he was appointed to Isleworth School, a prestigious appointment as only the best students were sent there on teaching practice. Gettins spent a year at the school before returning to Borough Road as Assistant Master of Method responsible for pedagogy. As a superb athlete he fitted in well. As already made clear, athleticism was a feature of college life at Borough Road which came to closely resemble life at Almond's Loretto – a pillar of the athleticism edifice.[38]

In addition to his teaching accomplishments, Gettins was a highly talented footballer. He was to play for a number of clubs: Middlesborough (with whom he won the FA Amateur Cup Final in 1895, the Northern League in 1897, and he played in their first ever Football League fixture against Lincoln City in 1899),[39] Reading, Spurs, Derby County, Brentford,[40] Richmond Association and Matlock Town. His talent was first recognized by Millwall Athletic (subsequently Millwall). And it was to be Millwall with which he was most closely connected, and which was his first and lasting love. He played for the club for 12 years making 71 appearances and scoring 69 goals. He was the only Millwall player who appeared in their two FA Cup semi-finals of 1900 and 1903 and he won two Southern League and two United League Championship medals with them. His ability was such that he was selected to play in the Amateurs v Professional International trial match in March 1896. Possibly because of this he was invited to tour South Africa with the famous Corinthians.

The Corinthians had been founded in 1882 by N. Lane ('Pa') Jackson, Honorary Secretary of the Football Association. The motivation for the formation of the club was clearly nationalistic as England had only won once against Scotland in twelve encounters. He made this clear when he wrote: 'At that period Public and University men provided most of the players for the England side, so I thought that by giving them plenty of practice together they would acquire a certain amount of combination.'[41] N. Ackland offers a view of the club's impact arguing that 'Within twenty years the Corinthians were to become the greatest and most attractive team that football had then known. With an intelligent nonchalance, and in their tailored shirts and well-cut shorts, they brought a quality and culture to the game.'[42] Besides an overt nationalism, the Corinthians were unashamedly elitist. Gettins may have been in awe of his social, though not necessarily academic, superiors – he had obtained his degree at the University of London in 1895 – but he had a passport to privilege. He possessed the one asset that all football teams desperately covet: he could score goals. Accordingly, he was selected for the 1897 Corinthians tour of South Africa. The tour was a great success and is noteworthy for being the first time an English team played outside Europe. The Corinthians won every match of their 23 game tour scoring 113 goals and conceding only 15.[43]

Gettins was not just a footballer. His further attraction to the Corinthians, incidentally, may well have been his exceptional, many faceted, athletic abilities so much admired in late Victorian England. He was an impressive all-round sportsman: an outstanding games player, an accomplished rower,[44] a talented shooter and a fine cricketer. He was the proletariat's C.B. Fry. As such, because of these social and sporting skills, he was acceptable not least to gentlemen[45] – where his fellow team mates to a man, were University graduates.

Gettins did not turn professional; he had far too much to lose. There would be no membership of the 'best' team in England, no more exotic tours and no more mixing with some of the most privileged sportsmen of his generation. Understandably, he used sport to overcome the social and educational handicaps of a working-class background and an elementary school education. His career reveals an ambitious man who gained a degree, won recognition for his sporting skills and used both to overcome a disadvantaged background. He was driven, it would seem, by ambition. He was a period Social Darwinist in the public school mould.[46] In a 'compendious' passage that could easily have come from the pen of Herbert Spencer or Hely Hutchinson Almond, he wrote:

> We have not yet arrived at the latter stage (of human evolution); we are still hunters, fighters, runners, diggers in the earth, and builders of houses – not philosophers. And more than ever, as intellectual, sedentary occupations absorb us, do we need a basis of sound physical health to carry us through the day's work; for though the struggle for existence is no longer as with our arboreal ancestors, a scramble for nuts in some primeval forest, where only the strongest survived, yet constitutional relics of those ages show themselves in us when we swing on the flying rings, balance on the parallel bars, or elbow our way to the first row of the pit on opening night.[47]

His plea was for action, not inaction. In all fairness, however, it should be added that he sincerely espoused the amateur ideal. He had no doubt about the value of football in life. In 1907 he set down his views in *Football*, a collection of essays by prominent footballers. In his chapter 'Football and National Life', he argued strongly against a national obsession with watching instead of *playing* football, for less spectating and more playing, 'There is, perhaps, little danger of any of Britain's sons *playing* too much football [but] ... there is a very real danger in the possibility of valuable time that should be devoted to the valuable things in life given up to not *playing* football, but to ... talking football an exercise ... as profitless as it is prevalent'. [original italics][48] And for him playing was a moral exercise performed modestly.

As a tutor at Borough Road Gettins practised what he preached. He always turned out for the college XI whenever he could, but although he played more and more games for Millwall, he remained modest about his achievements. When his brief biography, a common practice for all new tutors, was printed in the college magazine, the *B's Hum*, mention of his football achievements was absent. As the editor remarked: 'As an athlete, Mr Gettins has become famous wherever the association game is played, but by express desire we are debarred from making mention of his exploits as centre-forward.'[49] Gettins subscribed fully to what has been called the 'sportsmanship ethic' which gained acceptance in middle-class circles in the second half of the nineteenth century. The major features of this ethic were:

> First, playing for the side and not for self. Being modest and generous in victory and staunch and cheerful in defeat. Playing the game for the game's sake: there might be physical and moral benefits but there should be no other rewards and certainly not prizes or money. No player should ever intentionally break the rules or stoop to underhand tactics. Hard but fair knocks should be given and taken courageously and with good temper.[50]

He took this ethic onto the pitches of professional clubs as a pen portrait of him revealed: 'One of the few amateurs who have played consistently for a professional side. He ... is a very fine resolute forward not afraid of hard knocks and very quick to see and make use of openings. Is never flurried, seldom varies [*sic* and has been the utmost service to his side.'[51]

Football for Gettins, therefore, was a moral endeavour. In his own firm words: 'The first aim then of a game of football ... is not to win a league at all costs and by whatever means, but simply to play according to a few accepted rules that are not irksome in their limitations, and with all the skill and goodwill at one's command'.[52] He was a period avatar; he epitomized Corinthianism. He once declared: 'A player has no need of the incentive of payment, cup or medal to play ... To him the game is all.'[53] However, as John Lowerson has commented: 'The high moral seriousness so often claimed for the amateur ethic was paradoxically used to support pleasure in an almost Manichaean assumption about the inevitable fallen state of the ordinary world of the mass game.'[54] The cynic would say that there is more than a little of this in the Gettins's rubric. Nevertheless, there was sincerity as well as snobbery in his make up. And as the story of *Soccer's Missing Men* in due course, will make very clear, this sincerity was shared by others. Idealism can be for real!

Richard Holt, for one, is too zealous in his condemnation and too casual in his assertion that: 'The amateur code was in practice *frequently* a means of excluding working-class players from high level competition. Moral arguments were a means of class exclusivity.' (emphasis added)[55] In the case of Association Football, *many* working-class players were involved at the highest level of competition: the professional game! Indeed, in order for any amateur to play at this highest level, he would have to be as good as his professional, usually working-class team mate. In Association Football, amateurism, with regard to standards of performance, inexorably lost out to professionalism as time went by. This was because, in Derek Birley's words, 'professional competition brought higher standards, of effectiveness if not of chivalry, and required a degree of regimentation, rules, punctuality, commitment that did not fit in with the more casual amateur approach'.[56] This said, there were many working-class amateurs of high quality, indeed some of the highest quality in the amateur game. Furthermore, on occasion Holt clearly lacks subtlety as well as accuracy. To claim that moral arguments were 'a means of class exclusivity' is to fail to adequately recognize the genuine nature of the arguments of men like Gettins and to fail to do justice to a more complicated state of affairs than Holt simplistically describes and to indulge rather recklessly in sweeping generalization. More often than not, complexity characterizes reality.

Age makes spectators of us all, and in later life Gettins was a keen fan. The club he enthused about, above all others, was Millwall! In 1910, by which time he was Principal of a Training College in Liverpool, he was invited to become Vice-President of the newly formed Millwall Supporters Club. He accepted, proudly, replying: 'My Millwall days are among the best I have spent and my regard for those who have been responsible for its welfare, both the directors, and those less important folk who gather around the ropes, is undiminished.'[57]

His subsequent career was luminous. There was to be no elementary school drudgery for him. In 1898, barely two years after his appointment to Borough Road, Gettins took up a post as Master of Method at the Day Training College in Reading. He was no doubt delighted when the college achieved University College status in 1902, but the ambitious Gettins was not to remain there long either. In 1907, at the impressively young age of 33, he took up the post of Principal of the Day Training College of Liverpool University. When the First World War broke out Gettins, a Territorial, was immediately called up to work in the Army Service Corps. He was promoted from Captain to Major. He 'had a good war'. In 1918 he was awarded the Distinguished Service Order.

After the war, Gettins returned to Liverpool, not as Principal of the Training College, but as Bursar of Liverpool University. He apparently quickly moved to a position more to his liking and in 1920, took up a post in the Army Education Corps as Chief Education Officer at Sandhurst. In 1927, he was appointed Command Education Officer, Eastern Command. From 1931 until his retirement in 1933, in which year he was awarded an OBE, he commanded the Army School of Education at Shorncliffe.[58]

Gettins, it seems, achieved it all: sporting success, educational leadership, military honours, army promotion and an OBE. Would he have enjoyed his occupational and social success without his sporting talent? It is unlikely. Association Football gave him opportunities to go to places and to meet people that would have been denied to others. While his career outside of football proved that he was an able man, it was his career in football that gave him the chance to make the most of his opportunities. He provides a graphic illustration of the advantages that could accrue to a working-class player if he was good enough to remain amateur and play in the professional game and capitalize on his amateurism.

Gettins was a teacher training college student, tutor and principal, and, for a short while, an elementary schoolteacher. In all these positions he played for either famous amateur or professional clubs. As a principal, he became an enthusiastic supporter, with official responsibilities, of the team to which he had the closest attachment. In short, he made his mark on the English game, a mark characterized, not simply by a high level of skill, but also a high level of moral commitment. In this latter regard he played with purpose, above all, if his own words are to be believed, for a purpose – sound health, both moral and physical.

Gettins was concerned with spiritual well-being; others were more concerned with temporal well-being. At the end of the nineteenth and the beginning of the twentieth centuries, efforts were made by the players to organize themselves as a distinctive group of workers in order to campaign for better treatment by their employers – the clubs. Their action was part of a wider movement by skilled artisans and should not have come as a shock to the clubs, but it did. It was seen as a threat to power and profits. Many directors viewed their clubs as personal fiefdoms: the directors as barons, the players as villeins and the spectators as cottars. Such neo-medievalism was never going to be a long-term arrangement and it was challenged, vigorously, by way of the players' trade union.

The immediate reasons behind the establishment of a union were, briefly, as follows. With the introduction of professionalism in 1885 and the establishment of the Football League in 1888, it was apparent that there would be rich pickings for those shrewd enough to cash in, literally, on the innovations in the form of 'gate money'. The club owners, led by William McGregor, determined that there should be a maximum wage for players of £4 per week, arguing that this would prevent the poorer clubs losing their players since there would be no incentive for a player to change clubs as there would be no financial benefit in doing so. Thus, the League would remain competitive, and takings at the gate would remain healthy – and all the clubs would benefit. The idealism of the Football Association aided the owners in their fiscal machinations. As John Harding, author of a history of the Professional Footballers' Association, has explained: 'In the eyes of the F.A., football would always be a sport, never a business, while those who played it would always be "sportsmen", never workmen. That the pro-player *was* a workman with a legal contract and recognised as such (after struggle) by the law of the land, would make no practical difference. For the F.A., football was a world within a world and they were its rulers.'[59]

The most insidious aspect of the regulations in the eyes of the players was the clause that even after serving his contract a player was not free to move on unless the holding club agreed to release him, effectively tying the player to them. This scheme, known as 'retain and transfer', led directly to the formation of a players' trade union.

The first attempt to form a union came in 1893, but was unsuccessful because the stimulus, a threat of a unilateral cut in wages, was not implemented. Then in 1897, the players were angered that the Scottish League had agreed with the Football League to introduce the 'retain and transfer' scheme and to make it binding on both leagues. This action denied players in England the opportunity at the end of a contract to play in Scotland. The Football League also sought the same agreement with the Southern League (founded in 1893). In response, the Association Footballers' Union (AFU) was established. Its first secretary was John Cameron of Everton, but the new union struggled to attract members. In 1898 Cameron was transferred to Tottenham Hotspur and the search for a new secretary began. The man eventually chosen, Charles Saer, who played for Leicester Fosse, was an elementary school teacher.

Saer was born in St Clears, a small village in west Carmarthenshire, in 1871. He did not show any particular aptitude for sport as a child and it was not until he went to Bangor Normal Training College that he played football. Eventually, he became goalkeeper of the college eleven. After college, he taught in Blaenau Ffestiniog in a higher grade school, then left Wales and worked in Fleetwood in Lancashire, firstly as a teacher at Chaucer Road School, then as head teacher at Lord St. School and finally as head teacher at Milton School where he remained until his retirement. On arrival at Fleetwood, he played for a local amateur team for three seasons, then for Fleetwood Rangers. Towards the end of 1896 to 1897 season he joined Blackburn Rovers. In 1897, he spent a season with Leicester Fosse in the second division making 28 appearances. He was injured the following year and never played league football again. However, his abrupt departure from the professional game was also hastened by the fact that his School Board stipulated when renewing his contract in 1898 that he was to undertake no other paid occupation. Being a teacher was more attractive than being a professional footballer. As a senior teacher he was earning £85 per year and the maximum that a player could earn was £60!

In 1899, a year after he became Secretary of the newly established AFU, Saer came to national prominence with his proposal to amend the 'retain and transfer' scheme. The Football League was in negotiation with the Southern League with a view to absorb it. Saer argued at a committee meeting that this provided the Union with a perfect opportunity to flex its muscles arguing that it should press the League to amend the 'retain and transfer' scheme or the AFU would write to the FA urging that the Football League be refused permission to incorporate the Southern League. Saer's suggested reform of the existing 'retain and transfer' scheme was both modest and simple: clubs would have to offer a player a minimum of £52 for the ensuing season. If they did not offer this minimum no transfer fee could be charged. If a player refused the £52, half the difference between the sum offered would be the maximum fee chargeable for his transfer.

Saer's proposal was countered by Charles Sutcliffe, a member of the management committee of the Football League and Chairman of Burnley.[60] He argued that Saer's scheme would be unworkable as it would stop clubs from spending money on recruiting and nurturing talent and that it would lead to players 'playing for their papers', that is, refusing to play and forcing the clubs to sell them. The Football League met with the AFU, but the talks were inconclusive. No progress was made. This fact, along with others, without doubt dictated his subsequent action. At the Union's first Annual General Meeting in December 1898, Saer resigned as Secretary. The official reason given was that: 'Mr Saer had no alternative but to retire as his scholastic duties precluded the possibility of his devoting the necessary time to the office.'[61] No doubt there was some truth in this. His School Board was 'laying down the law', but it was not the whole truth. Saer had become increasingly disillusioned with professionalism. He was in dispute with Leicester Fosse over money he claimed the club owed him and had 'severed his connections with Stockport County (with whom he had been injured playing in a pre-season trial match) under circumstances which may cause Stockport County to appear before the F.A.'[62] Saer never played League football again, ended his connection with the professional game, resigned as secretary of the AFU and concentrated on his career as a teacher in Fleetwood.

By 1898, then, Saer had made his contribution to the professional game, on and off the field, while remaining the whole time a self-effacing elementary schoolteacher. He had never really sought the limelight. This was recognized when he was appointed Secretary in October:

> Mr Charles Saer has leapt into fame. The rapidity of his advance to renown has been unprecedented. Twelve months or so ago he enjoyed a quite local reputation as an expert goalkeeper. Today he is one of the best known names on football politics ... He is known by name rather than personality for albeit

> that he is a man of exceptional intellectual attainments, he is one of those who you have to seek to know and then know him by his acts. If it had not been for a few long headed men ... recognising what sterling qualities lay behind the barrier of quiet dignified restraint presented by this unobtrusive young Cambrian, he would probably have continued ever in retirement.[63]

Despite his sudden resignation and equally sudden departure from the professional game, Saer provides further evidence of the early contribution of the elementary schoolteacher to English professional football. He spent a very short time as union Secretary, but it was, according to his peers at the time, a post to which he brought imagination and inventiveness for 'once they installed him in office, and placed upon him the onus of steering a course for the disaffection-threatened union, it was not long before he showed what he was capable of, and had a definite policy shaped, a platform established. And footballdom today is ringing with his suggested reforms.'[64] Saer failed in his bid to amend the 'retain and transfer' system, but his importance lay in the fact that he helped revive a near moribund union, raised a crucial players' issue boldly and firmly with the clubs, the Football League and the Football Association and, as subsequent events would show, ensured a united union. Saer was important to the drive for recognition of players' rights. His significance to the game should not be underestimated. When the players needed a strategy they got one from a teacher, and when they needed a steady hand, again it was a teacher who provided it.

Charles Saer had no direct responsibilities to club directors, but Tom Maley was in a very different situation. He became a successful, if controversial, club manager. Maley, the son of an army sergeant, was born in Portsmouth in 1865. He trained as a teacher at Catholic St Mary's Training College in London from 1885 to 1886. He then settled in Scotland and quickly won a reputation as a fine footballer playing in turn for Cathcart, Hibernians, Partick Thistle and Third Lanark before becoming one of the founders of Glasgow Celtic playing in their first ever fixture, a 5-2 victory against Glasgow Rangers in 1888.

A brief consideration of the origins of the club permits an understanding of Maley's qualities including his desire to use his considerable footballing skills for the improvement of the lives of poor Irish Catholics in Glasgow. In 1887 Hibernian, an almost exclusively Irish Catholic club in Edinburgh, won the Scottish FA Cup. Before returning to Edinburgh (the game was played in Glasgow), their Glaswegian supporters arranged a dinner in their honour. During the after-dinner speeches the Hibernian secretary commented that a similar club in Glasgow would be a good idea. In the audience was a local elementary schoolteacher, Brother Walfrid, head teacher of St Andrews School, and Brother Superior of the Marist Teaching Order, in Glasgow. In November 1887, he held an inaugural meeting to establish Glasgow Celtic Football Club. The purpose of the club was to raise money for destitute Irish Catholics in the east end of Glasgow: 'After the deduction of the necessary expenses ... any remaining monies could be directed towards the East End Conferences of the St Vincent de Paul Society and thus the Poor Children's Dinner Tables in the parishes of St. Mary's, St. Michael's and the Sacred Heart.'[65]

Brother Walfrid had founded the club, now he needed some players. Only days after the club's creation, he travelled with two other committee members to the home of Tom Maley. Maley was not at home, but his younger brother, Willie, was. The visitors were so impressed by Willie that they asked him to join the club and it was he who persuaded Tom to join. It proved to be a fortuitous meeting, for not only did 'Handsome Tom', as he was nicknamed, play for the team, he also recruited several players from Hibernian. Furthermore, Willie Maley became the club's first manager, a post he held for 52 years before his enforced retirement at the age of 72 in 1940. Tom became a director of Celtic for a year in 1897, having previously been on the committee and indeed managed the club in a caretaker capacity in 1931 while his brother was recuperating from an illness.[66] The Maleys, incidentally, were an impressive footballing dynasty. Apart from Tom and Willie, their youngest brother, Alex, was manager of Clydebank from 1919 to

1921, Hibernian from 1921 to 1925, and Crystal Palace and Clydebank in 1927, while Charles Maley, Tom's son, was secretary of both Bradford City and Leicester City.

After a playing career of 20 years, Maley was ready for a new challenge. At 37, his playing days spent with various Scottish sides were over. But when playing he had another career. Throughout his lengthy football career he had remained a teacher. When he retired from playing in 1902, he was a teacher at Slatefield Industrial School in Glasgow but now wanted to try his hand at football management. He was interviewed for the post of secretary/manager at Everton early in 1902, but was unsuccessful. Nevertheless, the experience spurred him on to try elsewhere. As he himself said, 'Having, so to speak, sampled the goods, I was determined upon acquiring them, and so several months later found me in close association and contact with Manchester City.'[67] (Maley had played a single game for the club in 1896.) Maley successfully applied for the post of secretary/manager in July. His impact on the club was immediate. In 1902, the club had finished bottom of the First Division with only 28 points from 34 games. In Maley's first season as manager the club lost only five out of 34 games and were champions of the Second Division winning promotion back to the First Division with four points to spare over Small Heath. In 1904, City won the FA Cup beating Sunderland, Arsenal, Middlesborough and Sheffield Wednesday on the way to the final in which it beat Bolton Wanderers 1-0. In fact, the club narrowly missed out on 'the double', finishing runners up to Sheffield Wednesday. However, in Maley's case pride certainly came before a fall.

In the last game of the 1904/05 season, Manchester City played Aston Villa at Villa Park needing a win to secure the championship. Villa won 3-2. After the match rumours circulated that some Villa players had been offered bribes to throw the game. In August, Manchester City's star player, Billy Meredith, was suspended by the FA after Aston Villa's Alec Leake reported that Meredith had offered him a £10 bribe. Meredith initially denied the allegation, but an FA inquiry found him guilty and banned him from the game until April 1906. Meredith then changed his story admitting the offer of a bribe, but claimed that he was only acting under Maley's orders: 'On hearing this new evidence, the F.A. ordered a full investigation into the club's accounts. A whole manner of irregularities was uncovered, ranging from amateurs being paid, to ... senior players being paid more than the maximum weekly wage ... The chairman W. Forrest, along with manager Maley were banned *sine die* ... The club itself was fined £250, and the players, in total £900.'[68]

Maley fell from grace. Barred from football for life at the age of 41, Maley returned to teaching and became headmaster of St Mary's Catholic School, Calton, in Glasgow. He remained there until his ban was rescinded in 1911. A number of clubs were still interested in him and a friend arranged an interview with Bradford Park Avenue's Chairman, A.H. Briggs. 'What impressed me', explained Maley, 'was the intense desire he had to see the Bradford club grouped with the best clubs in the league and also his thoroughness and organising ability'.[69] He in turn impressed Briggs and became manager of Bradford Park Avenue. On hearing of his appointment one of his fiends remarked to him that 'it will take you a jolly sight longer than it did when you took Manchester up'.[70] It took three years. Maley achieved Briggs's aim and realized the dreams of the Bradford public by securing promotion to Division One. A contemporary wrote:

> Mr Maley has played the part of the strong man in Bradford football. He has been given considerable freedom in running the club, selecting the team and so on, and there are not wanting those who have dubbed him autocratic. The truth is, however, that he possesses that important quality, confidence in himself, and to-day he is in a position to laugh at his critics. He came to the Avenue to take the club into the First Division, he said he would do it and he has done it.[71]

Bradford Park Avenue, it seemed, had begun a most glorious period of its history and in its first season in the First Division finished a highly creditable ninth. However, for the next four years of war, the League was suspended and was not resumed until1919–20. Maley was an ardent supporter of the war and frequently appeared at football matches trying to recruit men for the front. Seven of his own players enlisted and two were killed in action, Donald Simpson Bell VC and Jimmy Smith, the club's prolific centre forward, who had scored 60 goals in 100 appearances. On the resumption of the League in 1919, the club finished eleventh. However, the next year Bradford was relegated to Division Two and in 1921–22 it was again relegated into Division Three (North). They narrowly missed promotion back to the Division Two in 1923 before Maley resigned in 1924, finishing his managerial career at Southport a year later. He returned to his beloved Scotland.

Maley died in 1935 aged 70. He may have blotted his copybook in England, but his humanity, compassion and concern for his fellow Glaswegians ensured that he retained a saintly image in Scotland: 'He was one of the best-known Catholic laymen in Scotland in his day and his funeral was attended by fifty priests and thousands of people.'[72] His footballing skills as player and manager were not forgotten. At his funeral the nation's footballing establishment also paid its respects. Both the President and Vice-president of the Scottish Football Association attended, as did the Secretary of the Scottish Football League: 'A wealth of beautiful wreaths were placed on the grave...Among them were tributes from ... Celtic F.C. and the Celtic players, Rangers F.C.; ... and numerous provincial clubs in addition to practically every known football legislative organisation.'[73]

Throughout his life Maley never lost his concern for the poor, nor his conviction that games were a means of providing both health and happiness for the disadvantaged in society. As a young man he helped establish a club whose *raison d'être* was the eradication of poverty. On his retirement, he became a governor of Slatefield Industrial School. It is recorded that 'he did everything possible for the comfort and health of the boys. Together with Mrs Maley and his family, he was constantly organising sports and swimming matches for the boys.'[74] Furthermore he was a devout Catholic, who raised thousands of pounds for Catholic charities and he 'tramped miles every Sunday to instruct Catholic children in their Faith'.[75]

Gettins, the idealistic amateur, was concerned with 'playing the game'; Maley, the realistic professional, was preoccupied with winning matches. No better examples can be found than these: On the eve of the 1904 FA Cup semi-final against Sheffield Wednesday, the club's directors, without Maley's knowledge, decided to drop two players. Maley was outraged and took on the Directors and spent hours that evening pressing them to allow him to select his side. He got his way. As one Director said to him: 'Well Tom if failure comes you'll get the blame, and if success comes we'll get the praise. You pay your money and you take your chance.'[76] City won the match!

Earlier in his playing career, in a hard fought game against Corinthians which Celtic was dominating, winning despite having three goals disallowed, the legendary 'Pa' Jackson complained to him at half time saying 'Look here T. E. M., if that right half of yours doesn't improve his methods and his language we shall have to cancel our fixture with you at the Oval.' Maley replied: 'My dear Mr J., unless your fellows improve their play and keep their goal a little more intact, it will be hardly worth our while going so far to play you!'[77] Finally, in the early years of Celtic, Everton's secretary, Dick Molyneux, tried to entice one of Celtic's best players, Peter Dowds to sign for them and had gone so far as to get a brake to take Dowds to Glasgow station and on to a train to Liverpool. What happened next is best expressed in Maley's own uncompromising words:

> We – my friend and self – drove after them and overtook them on the highroad, bored them so to speak into a hedgerow, and then having compelled them to stop ... sternly ordered Peter to get off and get up – off the Everton machine and on to the Celtic. This removal effected, we gave Dick and his pal the order to 'git'.
>
> Next day, a telegram reached Dowds from the late Fred Dewhurst, on behalf of P. N. E. [Preston North End] desiring Peter to meet him in a certain hotel in Glasgow. That wire I replied to. 'Peter can't come. I will', and signed it in full. Fred didn't wait to meet me.[78]

For Maley losing was not an option; winning was a necessity. He was no Corinthian. Today, he is more remembered for his part in a bribery scandal that rocked the footballing establishment than for his performances in football as a successful player and manager. Indeed, in a recent book chronicling the history of football management, Neil Carter's, *The Football Manager: A History*,[79] published in 2006, he does not receive a single mention in a book of 191 pages. This, considering that Maley was one of the founders of Glasgow Celtic, managed three clubs for 566 matches, was involved in one of football's biggest scandals, won the FA Cup, twice won promotion to the First Division, finished runner up in the First division, and whose funeral was attended by literally tens of thousands of people, is astonishing, unbelievable and, frankly, inexcusable.

Maley's contribution to the early moments of Association Football was spectacular, but he failed to match the probity of Gettins. While the degree of his culpability in the Manchester City bribery scandal remained a stain upon his character, it should be seen, however, in the fuller context of both a personal and professional life characterized by many sterling achievements. On his death, *The Glasgow Star* commented:

> Of his personal character one cannot speak too highly. He was one of God's gentlemen, endowed with a combination of qualities which won unfailingly the hearts of all and especially those of the young. A man with all the qualities associated with manhood, he was possessed in addition of a sweetness of disposition and a charm of manner which gained for him countless friends in every part of the country.[80]

Given that obituaries are required to be eulogistic there is, nonetheless, sufficient evidence on record to suggest that there was more than an element of truth in these generous words.

Gettins, Saer and Maley in their very different ways demonstrate the varied and significant contributions that elementary schoolteacher pioneers made to the early days of Association Football. While these men had much in common – their class and educational backgrounds, for example, were remarkably similar – their contributions to football were radically different. They were merely some of the pioneer footballing teachers. Space precludes details of others who were involved in the game in disparate, but distinctive roles, and who, for the most part, have disappeared from the history of Association Football. Incidentally, at least 75 elementary schoolteachers played for Football League clubs either as amateurs or professionals. Nine played for England. Four: Edward Johnson (St Peter's College), Jack Brodie (Wolverhampton Wanderers) Fred Dewhurst (Preston North End) and Evelyn Lintott (Queens Park Rangers) played with a fifth, James Haydock (Blackburn Rovers), being selected but unable to play through injury for England. Four others: Frank Monk (Glossop), and Joe Dines (Ilford), J.C. Kilkenny and E. Williams (Chelsea), played for England amateur side. What this reveals is that there was a greater penetration of the professional game by elementary schoolteachers than has hitherto been recognized and they were also to be found in significant numbers in a variety of other roles as administrators, and even more visibly as referees. Consideration of these roles, however, must wait for another time, and for the arrival of *Soccer's Missing Men*.

The schoolmasters considered in *Soccer's Missing Men*, and certainly many more not considered in it, have been largely overlooked, yet collectively they contributed to the early moments of the game at every level. Take, for example, administration: they served as county and league secretaries, council members, vice presidents and presidents. Furthermore, they provide, incidentally, further compelling evidence that the notion that football was codified, organized and administered and advanced largely by the products of the public schools, is ignorantly partial. The reality was far more complicated. For one thing, these men, through the training colleges and the network of schools and county associations and clubs, both professional and amateur, constituted an educational advance guard. With an enthusiastic commitment to the game fostered, in part, in their colleges, and imbued *inter alia* with, in many cases, the ideals of athleticism, and a desire to share and pass on these ideals, they took the game to their schools, clubs and communities. In short, they helped lay the foundations for a national football structure. Their stories should not be relegated to the footnotes of the history of the game, but rather restored to the main text.

English elementary schoolteachers with others, of course, took football to the world. They are part of a forged chain of global links which has bound the world together in the recent FIFA World Cup! But that is a story for another time.

Notes

1. The irony, of course, was that Reed is considered to be an excellent coach who had previously been employed by Charlton Athletic from 1996 to 1998 when the club won a famous Wembley Championship Play off final 7-6 against Sunderland. The next day Reed took up his appointment at the Football Association. Alan Curbishley, Charlton's manager from 2005 to 2006, the man who appointed Reed, wrote of him that

   > I think to many people in the professional game there's still a bit of stigma attached to someone like Les, who had not played professionally and had coached as part of the FA set-up. But as far as I'm concerned, not playing as a professional doesn't mean a thing: coaching is a different world and I knew Les had the sort of qualities I was looking for ... I had no doubt that Les would soon gain the respect of the players because they would be able to see just what a good football coach he was, and I knew he was excellent on a one-to-one basis improving someone's skills and their understanding of the game. Curbishley, *Valley of Dreams*, 102–3.

2. There is, of course, no one untold story of the emergence of association football. There are several. The diffuse roots are world-wide. Some deeply buried roots have recently been admirably uncovered (see Majumdar and Bandopadhyay, *Striving to Score*), while some English roots are now exposed in 'Soccer's Missing Men', and further roots are to be laid bare apparently in Eric Dunning and Graham Curry's *The Making of Association Football: A Sociological History of the People's Game*. The book is in preparation. It will be interesting to see what notice is taken in it of the role of elementary schoolteachers.
3. Walvin, 'Sport, Social History and the Historian', 5.
4. Series Editor's Foreword, Harvey, *Football. The First Hundred Years*, xvii.
5. See, for example, Mason, *Association Football and English Society*; Morris, *A History of Football*; Walvin, *The Peoples' Game*; Fabian and Green, *Association Football*; Harvey, *Football: The First Hundred Years*; and Kerrigan, *Teachers and Football.*
6. For a detailed account of the origins of the Football Association, see Fabian and Green, *Association Football*, Vol. 1. 47–54. Eleven clubs: Kilburn; Barnes; W.O. (War Office); Crusaders; Forest, Leytonstone; Perceval House, Blackheath; Crystal Palace; Blackheath; Kensington School; Surbiton and Blackheath Proprietary School met at The Freemason's Tavern in Lincoln's Inn Fields, London on 26 October 1863 and founded the Football Association.
7. Fabian and Green, *Association Football*, Vol. 1, 46.
8. Ibid., 47.
9. Charles William Alcock (1842–1907) was educated at Harrow and Oxford University. He was the secretary of the Football Association from 1870 to 1895.
10. Montague Shearman (1857–1930) was educated at St John's College, Oxford where he gained a reputation as both a scholar and an athlete. He was the author of two books on sport, *Athletics and Football* (1889) and with J. Vincent, *Football: its History for Five Centuries* (1885). He was knighted in 1903.
11. Shearman, *Athletics and Football*, 359.
12. For a full account, see Inglis, *League Football*; Butler, *The Football League*; Sutcliffe, *The Story of the Football League*.
13. Francis, *Seventy Five Years*, 20–1. The successful clubs were: Chatham 26 (votes), Luton Town 25, Millwall Athletic 25, Marlow 24, Swindon Town 24, Reading 22, West Herts 21, Woolwich Arsenal 19, Ilford 19, Chiswick Park 18, Old St. Mark's 15, Crouch End 12. The unsuccessful clubs were: Chesham 10, Wolverton 9, City Ramblers 8, Woodville 8, Uxbridge 7, St Albans 6, Westminster Criterion 2, Old St Stephen's 2, Upton Park 2, Tottenham Hotspur 1.

14. Ibid., 23.
15. Gibson and Pickford, *Association Football*, 170–1.
16. Francis, *League Football*, 23.
17. Harvey, 'Football's Missing Link', 92.
18. Ibid., 93.
19. Ibid.
20. Harvey, *Football.*
21. Ibid., 1.
22. The point needs labouring. There is at least one recent pretentious sub-title suggesting coverage of *the* unknown story. There are any number of aspects of football's history about which we know very little, as noted earlier (see note 3).
23. Series Editor's Foreword, Harvey, *Football*, xvii.
24. Harvey, 'Football's Missing Link', 93.
25. Kerrigan, *Teachers and Football*, passim.
26. Mason, *Association Football*, 2–3.
27. Dobbs, *Edwardians at Play*, 30.
28. See Mangan, *Athleticism*, passim.
29. See Hickey, 'Athleticism and the London Training Colleges'.
30. Hickey, 'Athleticism', passim.
31. See Mangan and Hickey, 'Athleticism in the Service of the Proletariat', 112–39; Mangan and Hickey, 'Globalisation, the Games Ethic and Imperialism', 105–30,
32. Mangan, 'Oars and the Man', 52–77; and Mangan, 'Lamentable Barbarians and Pitiful Sheep', 130–54.
33. Morris, *A History of Football*, 167.
34. Walvin, *The People's Game*, 61.
35. *The Book of Football*, 193.
36. *The Wolverhampton Wanderers Official Programme and Club Records*, 3.
37. For a closer analysis of the role, function and activities of the 'Poets', see Hickey, 'Athleticism', 106–46.
38. For a full consideration of athleticism in Loretto, see Mangan, *Athleticism*, 48–58.
39. Gettins played ten league games for Middlesborough between 1899 and 1903 scoring two goals. For details of Middlesbrough's early history see Appleton, *Hotbed of Soccer*, 77–87.
40. For details of Gettins career see Haynes *et al.*, *100 Years of Brentford*, 353–5. Although he only played a few games for Brentford, Gettins supplied the club with one lasting legacy: 'The "Bees" of Brentford got this name from the cry of encouragement given by students from Borough Road Teachers College to watch one of their number, J.H. Gettins, long ago.' Fabian and Green, *Association Football*, Vol.2, 340.
41. See Fabian and Green, *Association Football*, Vol.1, 386.
42. Ibid., 387.
43. See Raath, *Soccer through the Years*, 4–6.
44. In 1897 Gettins was in the staff boat that was only narrowly defeated by the students at the annual college boat race.
45. However, Gettins would probably have been affronted by the comment of fellow Corinthian, Frederick Pelly, about the state of Millwall Athletic's ground on East Ferry Road, opposite the Millwall Docks 'who remarked that he did not mind playing there but objected to falling on the pitch because "the smell wouldn't come off for weeks"'. Inglis, *The Football Grounds of Great Britain*, 263.
46. Mangan, 'Social Darwinism', 135–59.
47. Gettins, 'Football and National Life', in Corbett *et al.* eds, *Football*, 47.
48. In Corbett et al., *The Football Who's Who*, 139.
49. *B's Hum*, VIII., no.65 (Nov and Dec. 1896): 1.
50. Mason, *Association Football*, 223.
51. *The Football Who's Who*, 139.
52. Gettins, 'Football', 52.
53. Ibid.
54. Lowerson, *Sport and the English Middle-classes*, 183.
55. Holt, *Sport and the British*, 104.
56. Birley, *Land of Sport and Glory*, 238.
57. Murray, *Millwall Lions of the South*, 61.
58. Obituaries of Gettins were published in *The Times*, 8 June 1954 and *The Surrey Comet*, 12 June 1954. See also *Who Was Who*, Vol. V, 1951–60, 414. After his retirement Gettins became a member of the

Council of the British and Foreign School Society and became Chairman of the College Committee in 1942. See *B's Hum*, Whitsun 1955, 42 for details of his work for Borough Road after his retirement.
59. Harding, *For the Good of the Game*, 4.
60. Charles Sutcliffe (1855–1926) was born in Market Drayton and was one of the founders of Blackburn Rovers, member of the Council of Lancashire FA (1889), Vice-President (1901), President (1918). He was a prominent Football League Referee from 1891–1902, Vice President of the Football league (1898), and Member of Council FA. Sutcliffe was a solicitor and a Director of Burnley FC.
61. Harding, *For the Good of the Game*, 24.
62. Quoted in ibid, 62.
63. *Lancashire Evening Post*, 29 October 1898, 2.
64. Ibid.
65. Craig, *A Lion Looks Back*, 12.
66. Full details of Maley's career at Celtic can be found in MacBride, O'Connor and Sheridan, *An Alphabet of the Celts*, 236–7.
67. *Weekly Mail and Record*, 5 August 1916, 9.
68. Penny, *The Maine Road Encyclopaedia*, 175–6. See also Hayes, *Manchester City Football Club*, 86.
69. *Weekly Mail and Record*, 9 September 1916, 9.
70. Ibid.
71. See *St. Mary's Catholic College Centenary Record*, 47.
72. Ibid., 22.
73. *Daily Record and Mail*, 27 August 1935, 3. Maley's managerial career spanned over 500 games with three clubs. A healthy 44% wins.
74. *Glasgow Observer*, 27 August 1935, 14.
75. *St. Mary's Catholic College Centenary Record*, 122.
76. *Weekly Mail and Record*, 26 August 1916, 9.
77. Ibid., 10 June 1916, 9.
78. Ibid., 3 June 1916, 9.
79. Carter, *The Football Manager*.
80. *Glasgow Star*, 31 August 1935.

References

Appleton, A. *Hotbed of Soccer: The Story of Football in the North East.* London: The Sportsman Book Club, 1961.

Birley, Derek. *Land of Sport and Glory: Sport and British Society, 1887–1910.* Manchester: Manchester University Press, 1995.

Butler, B. *The Football League 1888–1988: The Official Illustrated History.* London: McDonald, 1988.

Carter, Neil. *The Football Manager. A History.* Abingdon: Routledge, 2006.

Corbett, B.O. *et al.*, eds. *Football.* London: Greening and Co., 1907.

Craig, J. *A Lion Looks Back.* Edinburgh: John Donald, 1998.

Curbishley, Alan. *Valley of Dreams.* London: Harper Sport, 1998.

Dobbs, B. *Edwardians at Play 1890–1914.* London: Pelham, 1973.

Fabian, A.F. and G. Green. *Association Football,* 4 Volumes. London: Caxton, 1960.

Gibson, A. and Pickford, W. *Association Football and the Men Who Made It.* London: Caxton, 1905.

Harding, J. *For the Good of the Game.* London: Robson Books, 1991.

Harvey, Adrian. *Football: The First Hundred Years. The Untold Story.* London: Routledge, 2005.

——— 'Football's Missing Link: The Real Story of the Evolution of Modern Football'. In *Sport in Europe: Politics, Class, Gender,* ed. J.A. Mangan, 92–116. London: Cass, 2000.

Hayes, D. *Manchester City Football Club: An A-Z.* Winslow: Sigma Press, 1996.

Haynes, G., G.E. White, R. Jex and Ian Westbrook. *100 Years of Brentford.* London: Brentford FC, 1989.

Hickey, C.F. 'Athleticism and the London Training Colleges: The Proletarian Absorption of an Educational Ideology'. PhD diss., IRCSSS, University of Strathclyde, 2001.

Holt, R., *Sport and the British. A Modern History.* Oxford: Oxford University Press, 1989.

Hopcraft, Arthur. *The Football Man. People and Passions in Soccer.* London: Collins, 1968; new edition, London: Aurum, 2006.

Inglis, S., *The Football Grounds of Great Britain.* London: Willow Books, 1987.

——— *League Football and the Men who Made It: The Official Centenary or the Football League, 1888–1988.* London: Willow, 1988.

Kerrigan, Colm. *Teachers and Football. Schoolboy Association Football in England, 1885–1915.* London: Routledge, 2005.

Lowerson, J., *Sport and the English Middle-classes, 1870–1914.* Manchester: Manchester University Press, 1993.

Macbride, E., M. O'Connor and G. Sheridan. *An Alphabet of the Celts: A Complete Who's Who of Celtic F.C.,* Leicester: ACL and Polar, 1994.

Majumdar, Boria and Kaushik Bandopadhyay. *Striving to Score: A Social History of Indian Football.* London: Routledge, 2007.

Mangan, J.A. 'Lamentable Barbarians and Pitiful Sheep: Rhetoric of Protest and Pleasure in Late Victorian and Edwardian Oxbridge'. In *Leisure in Art and Literature,* ed. Tom Winifrith and Cyril Barrett, 130–54. London: Macmillan, 1972.

——— 'Oars and the Man: Pleasures and Purpose in Victorian and Edwardian Cambridge'. *History of Higher Education Annual,* 4 (1984): 52–77.

——— 'Social Darwinism and Upper-Class Education in Late Victorian and Edwardian England'. In *Manliness and Morality: Middle-Class Masculinity in Britain and America, 1800–1940,* ed. J.A. Mangan and James Walvin, 135–59. Manchester: Manchester University Press, 1987.

——— *Athleticism in the Victorian and Edwardian Public School: The Emergence and the Consolidation of an Educational Ideology.* London: Cass Edition, 2000.

Mangan, J.A. and Colm Hickey. 'Athleticism in the Service of the Proletariat: Preparation for the Elementary School and the Extension of Middle-Class Manliness'. In *Making European Masculinities: Sport, Europe, Gender,* ed. J.A. Mangan, 112–39. London: Cass, 2000.

——— 'Globalisation, The Games Ethic and Imperialism: Further Aspects of an Ideal'. In *Europe, Sport, World: Shaping Global Societies,* ed. J.A. Mangan, 105–30. London: Cass, 2001.

Mason, Tony. *Association Football and English Society 1863–1915.* Brighton: Harvester, 1980.

Morris, M. *A History of Football.* London: Secker and Warburg, 1954.

Murray, J. *Millwall Lions of the South.* London: Indispensable Publications, 1988.

Penny, I. *The Maine Road Encyclopaedia: An A-Z of Manchester City F.C.* London: Mainstream Publishing, 1995.

Raath, P. *Soccer Through the Years. The First Official History of South African Soccer.* Cape Town: Castle Graphics, 2002.

Shearman, M. *Athletics and Football,* (3rd edition). London: Longmans, 1889.

St. Mary's Catholic College Centenary Record. London: St. Mary's College, 1950.

Sutcliffe, C.E. *The Story of the Football League, 1888-1938.* Preston: The Football League, 1938.

The Book of Football, 1906.

Tischler, S. *Footballers and Businessmen: The Origins of Professional Soccer in England.* London: Holmes and Meier, 1981.

Walvin, James. 'Sport, Social History and the Historian'. *International Journal of the History of Sport* 1, no.1 (May 1984): 5.

——— *The People's Game: The History of Football Revisited.* Edinburgh: Mainstream Publications, 1994.

Who Was Who, Vol. V, 1951–60, London: Adams and Charles Black, 1961.

Wolverhampton Wanderers Official Programme and Club Records, III, no.5 (Sept. 1922).

Exploring the sport spectator experience: virtual football spectatorship in the pub[1]

Mike Weed

Introduction

There has long been a link between the English public house (pub) and football. The pub has been a place in which to read about football, to talk about football, and to meet with friends before going to a live match. The pub provides a place where the holy trinity of alcohol, football and male-bonding come together. Pubs are the venues for the most vociferous of debates about the chances of the local or the national team in their forthcoming league, cup or international game, places in which to dispute the opinions or speculations of journalists about the team's latest signing or the identity of the next England Manager. In recent years, however, there has been a change in the role played by the pub. Its centrality in football culture certainly hasn't changed, but in the last decade or so it has increasingly become clear that the pub itself is now a significant and regular venue in which to watch live football. The number of pubs displaying boards and posters advertising the matches they will be showing is an indication that pub management companies and major brewers recognize the importance of this trend, but the football authorities also appear keen to promote the pub as a venue in which to watch matches. In September 2003, pub management companies, brewers and the football authorities jointly promoted 'National Pub Football Week'. This initiative has continued with further Pub Football Weeks being held in May 2004 and September 2005.

The emergence of virtual spectatorship in the pub

The evidence from market information sources, such as Mintel and Keynote, is that the market for pub sport spectating is significant. In fact, in 2002, more people (9.1 million) watched live sport on television in a pub or a bar than paid to watch live sport at an event (8.7 million).[2] This equals to 19 per cent of the population. While the data from earlier years is a little sketchy, and thus direct comparisons or any statistical trends analysis are difficult, it does not appear to be unreasonable to say that the use of the pub as a regular venue in which to watch football and sport in general has largely emerged and grown over the last ten to fifteen years. Given this timescale, it is possible to point to three factors that have driven this trend. One of these factors is fairly straightforward, and is simply the increasingly relatively cheap availability to pubs and bars of the technology to show sport on a big screen. The second factor is the move of live televised

Premier League football to the satellite broadcaster BSkyB in 1992. At this time there was a relatively low penetration of satellite and cable TV services into homes, with Weed estimating that between 5% and 8% of the population would have been able to access the first year of BSkyB's Premiership coverage at home.[3] Mintel has suggested that this 'led to increased numbers of consumers being forced to view live sport outside the home, with pubs and bars accommodating the bulk of this market'.[4] The third factor contributing to the growth of pub sport and football spectating is what has been referred to by some as the 'sanitisation' of Premier League football grounds as a result of the changes brought about by the 1990 Taylor Report on the safety of sports stadia. This report identified football clubs as having key responsibility for the safety and comfort of spectators, and included, as the prime recommendation, the conversion of all first and second division grounds to all-seater stadia by 1994, and of all Football League grounds by 1999. While the requirement for lower league clubs has since been relaxed, all Premiership grounds are now all-seater stadia. A range of authors such as Boyle and Haynes, and Williams,[5] and public figures such as Professional Footballers Association Chief Executive, Gordon Taylor and former Minister for Sport, Kaye Hoey, have commented on the change of atmosphere in all-seater stadia, with John Williams explicitly linking this to the enhanced attraction of the pub as a football spectator venue: 'Sky also offers young male fans, at least, the prospects of collective and participatory pub TV coverage, the "new terraces" in an age of what are, for them, "sanitised" and allegedly atmosphere-free all-seater grounds.'[6]

The development of a 'culture of pub supporting', has also found its way into popular culture writing, with Dougie Brimson, in his book 'The Geezers Guide to Football' writing that:

> The shift towards a culture of pub supporting has already started. It is cheaper and easier to simply go down the pub and watch the game while having a few beers. In most cases it will be with the same group of geezers and so the atmosphere will be as good if not better than at the actual game.[7]

While a 'culture of pub supporting' appears to have initially developed largely out of necessity as a result of a lack of access to live televised football matches in the home, it has now developed into an activity that is attractive in its own right. Despite the increased penetration of non-terrestrial television in recent years, pub sports spectating is increasing in popularity, with Keynote estimating that over a third of men regularly go to pubs to watch sport.[8]

An extended example perhaps serves to illustrate the popularity of the pub as a venue for 'participatory' football fandom. Weed presents an ethnography of the pub as a football spectator venue, and the description provided of the England vs. Argentina match during the 2002 World Cup is particularly vivid.[9] This match had long featured in the media as the most important first round fixture of the tournament. As the kick-off for the match was 12.30 p.m. on a Friday, many people had either booked time off work months in advance, or feigned illness to allow them to watch the match in the pub. In a bar in Sheffield with a capacity of 750, Weed describes the pre-match atmosphere as boisterous and alcohol-fuelled, with many people going on to drink late into the evening after the match.[10] Anti-Argentinian singing was widespread and often pervasive, with the IRA also featuring in the repertoire. In the usual course of events, the sound of around 700 drunken people inside a closed and confined space joining in unison in a rowdy and in some cases aggressive rendition of 'No Surrender to the IRA', would likely be cause for police intervention. Of course, in a bar, unlike at a ground, there is a plentiful supply of alcohol and no police or stewards to quell any racist or xenophobic chanting. The popularity of this nationalist chant is a somewhat strange feature of modern day England supporting, although it is unlikely that many of those joining in have any particular commitment to English Nationalism or to defeating the IRA, they simply want to enjoy communal singing and chanting. It is this communal desire to join in with the carnivalesque party atmosphere that appears to swell the numbers of 'hooligans' at international tournaments, and was a particular problem, as Weed has argued, at Euro 2000 in

Holland and Belgium. While this chanting may be uncomfortable, it is perhaps better that it takes place in a closed bar in England where there are no 'opponents' other than the virtual ones on the TV, than in the streets, bars and football grounds of another country.[11] However, it is an indication of the 'out-of-the-ordinary-ness' of pub football spectating that such chanting is tolerated. On a Friday or Saturday evening it is highly likely that security staff would intervene to prevent such chanting or to eject from the bar those involved.

However, notwithstanding the above, the atmosphere in the Sheffield bar was very intense, and some of the comments of those in the bar highlight this:

> It feels so loud in here, I s'pose that must be cos there's a roof on, which you don't have at the stadium – this is all enclosed. We're all England fans as well, and that contributes … I think you pick up on and join in the singing started by other people easier.

> Well, here in this bit down here [a lower section for which tickets had not been sold in advance] it's a bit like the old terraces, we're all packed in and you can feel you'self swaying with the chants and songs – there must be far more people per space than in a ground.

> Its got to be the beer hasn't it … eveyone's really tanked up cos they're not waiting till half time or whatever to get the next drink in – you can see the TVs everywhere. It's a good job we're all on the same side or there might be trouble.[12]

The Sheffield police had a significant presence in the city centre and had obviously realized that many people had been drinking heavily and were buoyed by the match result, in which England beat Argentina 1-0. The singing and chanting continued after the match and contributed to an atmosphere where the police decided to ask bars in the city centre to close for two hours in the early evening. While there had been no hint of any trouble, the police clearly felt this was a sensible preventative measure. Given the events of two years later, when there were a number of instances of disorder around UK following the screening of England matches from Euro 2004 in Portugal, this request seems to have been justified. Although there were no incidents during the 2002 World Cup, the potential for trouble surrounding 'big occasion' pub football spectating could certainly be anticipated from the observations during this tournament.[13]

Exploring the sport spectating experience

Sport spectating would appear, by definition, to be about watching a match, game, race or event live and in person. As a spectator one can become a 'vicarious' participant in the live event. In fact, in a conference paper around ten years ago, Baines refers to travel to watch sports events as 'the leisure pursuit of being there'.[14] While part of the pleasure of 'being there' is obviously the immediate pleasure and excitement of witnessing live events, a further motivation for live presence is the retrospective recall of the event upon returning. This is a concept that has long been recognized in the more general travel and tourism literature. MacCannell, for example, highlights the importance of 'returning' as a significant part of the travel experience, explaining that 'returning home is an essential part of being a tourist – one goes only to return'.[15] MacCannell believes that tourists travel with the expectation that they will have some kind of experience of 'otherness' that will set them aside from their peers on their return. In the football context, the experience of otherness is having 'been there' at a major international fixture or for a significant result or achievement for the team one supports. For years to come, such an experience will allow the spectator to recount to friends stories of, for example, 'I was there when we beat Germany in Charleroi at Euro 2000'. Such stories can often be the source of considerable status in some groups, and as such reinforce the importance of 'being there' live and in person as a key part of the sport spectator experience. There is considerable resonance between the idea that 'being there' enhances the experience of the event upon return, and John Urry's description of the motivation to 'collect places'.[16] Here, travellers will direct their 'gaze' onto more exotic and unusual places that they can 'collect', and thus display to their friends upon return through photographs, souvenirs and, most importantly of all, the re-telling of experiences. Travel to the 2002 World Cup in Korea and Japan, for example, might be regarded as such a 'collected place', that through merchandise and storytelling can be displayed to others long after the actual trip itself has ended.

The compulsion for proximity?

In relation to the excitement of witnessing live events, some writers have discussed the importance of physical presence. Boden and Molotch, for example, in their paper on 'The Compulsion of Proximity', describe the need to be in the company of others and to feel a physical proximity to the place (or in this case, the event) being visited.[17] This is reinforced by Urry who also discusses the significant role played by, 'intermittent moments of physical proximity, to particular peoples, places or events, [which] in significant ways … is felt to be obligatory, appropriate or desirable'.[18]

It would appear, therefore, that the two key features of the sport spectating experience are, first, a desire to experience physical proximity to the live event, and second, a desire to have an experience that can be re-told to others after the event. Given these features, how does the experience of watching football in the pub measure up to live football spectating?

The immediate response, of course, would be that watching football in the pub is a secondary experience to that of watching live at the event. Consequently, people only go to the pub to watch football when travel to the event itself (for whatever reason) is not possible and the match is not being shown on terrestrial television and so, for many, it is not available to watch at home. Certainly the discussions earlier in the essay indicate that the move of live televised Premier League football to the satellite broadcaster BSkyB in 1992 served as an initial stimulus for a growth in pub football spectating in the UK. This initial stimulus was largely due to the lack of penetration of satellite television into homes which thus 'forced' many fans to watch football in pubs and bars.[19] However, some have argued that there is another force at work related to the 'sanitisation' of football grounds in the wake of the Taylor report and the commodification and commercialization of football since the mid-1990s.[20] Williams describes pubs and bars as the 'new terraces' in which fans can celebrate their identity without the increasing restrictions of 'sanitised and allegedly atmosphere-free all-seater grounds'.[21] This perspective is further reinforced by some of John Bale's work on sports places and spaces.

From space to place: sport spectators as 'place-makers'

Bale describes three views of the 1992 European Nations Cup Final in which Denmark beat Germany.[22] He refers to three spectating environments: the first was the stadium, the 'real' game; the second was the homes of millions of European television viewers. In both of these environments Bale identifies constraints – in the stadium there are constraints on both behaviour and movement, as fans are allocated a seat, one viewpoint from which to watch the game, with a range of stadium regulations to limit their 'consumption', both of the game and of alcohol. Similarly, at home viewers are, 'confined in domestic space in which domestic constraints on behaviour are as rigid – if not more so – than those in the stadium at which the game is "actually" being played'.[23]

The third environment identified by Bale was both conceptually and geographically somewhere between the stadium and home – a huge television screen erected in the open space of the Faelled (in Denmark). Here Bale notes that the fans watching in this space took part in:

> a form of carnival, with drunken fans celebrating their small nation's victory over the German 'machine'. Who is to say that the experience of the Faelled was anything but the optimal sporting

> experience for late modernity – thousands watching in open spaces … standing in opposition to the panopticised confinement which the modern stadium enforces.[24]

Bale's view of the stadium would seem to resonate with Williams's view of sanitised stadia.[25] Furthermore, it also seems to reinforce the view, discussed earlier in the essay, that the end of open terraces, which allowed some freedom of movement, has been detrimental to the atmosphere at live football.[26] Therefore, it may be that the 'optimal experience' of this third environment may have much in common with the experience of pub football spectating, but what are the key elements of this experience?

The answer may lie in sentiments expressed by voices as diverse as the British Lord Chief Justice, John Williams of the Sir Norman Chester Centre for Football Research, former football hooligan and now popular culture writer, Dougie Brimson, and Mark Hastings of the British Beer and Pub Association. Weed has noted that each of these voices refer in some way to the 'collective enjoyment' or 'shared communal experience' that is part of the pub spectating experience, with the Lord Chief Justice noting that the experience is closer to that of actually attending the match in person than it is to watching at home.[27] It certainly appears to be the case that watching in the pub is qualitatively different to both watching at home and watching live at the stadium, the pub being a sort of 'third place',[28] akin to that referred to by Bale.[29]

The concept of a shared communal experience is at the crux of understanding the attraction of the pub as a sport spectator venue and, by extension, to understanding the nature of the sport spectating experience itself. Underpinning the desire for such shared experiences is 'the place-making quality of people as sports spectators'.[30] Bale describes how an open space can become a sporting place as a result of the addition of spectators, who create a cultural and historical 'fandom' associated with that place. This can happen temporally as over time certain spaces become enclosed sporting places (e.g. Lord's cricket ground or Old Trafford football ground). In fact, some sporting places become defined more by the culture associated with them than the space in which they exist, and it is this that allows some sports clubs to move their grounds to new spaces without losing the importance of the cultural place. However, spaces can also be transformed into sporting places temporarily as spectators (and, indeed, participants) bring the culture and history of a sport or sport event with them – consider, for example, the effect of the Monaco Grand Prix or the London Marathon on spaces that usually have nothing to do with sport. Here, the place-making quality of people has transformed an urban space into a sporting place. Similarly, the open space of the Faelled, described by Bale, was transformed into a sporting place by the Danish spectators during the 1992 European Nations Cup final.[31]

It seems reasonable, therefore, to apply these ideas about the transformation from space to place to pubs and bars. Here a social space is transformed into a sporting place by the addition of football spectators. One of the most obvious signifiers of this is the different spatial and social configuration of pubs and bars when football matches are shown, particularly the weakening of conventions about 'personal social space', with people being much more prepared to be in really close proximity to people they have never met before.[32] However, while pubs are temporarily transformed into sporting places, some pubs and bars also experience a temporal transformation over a period of time as they increasingly become known as places in which to watch football, and ones to which fans will gravitate, thus reinforcing their credentials as sporting places.

Dimensions of proximity

Whilst providing a useful context, the above discussion of transformations from social spaces to sporting places, and the comments about the restrictions imposed by modern stadia, still do not satisfactorily address the two key features of the sport spectating experience described earlier, namely: the need for a physical proximity to the event, and; the importance of the re-telling of the experience of being there. In addressing the need for proximity, it is perhaps useful to begin with a consideration of Gammon's work on sports 'Halls of Fame'. Here, Gammon describes two journeys: the first, the physical journey made to the attraction itself, and the second, an imagined journey that takes place once there.[33] There certainly seems to be a process similar to this taking place in relation to pub spectating. Activities such as the singing and chanting that take place inside the pub are an attempt to make an imagined journey to the event itself. However, some authors would argue that the experience of such 'imagined journeys' will always be secondary to physical travel because of the 'powerful compulsion to proximity'. This is explained further by Boden and Molotch:

> Different social groups require or feel obligated to experience at least intermittent moments of proximity, and this makes corporeal travel necessary. This means that virtual or imagined travel will only 'replace' such mode of physical movement if they can in part simulate the pleasures and benefits of such physical proximity.[34]

The question, therefore, would seem to be: what are the pleasures and benefits of such physical proximity? In a 2002 paper entitled 'Mobility and Proximity', Urry elaborates three bases for physical proximity: 'face-to-face', 'face-the-place' and 'face-the-moment'.[35] Face-to-face proximity refers to the need for people to come together to be with others in moments of 'intense co-present fellow feeling'.[36] Szerszynski includes festivals, conferences, holidays, camps, seminars and sites of protest as among such moments, and it would seem reasonable to include major sports matches in this list.[37] Indeed, the 'intense co-present fellow feeling', which Urry describes clearly resonates with the 'shared communal experience' identified earlier from a range of sources as being a key part of pub football spectating.

Urry describes how many places need to be directly experienced by physical presence, and it is this that he labels 'face-the-place' proximity.[38] In this respect, the earlier discussions of the place-making qualities of sports spectators are important. If, as discussed above, the distinctive features that make a space a sporting place are those that are brought by the people who occupy that space, and the culture and history they bring with them, then the place experience is related to the sporting nature of the place as created by sports spectators. Consequently, in respect of pub football spectating, the 'face-the-place' basis of physical proximity is provided by the transformation of the pub as a social space into a sporting place by such spectators. As such, 'shared communal experience' is as much a part of 'face-the-place' proximity as it is of 'face-to-face' proximity.

The final basis for proximity described by Urry is 'face-the-moment', in which timing is everything:

> This occurs where what is experienced is a 'live' event programmed to happen at a very specific moment. Co-presence involves 'facing-the-moment'. Examples include political, artistic, celebratory, academic and sporting occasions, the last being especially 'live' since the outcome is unknown. Each of these generates intense moments of co-presence … [and they] cannot be missed.[39]

Given the centrality of 'shared communal experience' in the 'face-to-face' and 'face-the-place' proximities described above in relation to pub football spectating, it would seem that the pub would provide an excellent setting in which to 'face-the-moment' of a live sporting event, albeit relayed through a technological medium. The tension as a player steps up to take a penalty kick differs only by degree (i.e., the numbers of those co-present) in a crowded pub or bar from that at the ground itself. The moment is being faced collectively by all present, and the joy or despondency at the outcome is a shared and communal emotion.

Re-telling the experience

The discussions above would appear to indicate that the need for proximity described by Boden and Molotch and elaborated by Urry is not to the sport event itself, but to other people sharing a communal experience in a space that has become a sporting place in which the 'moment' of the event can be collectively faced by all those co-present.[40] Armstrong and Young describe this as, 'the creative self-expression of spontaneous group association or partisan spectatorship. Such activities when manifested around football create a comradeship of fellow fans'.[41]

However, while the creation of such a 'comradeship of fellow fans' sharing a communal experience in a pub or bar may satisfy the need for proximity, the second element of the sport spectating experience, the importance of the re-telling of the experience of being there, has not yet been accounted for. Once again, however, this can perhaps be addressed by a consideration of the nature of proximity. If the need for proximity is not to the event itself, but to a sporting place where the moment of the event can be faced with a 'comradeship of fellow fans', then the experience that is re-told after the event can be the 'shared communal experience' of the collective enjoyment of the event in the pub. Such a phenomenon clearly existed among fans who watched the England vs. Argentina match during the 2002 World Cup in the pubs and bars in Sheffield:

The carnivalesque party atmosphere continued into the early hours, with many people who had never met before chatting to each other, not only about the football and the result, but also about their experiences of watching the match in the pub![42]

In fact, the importance of the re-telling of the pub spectating experience is reinforced and perpetuated by media coverage of major football and rugby tournaments in recent years. During the 2002 World Cup, the 2003 Rugby World Cup and Euro 2004, the vast majority of front page stories were focused on the places in which people watched the matches. TV news coverage sent reporters to pubs to report on the atmosphere generated. There were many more reports from pubs and bars than from the stadia, particularly on regional news programmes that were looking for a local angle. Such coverage legitimizes watching the match in the pub as a re-tellable experience, with stories about how many people were there, how loud the pub was, and how it was as good as being there at the stadium.

A tentative conclusion

The discussion in this essay might suggest that the nature of the sport spectating experience should be reconsidered. It would seem that sports spectators' need for proximity is not for proximity to the event, but to others sharing in the experience of watching the event. It would appear that 'spontaneous group association' is a key part of the sport spectating experience, and that the primary element of sports spectatorship can be redefined: rather than being about seeing the game, it is centred on sharing the experience.[43] As such, all the elements needed for the experience are present in pubs as sports spectator venues. The need for proximity is to the experience rather than to the game.

However, in turning to the implications that thinking about sports spectating in the way proposed in this essay has for our understanding of sports fandom, the 'longevity' of the experience might usefully be considered. As Bale's description of the Faelled in Denmark, and the big screens erected in city centres and other open spaces during the 2002 World Cup show, it is not just to the pub that sports spectators gravitate to share the experience of sport spectatorship.[44] The question remains, though, is this still a secondary experience to attending an event live and in person? Is it simply a way to provide a 'shared communal experience' for those who cannot attend the event? Despite the argument outlined above about the increasing legitimacy of the pub spectating experience as one that can be 're-told', such stories are never likely to rival the stories that can be told by those who were at the live event itself. As such, while pub sport spectating can perhaps provide an experience 'in-the-moment' to rival that of being present at the event itself, the longevity of such experiences, as measured by their re-telling after the event, is likely to be much shorter than 'live' event spectating. In this respect, 'I was at the Dog and Duck pub when England beat Germany at Euro 2000' will never be a story to rival 'I was there!'.

Notes

1. This essay draws heavily on material previously published in Weed, 'The Pub as a Virtual Football Fandom Venue: An Alternative to "Being There"?'
2. Mintel, *Leisure Intelligence: Themed Pubs and Bars.*
3. Weed, 'The Story of an Ethnography'.
4. Mintel, *Leisure Intelligence: Spectator Sports*, 5.
5. Boyle and Haynes, *Power Play*; Williams, 'The Changing Face of Football'.
6. Williams, 'The Changing Face of Football', 99.
7. Brimson, *The Geezers Guide to Football*, 166.
8. Keynote, *Market Report Plus: Public Houses.*
9. Weed, 'The Story of an Ethnography'.
10. Ibid.
11. Weed, 'Ing-ger-land at Euro 2000'.
12. Weed, 'The Story of an Ethnography', 89.
13. Weed, 'The Pub as a Virtual Football Fandom Venue'.
14. Baines, 'Sports Tourism'.
15. MacCannell, *Tourist or Traveller?*, 4.
16. Urry, *The Tourist Gaze.*
17. Boden and Molotch 1994.
18. Urry, 'Mobility and Proximity', 258.
19. Mintel, *Leisure Intelligence: Spectator Sports.*
20. Williams, 'The Changing Face of Football'.
21. Ibid., 99.
22. Bale, 'Virtual Fandoms'.
23. Ibid., 275.
24. Ibid.
25. Williams, 'The Changing Face of Football'.
26. Boyle and Haines, *Power Play.*
27. Weed, 'The Pub as a Virtual Football Fandom Venue'.
28. Lloyd and Jones, 'Where Everybody Knows your Name?'
29. Bale, 'Virtual Fandoms'.
30. Ibid., 272.
31. Ibid.
32. Weed, 'The Story of an Ethnography', 80.
33. Gammon, 'Fantasy, Nostalgia and the Pursuit of What Never Was', 65.
34. Boden and Molotch 1994, 272.
35. Urry, 'Mobility and Proximity', 262.
36. Ibid., 261.
37. Szerszynski, 'The Varieties of Ecological Piety'.
38. Urry, 'Mobility and Proximity', 261.
39. Ibid.
40. Boden and Molotch, 1994; Urry, 'Mobility and Proximity'.
41. Armstrong and Young, 'Fanatical Football Chants', 180.
42. Weed, 'The Story of an Ethnography', 90.
43. Armstrong and Young, 'Fanatical Football Chants', 180.
44. Bale, 'Virtual Fandoms'.

References

Armstrong, G. and M. Young. 'Fanatical Football Chants: Creating and Controlling the Carnival'. In *Football Culture: Local Contests, Global Visions,* ed. G.P.T. Finn and R. Giulanotti, 173–211, London: Frank Cass, 1999.

Baines, S. 'Sports Tourism: The Leisure Pursuit of Being There'. Paper presented at the *4th World Leisure and Recreation Association World Congress,* Cardiff, July 1996.

Bale, J. 'Virtual Fandoms: Futurescapes of football'. In *Fanatics: Power, identity and fandom in football,* ed. A. Brown, 265–278. London: Routledge, 1998.
Boden, D. and H. Molotch. 'The compulsion to proximity'. In *Nowhere, Space, time and modernity,* ed. R. Friedland, and D. Boden, 257–286. Berkeley: University of California Press, 1994.
Boyle, R. and R. Haynes. *Power Play: Sport, the Media and Popular Culture.* Harlow: Longman, 2000.
Brimson, D. *The Geezers Guide to Football: A Lifetime of Lads and Lager.* London: Mainstream Publishing, 1998.
Gammon, S. 'Fantasy, Nostalgia and the Pursuit of What Never Was'. In *Sport Tourism: Principles and Practice,* ed. S. Gammon and J. Kurtzman, 61–72. Eastbourne: LSA, 2002.
Keynote. *Market Report Plus: Public Houses.* London: Keynote Market Information, 2003.
Lloyd, E. and I. Jones. 'Where Everybody Knows your Name? The Health Club as the new "third place"'. Paper presented at the Leisure Studies Association Conference, *Journeys in Leisure: Current and Future Alliances,* Luton, July, 2001.
MacCannell, D. *Tourist or Traveller?* London: BBC Education, 1996.
Mintel. *Leisure Intelligence: Themed Pubs and Bars.* London: Mintel, 2003a.
——— *Leisure Intelligence: Spectator Sports.* London: Mintel, 2003b.
——— *Leisure Intelligence: Satellite and Cable TV.* London: Mintel, 2003c.
Szerszynski, B. 'The Varieties of Ecological Piety'. *Worldviews: Environment, Culture, Religion* 1, no.1 (1997): 37–55.
Urry, J. *The Tourist Gaze,* 2nd Edition. London: Sage, 2002a.
——— 'Mobility and Proximity'. *Sociology 36,* no.2 (2002b): 255–74.
Weed, M.E. 'Ing-ger-land at Euro 2000: How Handbags at 20 Paces was Portrayed as a Full-scale Riot'. *International Review for the Sociology of Sport* 36, no.4 (2001): 407–24.
——— 'The Story of an Ethnography: The Experience of Watching the 2002 World Cup in the Pub'. *Soccer in Society* 7, no.1 (2006): 76–95.
——— 'The Pub as a Virtual Football Fandom Venue: An Alternative to "Being There"'?. In *Football Fandoms,* ed. S. Brown and B. Majumdar. London: Routledge, 2007.
Williams, J. 'The Changing Face of Football: A Case for National Regulation?' In *Football in the Digital Age: Whose Game is it Anyway?* ed. S. Hamil, J. Michie, C. Oughton and S. Warby. London: Mainstream Publishing, 2000.

'No systematic doping in football': A critical review

Dominic Malcolm and Ivan Waddington

Introduction

Over the last two decades a growing amount of evidence has become available about the extent of illicit drug use in sport. Although much of this evidence has been anecdotal, some has come from relatively reliable sources like parliamentary or judicial inquiries at which evidence is given under oath. Although we cannot be sure of the precise level of drug use in modern sport, most writers agree that the phenomenon has increased markedly since the Second World War and in the last three decades in particular. Mottram has recently cited drug use as 'perhaps the biggest challenge facing sport today'.[1]

Although there has recently been a study of drug use by amateur footballers in Cameroon,[2] it remains the case that there are almost no systematic data about the extent of drug use in football. We do know that the use of performance-enhancing drugs in football is not new. In 2004 a BBC radio programme provided wide-ranging evidence of the history of the use of performance-enhancing drugs in English football.[3] The programme reported use by the Arsenal team of 'pep pills' prior to an FA Cup match against West Ham United in the 1924–25 season,[4] questions raised in the House of Commons in 1939 about Wolverhampton Wanderers' use of extracts from monkey testicles,[5] Stanley Matthews's description of his use of pills that were almost certainly amphetamines prior to an FA Cup fourth round tie in 1946,[6] and testimony from Manchester United players Albert Scanlon and Harry Gregg of their use of amphetamines during the 1950s. There was, indeed, considerable concern over the use of drugs in football at this time. In response to a Council of Europe investigation in 1963, football was identified by the British government as one of three sports (the other two being cycling and athletics) with the most severe problem of drug use.

Despite such historical evidence, officials of the Fédération Internationale de Football Association (FIFA) largely assume, and publicly state, that football is relatively free from drug use. Typically, FIFA President Sepp Blatter has argued that, 'from current data, the incidence of doping in football seems to be very low and we have no evidence of systematic doping in football'.[7] Gordon Taylor, Chief Executive of the Professional Footballers Association (PFA) in England, has similarly stated that, 'I'm almost certain that we have a clean sheet over performance-enhancing drugs'.[8] Articles co-authored by FIFA's Chief Medical Officer, members of FIFA's Doping Control and Medical Committees and the editor of the *British Journal of Sports Medicine,* also reflect the belief that performance-enhancing drugs are rarely used by footballers.[9]

Such a stance is not unique to football for, as Yesalis, Kopstein and Bahrke note, sports administrators, when faced with allegations of drug use in their sports, 'have often tended to deny that a major doping problem exists ... or have at least played down its magnitude'.[10] Yet the case of football is rather different. FIFA officials base their claim on the relatively low incidence of positive tests from players. Convinced of the rigour of their drug testing programme, they have cited a number of possible explanations for these 'favourable' test results:

- 'The stringent drug testing programme occurs during the entire football season in most countries;
- Football players worldwide understand that prohibited substances in sport will neither improve their physical performance nor their football specific skills and hence are reluctant to use agents that are not effective and subject to possible sanction;
- Ongoing education campaigns by FIFA for doctors, administrators, officials and players have encouraged a drug-free culture in football.'

A fourth possible explanation, though one that is quickly dismissed as 'unlikely', is that football's drug testing programme is 'insufficient to detect drug use'.[11]

The object of this essay is to critically evaluate these claims. This is no easy task for, as Mottram has noted, '[m]eaningful data on the prevalence of use of performance-enhancing drugs in sport are difficult to obtain' for, by its very nature, drug use in sport is a covert activity.[12] Yesalis *et al.* note that there are four major sources of information about the prevalence of drug use among athletes: investigative journalism, including the writings and testimonials of athletes and others involved in sport; government investigations; surveys; and results from drug testing. All four sources suffer from significant methodological problems. Yesalis *et al.* suggest, for example, that those who have used drugs and who serve as informants 'may project their own behaviour onto others in an attempt to rationalize their drug use', producing an overestimate of the level of drug use.[13] However, they argue – almost certainly correctly – that most of the methodological difficulties are more likely to lead to an *underestimate* of the level of drug use. In particular, they argue that:

> the responses of athletes to the questions of journalists, drug use surveys, or even government investigations may be influenced by the athlete's desire to respond to questions in a socially desirable manner, memory lapse, the illegal nature of the substances being surveyed, and a general distrust of those doing the questioning.

They also note that drug testing 'is hamstrung by significant limitations in technology', and conclude that, 'All these limitations would likely result in a significant under-reporting bias'.[14]

While each of the sources of information on drug use in sport raises particular methodological difficulties, the fact that we are not dependent on a single source enables us triangulate our findings, thus increasing the validity of our conclusions. As Goode has noted in relation to the problems of estimating the extent of drug use more generally in American society:

> As a general rule, the greater the number of *independent* sources of information that reach the same conclusion, the more confidence we can have in that conclusion. That is what we mean by triangulation: getting a factual fix on reality by using several separate and disparate sources of information. To

the extent that several independent data sources say the same thing, we can say that their conclusions are more likely to be true.[15]

To a greater or lesser extent, data on drug use in football can be gleaned from each of the four major sources identified by Yesalis *et al.* In examining these data sources, we made three important assumptions which should be noted. Firstly, we focused primarily on the European game. We did this because European football has supplied the majority of positive tests in recent years (72.7% in 2004, 74.4% in 2005),[16] but also because the press coverage of European football is both greater and easier to access, and because the prior research on drug use in football, and all legal investigations, have been European based. Secondly, we focused primarily on the use of performance-enhancing rather than recreational drugs across sport, as the former is generally perceived to be rather more serious than the latter. Thirdly, in our selection of data we have primarily been concerned with evidence of the *systematic* administration of substances, for analysts largely agree that drug use which is organized at an institutional level is more problematic than that which is individual and often therefore largely ad hoc. Moreover, our focus on systematic drug use directly addresses one of the key claims that FIFA officials make about drug use in football.

This essay examines each of these four data sources to assess more adequately the prevalence of the use of illicit drugs in football, before turning to consider some of the implications of these findings. It is our contention that there are both empirical and theoretical grounds for believing, first, that a significant minority of European elite footballers are using performance-enhancing drugs and that, second, some clubs have been involved in the systematic organization and delivery of doping programmes. We also argue that there are clear grounds to suggest that the use of performance-enhancing drugs is not as widespread in football as in many other sports, and that drug use is likely to be more common in some European countries than in others. We conclude by arguing that FIFA's limited analysis of evidence of the use of performance-enhancing drugs in football leads to an underestimation of the scale of the problem which the sport faces, and thus threatens the efficacy of their anti-doping programme.

Data on performance-enhancing drug use in football

Evidence from testing

Football was the first sport to conduct drug testing at a major event, introducing tests for the 1966 World Cup and thus pre-empting the first testing at an Olympic Games by two years.[17] FIFA has also been at the forefront of moves in international sport to use blood tests, introducing them in 2002 to supplement urine tests at the Japan-Korea World Cup.[18] These testing procedures have generated few positive test results. Two players were ejected from major football tournaments for taking drugs during the 1970s: Ernest Jean Joseph of Haiti in 1974, and Willie Johnston of Scotland in 1978.[19] Between 1994 and 2005, just four (0.12%) of the 3,327 tests carried out at FIFA competitions were positive;[20] most famously Diego Maradona, captain of Argentina at the 1994 FIFA World Cup who tested positive for ephedrine. Of the 22,500 drug tests worldwide in 2004, just 92 were positive, and the majority of these positive tests derived from the use of recreational drugs such as marijuana (39 cases) and cocaine (29 cases).[21] Figures released by the World Anti-Doping Agency (WADA) indicate that of 23,478 football-related tests performed by WADA accredited laboratories in 2005, 343 produced adverse findings.[22] Drug testing in international football, therefore, has revealed remarkably little evidence of the use of drugs in general, and the use of performance-enhancing drugs in particular. FIFA's Chief Medical Officer, Jiri Dvorak, concludes that, 'It can only be assumed that team sports such as football are not as prone to misuse of performance enhancing substances as are individual sports'.[23]

Drug testing programmes in domestic football leagues have similarly produced relatively few positive results for performance-enhancing drugs. Data from UK Sport, the body which administers drug tests in British football, indicate that, over the period from 1988 to 2001–02, there were 89 positive drug tests in football in Britain (these data include the results of testing on behalf of the Welsh and Scottish Football Associations, as well as the English FA). The most commonly detected drugs were Class 1A stimulants such as pseudoephedrine and metabolites of cocaine, of which there were 40 positive cases, and marijuana, for which there were 29 positive test results.[24] It is probably the case that the metabolites of cocaine were associated with recreational drug use rather than with drugs which were taken for performance-enhancing reasons. UK Sport figures indicate that the number of positive tests per year has gradually fallen – from 14 in 2003–04, 11 in 2004–05, to just 6 in 2005–06. Cocaine and marijuana cases remain the most common. Included within these figures are a number of high profile footballers who have tested positive for recreational drug use, most notably Mark Bosnich and Adrian Mutu of Chelsea in 2002 and 2004 respectively, and this has reinforced the impression that a culture of recreational, rather than performance-enhancing, drug use exists in English football.

However, between 1998 and 2002 footballers also produced six positive tests for anabolic agents. All these players initially escaped punishment or were given suspended punishments after successfully arguing, for instance, that the substance had been ingested inadvertently. However, the Rushden and Diamond's goalkeeper Billy Turley subsequently tested positive for a recreational drug, at which point his prior suspended two year ban (he had tested positive for the banned steroid nandrolone) was enforced.[25] Turley remains the only British player to have been punished for using a performance-enhancing drug. The only English league player to have been found guilty of taking performance-enhancing drugs since this time is Middlesborough's Portuguese international Abel Xavier, who tested positive for the anabolic steroid dianabol during a UEFA Cup tie in Greece in 2005. His initial 18 month ban was subsequently reduced to 12 months by the Court of Arbitration for Sport (CAS) and subsequently the club decided to reinstate his contract.[26]

Though the actual numbers cited suggest a definition of 'positive doping samples' which may be rather different from that used by UK Sport, Dvorak *et al.* demonstrate that a greater number of positive tests for drugs have occurred in other European domestic leagues. During 2004 and 2005 there were 30 positive tests in France, 21 in both Italy and Portugal, and 20 in Belgium compared to (according to FIFA figures) just one in England.[27]

At times 'clusters' of positive tests occur. For instance, between April and October 1997, five players, from a number of top French teams, tested positive for anabolic steroids.[28] In Italy in 2000–01 nine leading players in Serie A, and a number of more minor players, tested positive for nandrolone.[29] A number of these involved leading Dutch international footballers (notably Jaap Stam and Edgar Davids), and with the Dutch captain Frank de Boer also testing positive for nandrolone whilst playing for Spanish team Barcelona, there were suggestions that a common link might have been the Dutch national squad.[30] The fact that 31 first division players in Portugal also tested positive during a five month period in 2001 suggests however that the use of nandrolone at this time was more widespread.[31] That these clusters always involve performance-enhancing drugs suggests not only an improvement/increase in testing, but also that the drug use has an underlying pattern rather than being ad hoc.

Notwithstanding this evidence, the data from drug testing suggest that the use of performance-enhancing drugs in football is relatively rare. It is important to note, however, that there is a widespread recognition among informed observers that the number of positive test results merely represents the tip of a much larger iceberg. The Dubin Commission in Canada, for instance, concluded that 'many, many more athletes than those actually testing positive have taken advantage of banned substances and practices' and that 'positive test results represent only a small proportion of actual drug users'.[32] It therefore seems probable that this pattern of positive drugs tests merely scratches the surface of a more widespread phenomenon. Other sources of information support this claim and indicate how FIFA's approach to estimating the prevalence of drug taking in football can best be describe as myopic.

Testimonials of those involved in football

A number of allegations of doping made by players and managers suggest that the amount of positive drugs tests underestimates the extent of drug use in football. In 1999, Dr Wilfried Schiesslir (club doctor with German Bundesliga club Nuremburg) and Robert Louis Dreyfus (head of *adidas* and president of Olympique Marseilles) called for the liberalization of anti-doping laws in football because the 'current system of doping control is flawed'.[33] In 2002, Dr Michel D'Hooghe, chairman of FIFA's Medical Commission, argued that players across Europe were using erythropoietin (EPO), human growth hormone and anabolic steroids. He further claimed that 'high profile stars' had started to employ their own medical specialists and that doctors known to have been active in administering performance-enhancing drugs in cycling and endurance skiing were 'suddenly appear(ing) around football clubs all over Europe'.[34] Players such as Emmanuel Petit, Marc Overmars and Gianluca Vialli have made similar allegations that leading players in the game were using performance-enhancing drugs to cope with the physical demands of playing an increasing number of games. In 1999, for instance, Petit said that, 'If the present number of games continues, something is going to give. We will all have to take drugs to survive. Some footballers already do. I know that.'[35]

Perhaps more interesting, however, is the testimony of Arsenal manager Arsene Wenger. Speaking in 2004 Wenger claimed that some players joining Arsenal had displayed symptoms of EPO use. He said, 'We have had some players come to us at Arsenal from other clubs abroad and their red blood cell count has been abnormally high. That kind of thing makes you wonder.' He went on to exonerate the players, stating that, 'There are clubs who dope players without players knowing. The club might say that they were being injected with vitamins and the player would not know that it was something different.'[36] Wenger's comments are interesting in that they are based on tangible evidence derived from Arsenal's own blood testing programme. The evidence upon which Wenger based his suggestion that such players had been subject to club-administered doping regimes is, however, less clear.

That such organized and systematic doping occurs in European football is, however, indicated by the testimony of a number of retired players. Two former Marseilles players have publicly stated that the club provided players with performance-enhancing drugs. In his autobiography (published in 2002) Marcel Desailly stated that club chairman, Bernard Tapie, had instructed the squad to take pills before big matches and that whilst some team mates refused, Desailly himself took the tablets 'several' times. Whilst Desailly was not sure what these pills were, he recalled that the box of tablets contained the warning that: 'This medicine, above a certain dose, can be considered as a doping substance for high-level sportsmen.'[37] Four years later midfielder Jean-Jacques Edelie confessed to having agreed to take an illicit substance prior to the 1993 Champions League Final. Moreover, he argued that performance-enhancing drug use occurred in all but one of the clubs for which he had played, and that at Marseilles, 'we all (except Rudi Voller) took a series of injections and I felt different during the game, as my physique responded differently under strain'.[38] Only one Marseilles player (Christophe Dugarry) tested positive for a banned substance, and then some years later.[39]

In contrast to the Marseilles evidence, allegations of a systematic doping programme at Spartak Moscow football club arose directly from the positive test of a player. Yegor Titov tested positive for bromantan (a stimulant and masking agent) whilst playing for Russia against Wales in November 2003. The Russian media subsequently claimed that this drug had been administered as part of a systematic doping programme at Spartak, citing the sudden withdrawal of Spartak players on the eve of Russia's match against Ireland in September 2003 as suspicious. Two former Spartak players, Vladislav Vashchyuk and Maxim Demenko, subsequently provided testimony of their participation in this doping programme. Demenko recalled that, 'Small white pills were given to first team players before each game', and Vashchyuk said that doctors often used a drip to administer banned drugs.[40]

Finally, in 2006 *Le Monde* accused Spanish clubs Real Madrid, Barcelona, Valencia and Real Betis of having employed the services of Spanish doctor Eufemiano Fuentes. Fuentes was then being investigated by a Spanish judicial inquiry into doping in sport and was arrested in May 2006 on charges of crimes against public health. Though Barcelona and Madrid denied the allegations, and insisted that Fuentes had never been linked to their players either formally or informally, the journalist responsible, Stephane Mandard, claimed that he had seen Fuentes' handwritten notes mentioning the teams as having been treated by him.[41] These allegations support D'Hooghe's assessment of drug use in European football cited earlier.

Evidence from testimonials therefore suggests that organized doping programmes have existed at a number of leading clubs in several European countries. An interesting aspect of these testimonials is that none have come from players who have been found guilty of doping offences, but have been volunteered by those who have been neither accused nor convicted of taking performance-enhancing drugs. Indeed, the players have largely projected themselves as 'victims' in these scenarios, either given insufficient information or misled by doctors and football club administrators. Clearly some have stood to benefit commercially from such revelations (e.g. through increased sales of an autobiography), but this notwithstanding, these testimonials point to a relatively coherent and consistent picture: that in some European countries, leading football clubs have administered systematic doping programmes.

Government and judicial investigations

Across sport the most penetrating investigations of doping have come from government inquiries and quasi-legal investigations. It is widely acknowledged, for instance, that the Dubin Commission of Inquiry established in Canada following the positive drug test of Ben Johnson at the 1988 Olympic Games,[42] and the inquiry headed by Australian Senator Black,[43] have furnished us with the greatest understanding of the use of performance-enhancing drugs in sport. Neither of these looked at drug use in football, but there have been two inquiries – one in Germany and one in Italy – that are relevant here.

Post-unification inquiries into the state-sponsored doping programmes operated in Eastern Germany provide perhaps the most comprehensive and compelling evidence of doping in sport. These inquiries have shown that elite athletes were systematically doped by the East German state and were tested in the GDR prior to competition to ensure that athletes representing their country could evade official drug testing. As in other sports, the East German national football teams were 'required to use drugs in order to compete successfully against other nations'.[44] Research has, for instance, revealed records of drugs tests which demonstrated widespread and systematic use of amphetamines.[45] The use of performance-enhancing drugs within the national leagues was, however, officially forbidden by the East German state, in an attempt to promote greater playing equality between clubs. However, not all clubs complied with state orders, and used the knowledge developed at national level within their own club-based systematic doping programmes. Football, therefore, was no different from any other sport in communist East Germany, characterized by systematic doping programmes at both club and international levels prior to 1989.

The events surrounding inquiries into drug use in Italian football are rather more complicated. In that they have revealed doping offences involving leading players at a leading club, and in that they relate to democratic Western societies in which evidence of systematic doping programmes has been less common, they have perhaps produced more sensational findings.

Events were triggered by an interview with the then AS Roma manager, Zdenek Zeman, published in *L'Espresso Magazine* in July 1998.[46] Zeman stated that the use of performance-enhancing drugs was rife in Serie A, and suggested that football needed to 'come out of the pharmacy'. In particular he referred to two Juventus players, Gianluca Vialli and Alessandro Del Piero, whose muscular development had 'surprised him'. Given the implication of illegal drug use, Vialli and Del Piero started legal proceedings against Zeman. Debate in the Italian and international press generated pressure sufficient to lead the Public Attorney of Turin, Raffaele Guarinielo, to start an investigation. Guarinielo interviewed firstly Zeman and then Sandro Donati, a member of the Italian National Olympic Committee's (CONI) medical commission, leading to two significant findings.

On the basis of the interview with Zeman, Guarinielo ordered a raid on the Juventus premises which revealed that the club held 281 different pharmaceutical substances. The majority of these substances were not on the IOC's list of banned substances, though at least five anti-inflammatory drugs containing banned substances were found.[47] It was, however, the sheer quantity of pharmaceuticals found that raised suspicions for, as Gianmartino Benzi, medical advisor to Guarinielo, noted, 'the club was equipped like a small hospital'.[48] As a witness at the subsequent trial suggested, 'either the players were always sick or they took drugs without justification ... to improve performance'.[49]

Donati claims that his accusations of irregular testing procedures led Guarinielo to order that the IOC accredited Acqua Acetosa laboratory in Rome be searched.[50] Police discovered documents hidden in the building's air vents and the laboratory was closed. The president of CONI resigned and the director of the laboratory was sacked when it came to light that some of the doping controls conducted on footballers did not include tests for the detection of anabolic steroids or other hormones. It was later revealed that some documents relating to drug tests in football had disappeared,[51] and that laboratory technicians had been told not to publicize positive test results.[52] Further documents revealed that some 24 Parma players had abnormally high haematocrit levels, indicative of the probable use of EPO. Government raids on doping laboratories around Italy discovered 'a trail of abuse involving officers who had falsified documents and were guilty of fraud in relation to doping'.[53]

The steady accumulation of evidence led Gauriniello to bring charges against two Juventus club officials. In January 2002 Juventus managing director Antonio Giraudo and club doctor Riccardo Agricola were charged with supplying pharmaceutical products to several of the club's players between July 1994 and September 1998, a period in which Juventus won three Italian titles and the European Cup. It was acknowledged that the substances in question were legal, but that they were administered in such a manner as to produce the same effects as illicit substances.[54]

The trial lasted almost two years, during which some of the world's leading players, including Zinedine Zidane, Roberto Baggio, Del Piero and Vialli, were called as witnesses. The players stated that they had taken legal substances – for instance Zidane revealed that he had used creatine – but the testimony of two court-appointed independent witnesses proved crucial. Eugenio Muller, a pharmacologist, stated that there could be 'no therapeutic justification' for the club's administration of prescription-only drugs. Three drugs were cited in particular: Samyr, an anti-depressant, was taken by 23 players; Neoton, a drug containing creatine used for heart conditions, was taken by 14 players; and Voltaren, a pain killer and anti-inflammatory drug, was used by 32 players. In the case of Voltaren in particular, the drug was not used to treat isolated or occasional injuries; rather, according to Muller, its use was 'planned, continuous and substantial'.[55]

Juventus lawyers protested that the use of these substances was not illegal and club president Vittorio Chiusano argued that these were 'products widely used by many other Italian footballers'.[56] Post-trial revelations suggest that he was probably correct (see below), but new charges introduced during the trial relating to the use of EPO proved more damning. Club records produced in court indicated that Juventus' own blood testing programme revealed particularly high haematocrit levels from a number of players. On two occasions Didier Deschamps recorded increases of 20% in the space of a few months.[57] Deschamps' red blood cell count of 51.2% (45–47% is considered normal), would have been sufficient for cycling's international governing body (the UCI) to withdraw a cyclist from racing.[58] Reviewing these records, a leading haematologist, Giuseppe d'Onofrio, said that it was 'very probable' that Deschamps was among seven players who had taken small doses of EPO. D'Onofrio however was 'practically certain' that two other players – Antonio Conte and Alessio Tacchinardi – had used EPO to overcome bouts of anaemia, and other reports have suggested that the judge listed as many as 20 players involved in the 'chronic use' of EPO.[59] The court found this evidence compelling and in November 2004 Agricola was given a 22 month suspended jail sentence for supplying performance-enhancing drugs, barred from practising medicine for 22 months and fined 2,000 Euros. Giraudo was cleared of all charges and a third defendant, Giovanni Rossano, a pharmacist accused of supplying drugs on false prescriptions, agreed a plea bargain and was fined 5,000 Euros.

Though government and judicial inquiries into drug use in football have been few in number, where they have been undertaken, legally scrutinized evidence has been produced which indicates that organized and systematic doping programmes have occurred in elite European football. However, by their very nature, inquiries tend to provide us with depth rather than breadth of understanding and can therefore only point us towards the existence of relatively small pockets of drug taking in football. What is interesting about the Juventus trial is not simply that it provides almost incontrovertible evidence of a club-administered doping programme, but that the doping which it revealed is almost identical to that described in various player and manager testimonials. There are, therefore, good grounds for believing that such practices are more widespread.

Evidence from surveys

An alternative way of assessing how widespread is the use of performance-enhancing drugs in sport is through athlete surveys. A number of such surveys have been undertaken in different sports and different countries,[60] but there has been, to date, just one comprehensive survey of drug use in professional football, conducted by ourselves and colleagues in 2003.[61] With the aid and support of the English Professional Footballers Association (PFA), reply-paid postal questionnaires were sent to the home addresses of all 2,863 members of the Association. 706 questionnaires were returned, giving a response rate of just under 25%. Such surveys are not without their methodological problems, for it is clear that athletes have a great deal, potentially, to lose from the truthful reporting of illegitimate activities. As Mottram notes, elite athletes are generally reluctant to discuss drug use in their sport and thus low response rates are to be expected.[62] However, we obtained responses from players of different kinds (e.g. in terms of ages, playing division and frequency of first team appearances) suggesting that a representative sample was obtained. In an attempt to improve response rates the survey asked not about players' personal use of drugs but, less threateningly, asked them to estimate the prevalence of drug use in football and whether they personally knew players who used drugs. Whilst such surveys cannot be expected to give a precise indication of the extent of drug use in sport, it is important to bear in mind that the results will almost certainly underestimate, rather than overestimate, the real level of drug use.

A half of all players (49%) felt that there was no use of illicit performance-enhancing drugs in professional football. About a third (34%) felt that performance-enhancing drugs were being used by some players, though the great majority felt that their use was rare. In this regard, 23% of players felt that performance-enhancing drugs were used by under 2% of players; 8% felt that between 3–5% of players used such drugs and less than 1% felt that performance-enhancing drugs were being used by 10% or more of their fellow professionals (17% of players expressed no opinion).

Almost 6% of respondents (39 players in total) indicated that they personally knew players who used performance-enhancing drugs. Those who personally knew players who used performance-enhancing drugs were spread across all four divisions, with 18% playing for Premier League clubs, 24% for clubs in Division One of the Nationwide League, 36% for Second Division clubs and 21% for clubs in Division Three. Of the players who indicated that they knew players who used performance-enhancing drugs, most (68%) indicated that the drug-using players were at a previous club, though one in five indicated that the drug-using players were at their current club, and 12% indicated that they knew drug-using players at *both* their current and previous clubs. In all, four Premier League players, two First Division players, four Second Division players and four Third Division players indicated they knew players at their current club who used performance-enhancing drugs.

The research also found that the use of recreational drugs is considerably more widespread than is the use of performance-enhancing drugs. Only 29% of players felt that recreational drugs were not used by professional footballers. Almost 28% of respondents felt that recreational drugs were used by fewer than 2% of players, 13% felt that between 3–5% of players used recreational drugs, 9% felt they were used by 6–10% of players while 4% felt that recreational drugs were used by more than 10% of players (18% of players expressed no opinion).

Approaching a half of all players (45%) indicated that they personally knew players who used recreational drugs. Among Premier League players, 31% personally knew players who used such drugs, compared with 45% of players in the First Division of the Nationwide League, 44% of Second Division players and 52% of Third Division players. Of those who knew players who used recreational drugs, 15% indicated that the players who used such drugs were at their present club, 63% indicated the drug-using players were at a previous club while 23% knew players at *both* their current and previous clubs who used recreational drugs. In all, 16 Premier League players, 23 First Division players, 21 Second Division players and 39 Third Division players indicated they knew players at their current club who used recreational drugs.

These data provide clear evidence that performance-enhancing drugs are used in English professional football, though their use appears to be quite rare; by contrast, the use of recreational drugs is much more common. That player estimates of the proportion of footballers using performance-enhancing drugs are relatively low, and that players with personal knowledge of performance-enhancing drug users are spread across the divisions, suggest that in English football the doping of players as part of systematic, club-run, programmes does not occur, but rather those using performance-enhancing drugs normally act independently of their employers.

Discussion

Three main questions arise from our examination of the data relating to the use of performance-enhancing drugs in European football. First, how does doping in football compare with that in other sports? Second, are there grounds for believing that performance-enhancing drug use in football varies from country to country? And third, why is it that the scale of drug use in football as indicated by the testing programmes is much lower than that indicated by other sources?

The prevalence of doping in football relative to other elite sports

According to WADA, just 1.46% of drug tests in football proved positive in 2005, compared to an average of 2.12% for international sports in general, suggesting that drug use is less prevalent in football than in many other sports.[63] Moreover, a survey of 1,300 elite British athletes across nine sports (including football) conducted by the *Independent* in 1998, found that 54% of all athletes believed that up to 30% of competitors in their sport were using performance-enhancing drugs; 5% believed that between 30 and 60% were using drugs; and that 4% believed that over 60% of competitors were using drugs. In this survey, 20% of those from the sports of weightlifting and powerlifting admitted using anabolic agents, and 15% of those from rugby league admitted using testosterone.[64] Whilst almost a half of all PFA members felt that there was no use of illicit performance-enhancing drugs in professional football, no weightlifters or rugby league players, and just 3% of track and field athletes responding to the *Independent* survey made a comparable claim. Indeed in a more recent *Independent* survey, 84% of footballers in England expressed the view that the sport had no problem at all with the use of performance-enhancing drugs.[65]

Cross-sport comparison therefore suggests that the use of performance-enhancing drugs in football, or at least English football, is rather more limited than it is in other sports. One explanation for this disparity is the structure of football relative to other sports. All sports require a combination of physical ability and technical skill, and those sports which place a premium on the former rather than the latter are the sports in which the performance gains from the use of drugs are likely to be greatest.[66] Thus participants in those sports which are based largely on physical strength and power – e.g. weightlifting, cycling, athletics – are most likely to use performance-enhancing drugs, whilst those sports which are primarily skill-based, such as golf or football, are likely to have lower rates of performance-enhancing drug use. Sepp Blatter has similarly argued that, 'footballers have absolutely nothing to gain from taking drugs because – in contrast to other sports – they need a vast array of qualities and skills to succeed in the game, such as strength, endurance, speed, intelligence, tactical understanding and ball control'.[67]

Whilst such structural properties of different sports are clearly important factors influencing not just whether or not participants are likely to use performance-enhancing substances, but also the types of substances they use, the relative strength and skill requirements in a sport are not static, but vary over time. In this regard it is not the case, as Blatter claims, that 'footballers have absolutely nothing to gain' from taking drugs for, in addition to the data on the use of performance-enhancing drugs discussed above, there is growing evidence to suggest that footballers use significant quantities and varieties of legal pharmaceutical products in search of improved performance. For example, the survey of members of the English PFA found that 58% of players used vitamin pills, 37% used creatine and 24% used protein powders.[68] Dvorak has stated that creatine is 'widely used' by footballers in Italy, France, Portugal and Spain (interestingly the English league was not mentioned in this list) and has further commented that he has been struck by 'how much medication is used at FIFA tournaments'.[69]

In the wake of the Italian judicial inquiry, two further 'scandals' provided supporting evidence for this point. In April 2005, film footage was broadcast which showed Parma footballer Fabio Cannavaro using a drip on the eve of the 1999 UEFA Cup final. It was later claimed that the drip contained Neoton,[70] a drug cited in the Juventus trial. Juan Sebastion Veron indicated that the club made the substance available to all the players and he further asserted that 'All the teams (in Italy) use it.'[71] Secondly, in 2005 Florentine public prosecutor Luigi Bocciolini opened an investigation into the deaths of three former Fiorentina players whose deaths were suspected of being linked to their use of drugs. Suspicion stemmed from Guariniello's investigation which revealed an apparently high incidence of cancer, leukaemia and diseases of the nervous system amongst players who had appeared for top Italian clubs. In addition, former Fiorentina player Nello Saltutti told Guariniello that before every match 'they gave us medicines, telling us they were vitamins'.[72] One such drug was Micoren, banned by the IOC in 2000. Despite warnings that prolonged use of Micoren could have adverse effects on the arteries, Saltutti claimed to have used it approximately 300 times during a 500 match career. In 2003, at the age of 56, he died of a heart attack.

Whilst, on the one hand, a clear distinction should be drawn between these events and the illegal use of drugs to enhance sporting performance; on the other hand, their use demonstrates a perceived need amongst footballers to enhance physical performance, and a willingness on their part to use medical substances to obtain that goal. Moreover, the evidence quite consistently points towards the use of products that build stamina and improve cardiovascular fitness. It might be concluded, therefore, that whilst the physical requirements of football mean that drug taking to enhance performance may not be as widespread as it is in sports such as cycling and weightlifting, this is not to say that footballers have no use for such substances. Moreover, recent developments in the way that the game is played – in particular, the increasing pace of the game and the increased number of games players at top clubs are expected to play in a season – suggest that the demands for these substances might well be increasing and thus that patterns of drug use in football may converge with those in other, more strength- and power-based, sports in future.

The use of performance-enhancing drugs in football in different European countries

The evidence reviewed here suggests that the use of performance-enhancing drugs and the administration of systematic doping programmes vary across Europe, but are particularly uncommon in England. Can such a contention be justified?

Waddington argues that the increased use of performance-enhancing drugs in sport is the product of the conjuncture of two social processes: the medicalization of social life in general and of sport in particular, and the 'increasing competitiveness' (i.e. de-amateurization, politicization and commercialization) of sport.[73] However, the degree to which these two processes have converged appears to vary from sport to sport and from nation to nation. One notable aspect of the development of sports medicine has been the relative slowness with which it became established in England.[74] Moreover, research conducted into the contemporary provision of sports medicine in English professional football has indicated that football club doctors are most usually family doctors, recruited on the basis of family or personal connections with the club. This research similarly pointed towards an 'old boy's network' of recruitment amongst physiotherapists at football clubs. Significantly, few of the medical staff working in professional football clubs have specialist qualifications in sports medicine or much experience of practising medicine in other sports contexts.[75] In sum, this research indicates that the medical care of players has generally been viewed as a relatively low priority in English football. In this sense, it might be argued that, by comparison with the situation in some other European countries, English football has been relatively untouched by the broader medicalization process and, we suggest, this has had the unintended consequence of also limiting the extent of the application of sports medicine in general, and the use of drugs in particular, as part of the search for improved performance.

An important caveat to this argument, however, is to note the international nature of football, and the increasing heterogeneity of English football in particular. The English football league is the most cosmopolitan in the world,[76] and particularly notable has been the influence not just of overseas players, but also of overseas managers in recent times. If doping is more prevalent and more organized in some continental countries, then it follows that the recruitment by English clubs of players and managers from clubs in those countries in which drug use is more common and more organized may have some unintended consequences; in particular, it may lead to the increased use not only of legitimate sports medicine practice, but also to the increased use of illegal performance-enhancing practices.

Doping control in football

Finally we might ask why it is that the scale of drug use in football as indicated by testing programmes is much lower than that indicated by other sources. Firstly it should be re-emphasized that drugs tests clearly do not reveal the true extent of doping in any sport. For example, though we now know that illegal drug use was widespread during the 1998 Tour de France, not one rider tested positive for performance-enhancing drugs during the event.[77] However, whilst general criticisms can be made of the ability of doping control programmes to reveal the prevalence of drug use, particular criticisms can be made of the doping control programmes in football. These criticisms can be combined under the following headings: failures in testing procedure; attempts by clubs to circumvent drugs testing; and the inability of football administrators properly to enforce doping controls.

As revealed in the Juventus inquiry, during the 1990s there appear to have been specific instances of malpractice by testers which served to obscure the extent of drug use, or to cover up those positive tests which did occur. It is interesting to note that the re-opening of the Rome laboratory in 2000 coincided with an unparalleled number of positive tests in Italian football in the following season. Italian football now conducts an extensive doping control programme entailing three times as many tests as in English football,[78] including the testing of two players from each side after every Serie A match.[79] As stringent as this testing programme appears, it is not mandatory for players to take these tests. Though regulators state that a test refusal will make a player ineligible for the national side, Lazio midfielder Rino Gattuso was selected to play for Italy in March 2005, just one week after declining to take a urine test.[80]

Testing procedures in English football are similarly problematic. Though the Football Association rightly argues that football is the most tested sport (there were 1,516 tests carried out between April 2004 and March 2005),[81] such is the scale of the professional game in England, and such is the distribution of tests throughout different levels of the game, that the testing programme appears to have only a limited deterrent effect. For instance, tests are rarely conducted after professional football matches, with only eight of the 380 Premiership matches in 2000–01 subject to doping controls.[82] The survey of PFA members indicated that only about a third of professional footballers are likely to be tested during the course of a season, and that a substantial majority (60%) not unreasonably felt that they were unlikely to be tested in the next 12 months. This compares very badly with other sports in the UK. For instance, a Sports Council survey (1996) found that 77% of elite track and field athletes had been tested by in the UK and 37% had been tested by other agencies in the previous year.[83] In line with these findings, former Liverpool manager Gerard Houllier noted that clubs are likely to be visited only two or three times a year, and he called for more frequent testing.[84]

Concerns have also been expressed about the rigour of the testing procedures in English football. In October 2003, England and Manchester United defender Rio Ferdinand failed to present himself to doping control officers at the club's training ground. Ferdinand claimed that, due to the stress of moving house, he had forgotten that he had been required to provide a sample. Ferdinand was subsequently suspended from football for eight months for his failure to undergo the drugs test (failure to comply with testing is deemed an offence equivalent to testing positive for a performance-enhancing drug) but, more interestingly for present purposes, the inquiry into this incident revealed how lax procedures had been. The Ferdinand case revealed that at this time there was no requirement upon testers to accompany footballers until they provided a sample. Rather, testers were forced to act through club medical officers who then presented players for testing.[85] Such an arrangement is unusual in sport, for it presents the opportunity for players, in collaboration with the club's medical staff, to avoid testing positive (e.g. through the administration of a masking drug). Thus, whilst doping control in English football may appear relatively comprehensive, the sampling and testing procedures have been such that users of performance-enhancing drugs could have evaded testing positive.

A further point of concern is the extent to which clubs perform their own testing programmes. Evidence presented in the Juventus inquiry demonstrated that Juventus had an internal drug testing programme and Lazio has similarly stated that it regularly drug tested its entire squad.[86] However, internally administered testing programmes appear to be even more widespread amongst English clubs. It has been claimed that 'almost all of England's top clubs require players to give samples several times a season' and that 'all test results are kept secret'.[87] The objection to clubs performing their own drug tests is that this information may enable them to shelter some players from official doping controls (as the East German state did prior to 1989), and indeed, two English clubs, Arsenal and Chelsea, have been sanctioned by the FA for their illegal testing of players.[88]

Finally, it should be noted that various governing bodies of football have been criticized for their limited commitment to, and enforcement of, anti-doping policies. In particular, FIFA have clashed with WADA, the role of which is 'to promote, coordinate, and monitor at the international level the fight against doping in sport in all its forms'. Most analysts have seen WADA as a very significant development in anti-doping policy. Houlihan, for example, sees it as, 'play(ing) an important part in raising the level of confidence in drug testing procedures',[89] but throughout its history FIFA, alongside cycling's UCI, has been WADA's 'sternest critic'.[90] FIFA has continually resisted WADA's attempts to standardize doping procedures and penalties across sports and across national boundaries. FIFA argues that the imposition of mandatory suspensions is legally problematic as it fails to take into account the extent of the offender's guilt, and thus contravenes the principles of Swiss sanction law.[91] The objection that bodies like the International Olympic Committee (IOC) have to this position is that such clauses mean that standardized minimum penalties cannot be enforced and indeed bans in football (12 months for Abel Xavier) seem to be shorter than in some other sports, e.g. athletics (24 months for Dwain Chambers). IOC president Jacques Rogge has been critical of the lenient penalties in football, and when FIFA continued to refuse to sign up to the WADA code it came perilously close to being dropped from the 2004 Athens Olympic Games. Eventually, in May 2004, FIFA and WADA signed a 'cooperative agreement' in which WADA agreed to fully respect FIFA's stipulations of individual case management and flexibility when imposing sanctions, whilst FIFA accepted WADA's right to refer football related cases to CAS. Whilst the differences between WADA and FIFA have largely now been settled, in 2006 WADA President Dick Pound was still citing cycling and 'some elements within FIFA' as the only problematic governing bodies in international sport.[92]

Inconsistencies between FIFA and other international governing bodies of sport are further compounded by FIFA's inability to gain compliance from national football federations. Sepp Blatter rebuked English FA Chairman Geoff Thompson over his handling of the aforementioned Rio Ferdinand case,[93] and since this time FIFA has taken harder action against the national associations of France, Italy and the Netherlands who have been fined between £4,500 and £6,000 for failing to adhere to FIFA's minimum punishment for doping infringements.[94] Not only is FIFA out of step with the majority of the world sporting community over punishments for the illegal use of performance-enhancing drugs, but the considerable autonomy wielded by national governing bodies of football provides significant inconsistencies within football itself.

Conclusion

The use of performance-enhancing drugs in football is a problem the significance of which has not previously been fully recognized by the game's administrators. Whilst Dvorak *et al.* argue that 'any estimation of the problem can be considered as merely an unscientific hypothesis or speculation',[95] it is not the case that all estimations are equally speculative. Whilst FIFA medical officials base their estimation of the scale of drug use in football solely on the basis of drug testing results, our triangulation of sources is likely to provide a more accurate assessment. Whilst we recognize that there are considerable methodological difficulties with each of the data sources drawn upon here, the fact that they provide relatively consistent and coherent evidence leads us to believe that we can have a relatively high level of confidence in the accuracy of our depiction of this phenomenon. Moreover, it should be re-iterated that as Yesalis *et al.* note, it is almost certainly the case that the sources used are likely to lead to an underestimate, rather than an overestimate, of drug use in the sport.

We should, however, be circumspect in our claims for we think that there are both empirical and theoretical grounds to think that the use of performance-enhancing drugs in football is not as widespread as it is in other sports. However, it is worth reflecting on the factors which FIFA's Chief Medical Officer, Jiri Dvorak, and others have forwarded as possible explanations for the relatively low use of performance-enhancing drugs in football.[96] It will be recalled that Dvorak *et al.* suggest that the stringent nature of the drug testing programme, the perception amongst footballers that such drugs are ineffective ways of improving performance, and the success of educational campaigns which have fostered a drug-free culture in football may all contribute to the occurrence of relatively few positive tests in the game. However, our analysis indicates that footballers do not see the drug testing programme as particularly stringent, and that footballers actively seek out substances which they think will increase their physical capabilities. The prevalence of recreational drug use in the game would also suggest that football does not have a 'drug-free culture'. Indeed the most likely explanation for the apparent lack of drug use in football is the very explanation that Dvorak *et al.* dismiss out of hand; that is to say, the existing testing programme is simply not very effective at detecting drug use.

Notes

1. Mottram, *Drugs in Sport*, cover notes.
2. Ama *et al.*, 'Football and Doping'.
3. BBC Radio 4, 'Monkey Glands and Purple Hearts', 8 March 2004.
4. Joy, *Forward Arsenal*, 32–3.
5. *Hansard*, 27 April 1939.
6. Matthews, *The Way It Was*, 216–18.
7. Blatter, 'FIFA's Commitment to Doping-Free Football'.
8. Samuel, 'English football should not be on such a high over record for catching the game's drugs cheats', *The Times*, 19 October 2005.
9. Dvorak *et al.*, 'FIFA's Approach to Doping in Football'; Dvorak, McCrory and D'Hooghe, 'FIFA's Future Activities in the Fight Against Doping'.
10. Yesalis, Kopstein and Bahrke, 'Difficulties in Estimating the Prevalence of Drug Use Among Athletes', 45.
11. Dvorak, McCrory and D'Hooghe, 'FIFA's Future Activities in the Fight Against Doping', 58.
12. Mottram, *Drugs in Sport*, 357.
13. Yesalis, Kopstein and Bahrke, 'Difficulties in Estimating the Prevalence of Drug Use Among Athletes', 45.
14. Ibid., 56.
15. Goode, *Between Politics and Reason*, 14.
16. Dvorak *et al.*, 'FIFA's Approach to Doping in Football', 5. The distribution of positive tests, however, is probably not unrelated to the global distribution of FIFA/WADA accredited laboratories, two-thirds of which (20 out of 33) are in Europe.
17. Houlihan, 'Doping in Sport', 225.
18. FIFA, *Activity Report*, 79.
19. Cashmore, *Making Sense of Sports*, 143.

20. Dvorak *et al.*, 'FIFA's Approach to Doping in Football', 4.
21. *FIFA Magazine*, June 2005, 68. Cocaine is a stimulant and therefore technically a performance-enhancing drug. However it is more widely used as a recreational drug, both within and outside of sport.
22. WADA, *Adverse Analytical Findings*.
23. Dvorak *et al.*, 'FIFA's Approach to Doping in Football', 4.
24. UK Sport, *Anti-Doping Report 2001/2002*.
25. *The Guardian*, 24 December 2004.
26. *The Times*, 20 October 2006.
27. Dvorak *et al.*, 'FIFA's Approach to Doping in Football', 5.
28. Malcolm, 'White Lines', 18.
29. 'Testing times for football', BBC Sport, 9 May 2001. http://news.bbc.co.uk/sport.
30. 'Dutch launch drug probe', BBC Sport, 9 May 2001. http://news.bbc.co.uk/sport.
31. *The Observer*, 31 March 2002.
32. Dubin, *Commission of Inquiry*, 349–50.
33. '"Legalise drugs" – adidas boss', *The Observer*, 17 October 1999.
34. Campbell, 'Is football in denial over drugs?', *The Observer*, 31 March 2002.
35. Ibid.
36. Lichfield and Harris, 'Football: Wenger suspects foreigners of doping', *The Observer,* 31 March 2002. *Independent*, 8 October 2004.
37. Campbell, 'Is football in denial over drugs?', *The Observer*, 31 March 2002.
38. 'Marseille doping scandal rocks Milan', *Channel 4*, 21 January 2006. http://www.channel4.com.
39. *The Guardian*, 30 June 1999. Dugarry was subsequently acquitted of a doping offence due to a testing technicality (*The Observer*, 17 October 1999).
40. *Mosnews*, 3 May 2005. http://www.mosnews.com/
41. *International Herald and Tribune*, 9 December 2006.
42. Dubin, *Commission of Inquiry*.
43. Australian Parliament, *Drugs in Sport*.
44. Spitzer, 'Sport and the Systematic Infliction of Pain', 112.
45. Spitzer, *Doping in der GDR*, 351.
46. Grayson and Ioannidis, 'Drugs, Health and Sporting Values', 247.
47. *The Times*, 1 December 2004.
48. Dunne, 'The drugs scandal that blackens the name of Juve's team of the nineties', *The Independent*, 1 December 2004.
49. 'Justice of the pieces', *Sports Illustrated*, 7 December 2005. http://www.SI.com.
50. Donati, *Anti-doping*.
51. *The Times*, 27 November 2004.
52. Grayson and Ioannidis, 'Drugs, Health and Sporting Values', 247.
53. Donati, *Anti-doping*.
54. 'Juventus doping trial opens', BBC Sport, 31 January 2002. http://news.bbc.co.uk/sport.
55. Dunne, 'The drugs scandal that blackens the name of Juve's team of the nineties', *Independent*, 1 December 2004.
56. 'Juventus doping trial opens', BBC Sport, 31 January 2002. http://news.bbc.co.uk/sport.
57. Donati, *Anti-doping*.
58. *The Times*, 1 December 2004.
59. *Independent*, 1 December 2004; *Independent on Sunday*, 27 March 2005.
60. Scarpino, Arrigo and Benzi, 'Evaluation of Prevalence of Doping'; Anshel, 'A Survey of Elite Athletes'. See also Waddington, 'Changing Patterns of Drug Use'.
61. Waddington *et al.*, 'Drug Use in English Professional Football'.
62. Mottram, *Drugs in Sport*, 370.
63. WADA, *Adverse Analytical Findings*.
64. *Independent*, 9 December 1998.
65. Ibid., 12 April 2006.
66. Malcolm, 'White Lines', 19.
67. *FIFA Magazine*, March 2004, 3.
68. Waddington *et al.*, 'Drug Use in English Professional Football'.
69. Dvorak, 'There is Nothing to Gain from Using Drugs', 18–19.
70. *International Herald and Tribune*, 30 April 2005.

71. 'Veron in Cannavaro Video'. http://www.ergogenics.org/neoton.html.
72. 'Football: Italy's drug scandal: Outside help Sought in Juve case', *Guardian*, 3 March 2005.
73. Waddington, *Sport, Health and Drugs*, 127–8.
74. Waddington, 'The Development of Sports Medicine'; Malcolm, 'Unprofessional Practice?'.
75. Waddington, Roderick and Naik, 'Methods of Appointment and Qualifications of Club Doctors'; Waddington, 'Jobs for the Boys'.
76. Maguire and Pearton, 'Global Sport'.
77. Waddington, *Sport, Health and Drugs*, Chapter 9.
78. *The Times*, 19 October 2005.
79. *The Observer*, 31 March 2002.
80. *Independent on Sunday*, 27 March 2005.
81. *The Guardian*, 18 June 2005.
82. *The Observer*, 31 March 2002.
83. Sports Council, *Doping Control in the UK*.
84. *The Guardian*, 25 February 2004.
85. Ibid., 19 October 2004; *Independent on Sunday*, 30 November 2003.
86. BBC Sport, 21 April 2001. http://news.bbc.co.uk/sport.
87. Campbell, 'Premiership players are drug tested in secret', *The Observer*, 23 March 2003.
88. Ibid., 23 March 2003; *The Guardian*, 9 September 2005.
89. Houlihan, *Dying to Win*, 172.
90. *The Guardian*, 4 March 2003.
91. *FIFA Magazine*, September 2004, 68; Dvorak *et al*., 'FIFA's Approach to Doping in Football', 10.
92. *The Guardian*, 19 September 2006.
93. Ibid., 17 December 2003.
94. *FIFA.Com*, 28 September 2004; *The Guardian*, 19 October 2004.
95. Dvorak *et al*., 'FIFA's Approach to Doping in Football', 4.
96. Dvorak, McCrory and D'Hooghe, 'FIFA's Future Activities', 58.

References

Ama, P.F.M., B. Betnga, V.J. Ama Moor and J.P. Kamga. 'Football and Doping: Study of African Amateur Footballers'. *British Journal of Sports Medicine* 37 (2003): 307–10.

Anshel, M.H. 'A Survey of Elite Athletes on the Perceived Causes of Using Banned Drugs in Sport'. *Journal of Sport Behaviour* 14, no.4 (1991): 283–307.

Australian Parliament. *Drugs in Sport: an Interim Report of the Senate Standing Committee on Environment, Recreation and the Arts*. Canberra: Australian Parliament, 1989.

Blatter, Sepp. 'FIFA's Commitment to Doping-Free Football'. *British Journal of Sports Medicine* 40, Supplement 1 (2006): 1.

Cashmore, Ellis. *Making Sense of Sports*. London: Routledge, 1996, 2nd edition.

Donati, Sandro. *Anti-doping: The Fraud Behind the Stage*. Vingsted, Denmark: Sports Intelligence Unit, 2001. Reproduced, www.ergogenics.org/donati.html.

Dubin, The Hon Charles L. *Commission of Inquiry into the Use of Drugs and Banned Practices Intended to Increase Athletic Performance* Ottawa: Canadian Government Publishing Centre, 1990.

Dvorak, Jiri, Paul McCrory and Michel D'Hooghe. 'FIFA's Future Activities in the Fight Against Doping'. *British Journal of Sports Medicine* 40, Supplement 1 (2006): 58–9.

Dvorak, Jiri. 'There is Nothing to Gain from Using Drugs'. *FIFA Magazine* (March 2004): 16–19.

Dvorak, Jiri, T. Graf-Baumann, M. D'Hooghe, D. Kirkendall, H. Taennler and M. Saugy. 'FIFA's Approach to Doping in Football'. *British Journal of Sports Medicine* 40, Supplement 1 (2006): 3–12.

FIFA. *Activity Report, April 2002–March 2004: 54th Ordinary FIFA Congress, Paris*. Zurich: FIFA, 2004.

Goode, Erich. *Between Politics and Reason: The Drug Legalization Debate*. New York: St Martin's Press, 1997.

Grayson, Edward and Gregory Ioannidis. 'Drugs, Health and Sporting Values'. In *Drugs and Doping in Sport: Socio-Legal Perspectives*, ed. John O'Leary, 255–68. London: Cavendish Publishing, 2001.

Houlihan, Barrie. *Dying to Win: Doping in Sport and the Development of Anti-doping Policy*. Strasbourg: Council of Europe Publishing, 2002, 2nd edition.

________ 'Doping in Sport: More Problems than Solutions?' In *Sport and Society: A Student Introduction*, ed. Barrie Houlihan, 218–34. London: Sage, 2003.

Joy, Bernard. *Forward Arsenal: The Arsenal Story, 1888–1952*. London: Phoen House, 1952.

Maguire, Joseph and Bob Pearton. 'Global Sport and the Migration Patterns of France '98 World Cup Finals Players: Some Preliminary Observations'. In *The Future of Football: Challenges for the Twenty-First Century,* ed. Jon Garland, Dominic Malcolm and Michael Rowe, 175–89. London: Frank Cass.

Malcolm, Dominic. 'White Lines, Grass and the Level Playing Field'. In *Singer & Friedlander Review of 1997–98 Season,* ed. Patrick Murphy, 17–19. London: Singer and Friedlander, 1998.

________ 'Unprofessional Practice? The Power and Status of Sports Physicians'. *Sociology of Sport Journal* 23, no.4 (2006): 376–95.

Matthews, Stanley. *The Way it Was: My Autobiography.* London: Headline, 2000.

Mottram, David R. ed. *Drugs in Sport.* London: Routledge, 2005, 4th Edition.

Scarpino, V., A. Arrigo and G. Benzi. 'Evaluation of Prevalence of Doping Among Italian Athletes'. *Lancet 336* (1990): 1048–50.

Spitzer, Giselher. *Doping in der GDR: Ein historischer Uberblick zu einer konspirativen Praxis.* Klön: Bundesinstitut für Sportwissenschaft, 2000.

________ 'Sport and the Systematic Infliction of Pain: A Case Study of State-sponsored Mandatory Doping in East Germany'. In *Pain and Injury in Sport: Social and Ethical Analysis,* ed. Sigmund Loland, Berit Skirstad and Ivan Waddington, 109–26. London: Routledge, 2006.

Sports Council. *Doping Control in the UK: A Survey of the Views of Elite Competitors 1995.* London: Sports Council, 1996.

UK Sport. *Anti-Doping Report 2001/2002.* London: UK Sport, 2002.

WADA. *Adverse Analytical Findings Reported by Accredited Laboratories: Overview of results.* http://www.wada-ama.org/rtecontent/document/ LABSTATS_2005.pdf.

Waddington, Ivan. 'The Development of Sports Medicine'. *Sociology of Sport Journal* 13, no.2 (1996): 176–96.

________ *Sport, Health and Drugs: A Critical Sociological Perspective.* London: E&FN Spon, 2000.

________ 'Jobs for the Boys'? A Study of the Employment of Club Doctors and Physiotherapists in English Professional Football'. *Soccer and Society* 3, no.3 (2002): 51–64.

________ 'Changing Patterns of Drug Use in British Sport from the 1960s'. *Sport in History* 25, no.3 (2005): 472–96.

Waddington, Ivan, Martin Roderick and Rav Naik. 'Methods of Appointment and Qualifications of Club Doctors and Physiotherapists in English Professional Football: Some Problems and Issues'. *British Journal of Sports Medicine* 35, no.1 (2001): 48–53.

Waddington, Ivan, Dominic Malcolm, Martin Roderick and Rav Naik. 'Drug Use in English Professional Football'. *British Journal of Sports Medicine* 39, (2005): e18.

Yesalis, Charles E. III, Andrea N. Kopstein and Michael S. Bahrke. 'Difficulties in Estimating the Prevalence of Drug Use Among Athletes'. In *Doping in Elite Sport: The Politics of Drugs in the Olympic Movement,* ed. Wayne Wilson and Edward Derse, 43–62. Champaign, IL: Human Kinetics, 2001.

Tackling the anxieties of the English: searching for the nation through football

Jessica S.R. Robinson

> England itself has changed and in recent years
> Football seems to have held a mirror
> up to the changing face of England.[1]

Introduction

UK

Union Flag

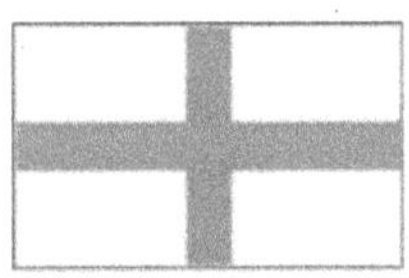

ENGLAND

St George's Cross

ROYAL NAVY

White Ensign

On 28 May 2005, England's national association football team played an international 'friendly' against the USA national team in Chicago. Soldier Field was filled with England fans, many of whom, unlike their American counterparts, had decorated the stadium with flags. Hundreds of St George's Crosses, and a sprinkling of 'Union Jacks' were displayed in a ground intended for the other kind of 'football'. Curiously, many chose to display the White Ensign, the flag of the Royal Navy.[2] It takes the form of a larger England flag with a Union Flag superimposed on the upper left-hand corner of the St George's Cross. A number of fans also chose to write the name of a local football club across the flag, demonstrating allegiance to clubs as internationally renowned as Arsenal and Manchester United, to those as obscure as Crook Town, a team that languishes in the second division of the Arngrove Northern League. On display in a country where their flag is sacred and 'soccer' relatively insignificant, these piecemeal attempts at hijacking a flag to stress the complexities of national allegiance through football 'fandom' seemed to call up confluence of what might be termed English identity and sport.[3]

This is a new development in the public display of Englishness. In the 1980s, when England and football hooliganism were seen as synonymous, England's travelling fans arrived draped in Union Flags.[4] The St George's Cross did not appear until the late 1990s, and especially at FIFA World Cup 2002,[5] and so in this period there was no need whatsoever for the White Ensign. England meant the 'Union Jack'. Between 1980 and 2000 how the English viewed themselves, and how they viewed football, radically changed. The flag as a symbol of nation is being used as a seemingly uncomplicated statement – one of belonging without assertions of ownership. The flag of the 'United' Kingdom, of the Empire, was no longer an appropriate, meaningful and unproblematic symbol for the national team of a multicultural England.[6]

I will argue in this essay that the English had entered a new era where the longstanding England/Britain conflation became cause for anxiety. It was no longer taken as a given that 'Englishness' was equivalent to 'Britishness', with the 'Celtic fringes' merely providing an uncomplicated element of 'noble savage' (or uncivilized brute), in a state of cultural hegemony.[7] It has become possible to ask: who are the English? Are they just the non-Celt Britons? Is there an English ethnicity? Can this be defined by class, culture, origin, race, politics or history? What exactly makes the English different?

The choices about changing the flag and displaying it can be seen to embody the true tensions of England and Englishness that have emerged in the last half of the twentieth century. The tensions as to what constitutes a nation – is it just the interplay of political, cultural and ethnic distinctions and definitions?; of what should be the state, that is, the political state of the United Kingdom of Great Britain and Northern Ireland, alongside emerging political powers in the Celtic nations; as well as of the regional affiliations that plague the growing concern in England as to what it actually means to be English, and what it means to be British – are more fraught now than ever. For even though England and Britain can no longer be assumed to be the same thing, the two are complexly and inextricably linked, as was demonstrated by the new choice of flag in which the two 'national' symbols became one, yet remained distinct.

For the purposes of this essay, I take Englishness to be the cultural space that the non-Celtic people of the United Kingdom forge for themselves. I am interested in the white majority, and their perceptions of their Englishness. This includes a set of ideas, practices, beliefs, experiences, genealogy and history, all of which are essentialized and reified in the identity and ethnic rhetoric of the people of England. It is a process of self-conscious differentiation and is intimately bound up with England's imperial past and its 'after Empire' present. What constitutes the cultural community of England is determined through Englishness.

Sahlins,[8] quoting Brumann, notes that while anthropologists may not like it, people *want* culture. They want the bounded, reified, essentialized and timeless culture that anthropologists often now reject. While at the same time, Sahlins notes, this all too stabilizing identity rhetoric is too 'negotiable' and too 'easily manipulated'.[9] It is this paradox that lies at the core of Englishness today. Anxieties are emerging as the English negotiate and manipulate some of the seemingly bounded and timeless dimensions of who they think they are. Football has become one space where the English can engage in the manipulation of class and the confrontations of race as white England seeks, but not necessarily succeeds, to become classless and multicultural.

In this essay, I will argue that assumptions about England and the English nation, and especially of football and its role in establishing English national identity, rest on a false premise about what constitutes *all* nations. That in order to understand the current anxieties of Englishness expressed through nationalism we must look to imperialism. This is not an analysis of history, but of ideologies. It is assumed that the ideal for Britain today is to be a multicultural and classless society. This claim can be understood by considering the rise of English football over the last decade, as it has shifted from the game of the working classes to a game of working out 'classlessness'. A forced, if often unconscious, confrontation with their historical understanding of the term 'international' has become more important as the English battle with sense of nation, 'after Empire' post-colonialism of 'after Empire', class and multiculturalism. 'England' is coming to mean something new.

Becoming 'After Empire' – post-imperial/post-colonial Britain

The emerging nation – why England is not Britain

The growth of nation and nationalism is intimately connected with experiences of colonization.[10] Hobsbawm has noted the relationship between the end of empires and the emergence of nationalism, eventually leading to the recognition of nation states.[11] Questions of a British or an English nation are equally tied to issues of imperialism and colonialism. The twentieth century has been regarded as the era of post-colonialism, both politically and ideologically, as countries (particularly in Asia and Africa) have emerged from the British Empire as independent nation-states. This century effectively saw the end of an overseas Empire with the sun finally setting on the British Empire in 1997 when their 'lease' on Hong Kong finally expired. While the development of post-colonial and subaltern studies, especially in political science and anthropology, has provided a space to think about the end of Empire.[12] However, to think only from the side of the subaltern experience conceals much of the complexity of British imperialism. In order to understand contemporary England and her concerns with class and race we need first to consider the relationship between colonizer and colonized, and the implications of post-imperialism from the English perspective. Moreover, what is and is not considered post-colonial is in itself a less clear issue bound up with significant political claims; the concept itself is a recent phenomenon, even though the ebbs and flows of Empires have existed throughout history. What does being post-imperial imply for Britain?

England and the Union

The British Empire began at home with the assimilation and conquering of the Celts.[13] The first *nation* to become a part of the 'inner Empire' was Wales in the thirteenth century,[14] followed by various degrees of influence in Ireland and Scotland throughout the Middle Ages. Certainly, by 1707, the Act of Union between England and Scotland formed the Kingdom of Great Britain, and 1801 saw Ireland brought into the merger of Kingdoms. It would be incorrect, however, to conclude that the non-English nations of the UK were as subject to imperialism as those in the 'outer Empire'. Many of the imperialists themselves were Scottish or Welsh, usually of the upper classes. Nevertheless, the political rights of these nations to almost all levels of independence were actively suppressed.

From the eighteenth through to the twentieth century, when other peoples were beginning to imagine themselves as nations, the English defined themselves through Empire. With their 'inner Empire' in the United Kingdom and their 'outer Empire' overseas 'imperialism(s)' trumped 'nationalism(s)' as the foci for English identity, and the English did not consciously reflect on the English nation or English nationalism.[15] The beginning of the end of Empire for the British started in earnest in 1922 with Irish independence, and continued most deliberately after the Second World War. The loss of India in 1947 was a significant challenge to the Empire, followed by most African nations in the 1960s, but the true end of British imperialism, as I noted above, did not occur until the very end of the century.

When Tony Blair's Labour government was elected in 1997, it was a landslide victory. The party of the working classes had transformed itself into the model of 'middle England'. With the slogan 'Cool Britannia', they embraced multiculturalism, and Blair pronounced 'We are all middle class now'. Most importantly, politically at least, was their mandate to have referenda on devolution in Scotland and Wales. The success of the referenda in 1998 meant that, in July 1999, her Majesty's Government of Great Britain and Northern Ireland formally transferred some powers to a parliament in Scotland and an assembly in Wales. At that moment, they made a commitment to the rights of nations as nations. The powers devolved were not massive, and by no means challenged the sovereignty of Parliament in Westminster, but the political recognition of the nation (rather than the region) should not be underestimated. The Good Friday Agreement in 1998 was a commitment to constitutional change in Northern Ireland and acknowledged the distinct rights of Northern Ireland to some extended levels of self-rule. Where did this leave the English? There was no provision for a national assembly for England and few calls were made for one. Devolution left Englishness – and by extension both England and Britain – unclear and unmarked.

England is a nation?

Devolution has led to greater individual and independent powers in the non-English nations of Britain, but calls by the Scottish Nationalists for full independence in recent years act to further show that they are still a long way from being independent political *states*. The debate is problematized because the relationship between nation and state, especially in Britain, is very much a blurred one. The British 'home nations' of England, Scotland, Wales and Northern Ireland challenge the definition of nation that we are most comfortable with today. Although they claim recognition as nations, rather than regions, they do not fit into the model of the nation-state. The idea of 'home nations' different from each other has a long history in the British Isles.[16] Prior to the Second World War 'nation' was not associated with 'state', but with 'race'.[17] What made the English, Scottish, Welsh and Irish different from each other were that they were distinctive races of peoples. While the definition of 'race' has altered as radically as the definition of 'nation', the idea and belief that the English, Scottish, Welsh and Irish are distinctive peoples has prevailed. Definitions as to what constitutes 'nation' are therefore contextual: in one instance it may be political will, in the next it may be a distinctive history and culture. It is Britain, the state, that unites the 'nations' as the political unit; the UN member and the Olympic representative, appears to best fit the global model of what constitutes a nation. Yet within the UK, certainly in Scotland and Wales, distinctive nationalisms exist.

For many, especially in England, the distinction between Englishness and Britishness is by no means clear-cut. This was unproblematic in the first part of the twentieth century when 'England' was the label for Britain as much as it was for England. England was an unmarked category. However, just as it became unacceptable (not to mention inaccurate) to speak of the whole population as English*men*, it became recognized as equally problematic to speak of England and mean Britain. Yet, paradoxically, within England, English and British do still blend into each other. This was exemplified in the study of English culture by the journalist Aslet in the late twentieth century that uses English and British as if they were still interchangeable.[18]

The historical experiences of imperialism, of colonization and de-colonization of an Empire that was coordinated from London, but operated in the name of the British as a whole, has led to multiple shifts in how England/Britain can, has been, and should be understood. Constitutional change in the United Kingdom in the last 30 years, starting with the Treaty of Rome 1976, which marked the UK's entry into the European Union; and including devolution in Scotland, Wales and Northern Ireland in 1999 and legislative changes since 9/11, have all led to a greater focus on who and what are the English.

Following Anderson's famous definition of the nation as 'an imagined political community – and imagined as both inherently limited and sovereign',[19] it is Britain and not England (or Scotland, Wales or Northern Ireland) that is the nation. However, when we turn to Smith's definition: 'a nation is a named community of history and culture, possessing a unified territory, economy, mass education system and common legal rights',[20] England's claim as a nation distinct from Scotland and Britain (but perhaps not Wales) is wholly justified.[21] What scholars of the nation have found is the need to talk in 'ideal types' because no one formula fits all. Renan's argument against definitions of nation that effectively constitute an 'ideal type' is compelling because he demonstrates that some regions have the components of the ideal types and yet do not constitute a nation (such as Tuscany), while some nations are still considered such without the components of the ideal types (such as Switzerland).[22] Kumar identifies five kinds of nationalism – political, civic, cultural, ethnic and imperial.[23] However, his discussion of Englishness and the nation from the eleventh to the twenty-first century fails to engage with the idea that anything other than the nation-state is truly national. I believe that in order to understand how the English have engaged with a kind of national identity we need to more carefully consider the role that ethnic, civic and cultural ideas of nation (distinct from the political) have played important roles in the shaping of the modern nation – which is undoubtedly now tied to the political.

The question of political will has been the central tenant of theories of nation and nationalism.[24] This places England in a difficult position. While Scotland and Wales are now able to assert an independent political will (albeit limited) outside the UK state, England cannot. Rather than argue how England (and Britain) does or does not fit into an 'ideal type' of nation, it is perhaps more profitable to track the production and mobilization of the English 'nation' as a discourse, as types of commitments and as an evolving form. To understand the relationship between nation and state in England we may more profitably look to the historical evolution of the term, rather than to expressions of nationalism elsewhere in the world (even as close to home as Scotland and Wales). In the age of nationalism, England has not experienced great ruptures, but rather evolutions, which makes it distinctive from most other nations. It was 'after Empire' when being a nation came to be important for the English. To be a nation among nations was a radical loss of power and influence, and outside of sport, the English cannot even claim this status. They are a nation, but not like anyone else's.

Kelly and Kaplan argue that those who use Anderson's 'imagined community' approach to the study of the nation have mistakenly projected the post-Second World War nation state of the UN onto the existing nations and nationalisms of previous centuries.[25] The anxieties following the Second World War made deep, horizontal comradeships between nations a necessity.[26] It was this 'global moral absolute' that meant Britain needed to appear as a nation-state, rather than an Empire. Presenting oneself as an equal national player in the UN became a necessary diplomatic move on a global scale, even though it did not necessarily reflect the feeling at home. However, rather than erase the existing 'home nations', they became eclipsed in the international view through the role of Britain in the UN. As the 'British Empire' had always eclipsed its separate units (in both the 'inner' and 'outer' Empires), assertions of Britishness on a world stage in 1945 seemed unproblematic. At this moment in time Britain was still an Empire.[27] It was only as time progressed, and the 'outer Empire' decolonized, that Britain really began to take the form of the 'globally imposed model of nation-state' at home.[28]

While Anderson's analysis of how the 'imagined community' became the nation may not be helpful in establishing how England is a nation distinct from Britain,[29] the idea of 'imagined' remains central. England exists more in imagination than it does anywhere else, as England lacks many of those political or cultural institutions that are usually taken to embody the nation (state). Whatever role the English play in the United Nations they do so as part of the United Kingdom. At the Olympic Games, whose opening ceremonies are an important space for marking and celebrating nationhood,[30] England competes as part of Great Britain.[31] As a consequence, trying to locate England as a nation in post-devolution UK is not an easy task.

Where is England?

Since 1996 one thing has become increasingly apparent. The one place where England exists as England is on the international sports field. England's football, rugby and cricket teams do not represent the UK. When tracing the relationship between England and Scotland, international sport is often cited as an example where this relationship is played out. The Scottish attitude of 'anyone but England' to win an international sports match has been noted by commentators on English and British identity, as well as by sport sociologists.[32] This is a place where Englishness and Britishness no longer merge. This has been further marked in recent years with the growth in popularity of displaying English flags during international sports tournaments. This almost aggressive assertion of allegiance to the national team has filtered out into everyday life, with more and more flags displayed on buildings, cars and clothing, even beyond the sporting context. Nevertheless, this expression of football fandom was almost unknown during Italia '90 (FIFA World Cup 1990), but has become an expected display since Euro 1996. If only for a few weeks every other year, football supporters themselves become a symbol of the nation.

If England is realized on the international sports field, why is it that football rather than rugby or cricket has become the symbol of the English? I propose that the answer to this lies in the question of Empire. While England's greatest opponents in football are perceived to be Germany, France, Italy, Argentina and Brazil, its greatest opponents in cricket are Australia, the West Indies, India and Pakistan. In rugby it competes against France and Italy, but fears New Zealand and South Africa. What is significant here is that only in football does England's serious competition come from countries that were never part of the British Empire.[33]

Indeed, the obsession with football is seemingly all consuming, win or lose, but the glorification of cricket or rugby comes only in times of victory. Every stage of international football competition is poured over by the British public, even when defeat seems imminent. Cricket and rugby may have elicited flag waving in the aftermath of World Cup or Ashes victories, but not to the level that football achieves even when England lose. Even the wives and girlfriends of England football players are celebrities in their own right to such an extent that during the World Cup 2006 the English tabloid press developed the acronym WAGs to refer to the wives and girlfriends of the squad, devoting many column inches to their antics.[34]

Beating a German football team may lead to calls for a public holiday (as they did in the qualifying rounds for FIFA World Cup 2002), however, beating an Indian or West Indies Cricket team never produces as explicit jingoism or racism in the media that beating international football teams does. In cricket the press celebrates an English victory,[35] but in football, and especially against Germany it is as much about the opponent's loss. The very different historical relationship with their opponents in cricket may explain this, making it a somewhat bittersweet victory that evokes memories of Empire.

Newspaper reports on current world events tend to sidestep issues of Britain's former imperial influence in many areas; an especially notable omission is discussions of Iraq or Israel's British colonial past. In contrast to this, discussion of the Second World War is still a common trope, mentioned almost daily in the British media. However, if media coverage were taken to reflect the most influential and significant British expression of power and dominance, one could easily assume that the FIFA World Cup victory for England in 1966 was her most important international moment!

In 2006, as the World Cup approached, it seemed that every other vehicle in England was, quite literally, flying the flag of St George. Almost every store on the high street, from the family-run newsagent to the monolithic department store Marks and Spencer, had some kind of display in white and red. But curiously the white ensign, so ubiquitous at the football games themselves, is absent. 'England' may be written on these high street flags, but 'Crook Town', 'Liverpool' and 'Chelsea' that denotes the regional affiliation of these fans is not on display. That the manipulation of the flags has taken on a kind of discursive role and one that comes into being almost exclusively in sporting events is particularly significant. Whether they are English or British, or that it matters just as much to identify with a region, a city or even a small town, is a debate that occurs on the terraces. It complicates a simple division between Britishness and Englishness that is a central dimension of the current climate of national identity crisis. Regional identities are important, and while a nascent nationalism is evident in the streets and pubs of England as they fly their St George's cross, the *negotiation* seems to be occurring more on the terraces.

In the last few decades scholars of sport have shifted their analysis from discussion of the game itself further towards debates over 'meaning'. Sport is increasingly analysed as a 'reflection of social and political forces', or as a 'lens' to better understand the society under review.[36] However, I argue that football for the English is an important location for working out and expressing ideas and identities not because it is a metaphor, but because it is a mechanism. It does not 'reflect' a distinctly English institution – it *is* one. English football, just like the St George's cross, is one of those rare things that cannot be mistaken as British. English football does not reflect England, but actually brings it into being. In almost no other area is the distinction between England and Britain as absolute and clear-cut. England has no distinctive political manifestation (Parliament is British), it has no national dress, no national anthem and even its patron saint is neither English nor uniquely its own. The English (as opposed to the British) have few of the cultural or political trappings that have come to be associated with the nation. However, in sports, and especially in football, an England team represents England, not Britain, making football *the* location to examine an emerging national consciousness – whatever that may be. As Hobsbawm has noted, 'the imagined community of millions seems more real as a team of eleven named people. The individual, even the one who only cheers, becomes a symbol of the nation himself.'[37] In football, if nowhere else, the English *are* England.

The national game: international or intranational football?

Football is a national obsession for the English. Then again, it could just as easily be claimed that football is the national obsession of the Scottish,[38] and also the Italians, the Brazilians, or the Argentineans.[39] As Markovits and Hellerman point out, it is *not* having football as a national obsession that makes America unusual.[40] But the British obsession with football has a distinctive flavour because it is the British who invented the game (some claim the game originated in Scotland, all note that its modern institutionalized form was developed in England)[41] and still control the rules of the game. It has been claimed that international competitions merely provide a space for expressions of jingoism.[42] However, if we read the headlines of the tabloid press when England face Germany, or accounts of the chants from international matches, this does not seem to be the case, rather, the roots of this seeming jingoism, the form it takes and the obsession with beating the German national team lie in the anxieties about Englishness. Claims of origins and authenticity are far reaching claims that make the British relationship with organized sports generally, and football particularly, complex, and influence where the game is played, who plays the game and how they play the game.

Britain gave football to the world, but it took a while for them to accept this role.[43] England, and the other UK Football Associations, have had a troubled relationship with the international game. They refused to join FIFA (Fédéderation Internationale de Football Association) when it was formed in 1904.[44] The British FAs were reluctant to become involved in the international game, and they refused to take part in the first FIFA World Cup in 1930. Some of this may be explained in terms of the understanding of the term 'international' in the British game. In 1882 the 'home nations' formed the International Football Association Board (IFAB) to 'standardize the rules of the game and agree on definitions … also to regulate the intricacies of relations within a United Kingdom'. 'International' games played in the UK were between the 'home nations', and rivalries between England and Scotland were particularly fierce.

The negotiation of sport rules or 'laws' as an expression of the tensions of 'inner Empire' was also expressed in Rugby Union. The International Rugby Football Board (IRFB, now known as the International Rugby Board [IRB]) was founded in 1886 by Scotland, Wales and Ireland. England was not a founder member. Until 1885 England had made the Rugby laws. After a disputed try in an England-Scotland international the home unions founded the IRFB and refused to play England until they joined, which they did in 1890. This original conflict is perhaps one reason Rugby is the dominant national sport in Scotland and Wales, while football is much more important to England.

This question of what 'international' means remains a considerable issue within British football. As the UK looks towards 2012 and hosting the Olympic Games, the role of the most followed sport once again comes to the fore. As it is the UK that competes in the Olympic Games and not England, Scotland, Wales and Northern Ireland, an all British football team that could compete in this ultimate arena of international sport has once more become an issue of debate. In Rugby this is not a problem. While Rugby has not been an Olympic sport since the 1920s, the British and Irish Lions, a team made up of the original home nations, has played international tours since 1910 without challenging the independence of the separate nations' Rugby Unions.[45] Contemporary definitions of nation that map onto the state suggest that a move towards a temporary UK Olympic team in football would challenge the independence of the distinct Associations. If the separate FAs are able to agree to field such a team (an event that currently seems unlikely) it would potentially weaken the British (not English) control over the international game. Just as the Scottish teams remain outside of the Premiership in the domestic game, they must remain outside of a UK team if the British want to retain the right to four of the eight seats on IFAB (the other four representatives are from FIFA). To present a British team in an international arena would be a challenge to both political and cultural independence that is expressed both in and through football in the UK. By effectively controlling the standard rules of the game, football retains a distinctly British flavour. Although FIFA acts as judge and jury in interpreting the rules, it is Britain through domination of IFAB that is the 'law' maker.

The full implications of 'international' in UK football are often ignored in the sociology and history literature. England and Britain are assumed to be interchangeable. Sugden and Tomlinson's study of FIFA discusses the relationship between Britain and FIFA while mentioning the existence of separate Football Associations, and ignores the implications of an 'international' dimension *within* the UK.[46] They note that England was not part of FIFA from 1920–1947 but do not take into account the official 'international' games played between the home nations. Even studies of an explicitly English game use examples and statistics from Scotland as more than comparison.[47] Studies of 'British Sport' mention the role of the International Board as central to the formulation and regulation of the international rules of football, but do not examine the significance of separate national teams within one, generally regarded, nation state.[48] Some go as far as to mention the intensity of England-Scotland rivalries, and the fact that '"Anyone but England" is an instantly unifying Celtic cry', but then go on to assume that football plays the same role in identity formation on all sides of the borders.[49] Even the most cursory glance at the role of sectarianism in Scottish football presents a world very alien to the English experience. They do not examine how football may express the 'international' *within* a multinational state. America is mocked for being a country 'that plays incomprehensible versions of rounders, rugby and netball and calls them World Championships',[50] but Britain's international 'home' matches are almost never held up to examination.

Understanding both Britishness and Englishness can only come from realizing – as has already been argued – that Britain is not a nation state, but a state of nations. The distinction is demonstrated explicitly through the need for separate football associations. The FAs were formed in the 1860s–80s, which Kelly and Kaplan have argued was a period when the concept of nation mapped onto 'race' rather than state.[51] These nations were seen to be home to distinctly different peoples. The first international match was played between England and Scotland in 1872. This was almost

30 years before international matches between other nations began: the first was played between Argentina and Uruguay in 1901. The idea of international matches was fully established within the UK as a space for working out rivalries and tensions, particularly for the Scottish and Irish who felt unjustly dominated politically and culturally by English Imperialism.[52]

Those who study English sport and assume it is British, and those who study international sport and assume that the UK exists merely as a nation among nations, miss the fundamental anomaly that the English case presents. We can neither understand English/British sport nor the complexities of English/British nationhood without realizing that there is an 'international' dimension *within* the United Kingdom. Further, this international dimension relies on a kind of diplomacy forever tackling tensions that are figured by ethnic, cultural, racial, political and temporal factors that the assumed cultural hegemony of 'Britain' masks. To speak of the 'home internationals' as such is not an anachronism, but an indication of that anomaly. The UK nations do not fit with the generally regarded model of nation-state – they are nations but not fully-fledge *nation-states*. In order to understand these nations we need to develop a new, more sophisticated analytic framework that allows us to move beyond the marriage of nation with state and the assumption that achieving and expressing nation status is about gaining power.

Changing attitudes towards the relationship between Britishness and Englishness can be seen in how fans react to this definition of international. Buford's infamous account of his time *Among the Thugs,* a narrative account of football hooliganism in the 1980s and up to the FIFA World Cup 1990, describes England fans carrying Union Flags. He describes England fans who saw themselves as representing Britain. They were not carrying the flag of England. It was not until the late 1990s, and notably Euro '96 held in England, that English football became associated with the English flag. By this time Scotland and Wales had devolution in their grasp and the distinction between England and Britain had become more relevant.

During this era the English became aware that what they meant by nation might not map onto what everyone else meant. It was in this same period that a great deal of popular literature questioning a distinctly English identity was produced.[53] Football played an important role in maintaining the knowledge that England, Scotland and Wales were separate nations in the period when the English assumed that English and British were the same. This became especially noticeable when England failed to qualify for the FIFA World Cup finals in the 1970s and 1980s, but Scotland did. English superiority could not be assumed. Welsh football became a feature in the English consciousness in the 1990s when star Manchester United player Ryan Giggs chose to play for Wales rather than England. Whether this was a loss for the England team or a gain for the Welsh was something that was never quite worked out, but was certainly considered. An explicit assertion either way would have been seen as a challenge to the shared British identity of England and Wales, which in public forums, would not have been acceptable. The multiculturalism that defines the current era does not allow for overt attacks on the other nations of the UK, and to deny the right of the Welsh to a talented football player such as Giggs would be considered such an attack.

On the surface multiculturalism may appear to be a race question; however this is not the case. The question of culture in all its dimensions is up for grabs. The influence of immigration, especially from the former Empire, has no doubt made questions of race and religion as cultures perhaps the most visible, but the implications of multiculturalism, however, can also be seen to stretch into questions about gender cultures, nationalisms as cultures, sexuality cultures, regional cultures, and, perhaps most intriguingly, is the implication of class as culture. For the English/British one of the greatest means of differentiation, historically, has been class. The negotiation of class in the face of multiculturalism is a central component of the emergence of a new sense of Englishness to which I now turn.

I have argued that to assume homogeneity within Britain ignores important distinctions and historical and cultural divides between the English, Scottish, Welsh and Irish. To assume homogeneity within England is equally problematic. The question of class is a hugely significant factor, and social position leads to different experiences of what Englishness or Britishness means. The predominant narrative in the history of sport, which could be termed the conventional curriculum, tends to trace the role of upper and middle classes who institutionalized the games through the public schools.[54] Alternatively, other historians take a Marxist approach focusing almost exclusively on football and its role as the game of the working classes.[55] Football, however, has transformed in recent years.[56] It can no longer be considered the game of the working man. The best selling memoir, *Fever Pitch*, written by the Cambridge graduate Nick Hornby in 1992, started a trend for a middle class acknowledgement of the love of the game. Politicians on both the left and the right claimed to follow teams, such as the former Prime Minister John Major and the cabinet minister Tony Banks. Intellectuals wrote newspaper columns for the broadsheets, with the feminist Germaine Greer's views on Euro '96 and the novelist Will Self's response to the FIFA World Cup 2002.[57] Not only did British sports act to mediate between the 'outer Empire' and the imperial centre through the spread of the 'Games ethic' and Muscular Christianity, not only did the ideals of 'Olympism' allow disparate nations to come together, but, today within the UK, sport, especially football, has allowed a space for the English and the Scottish to express their rivalries and the English to work out what it means to be ideologically 'all middle class now', in a time 'after Empire' where England exists as part of an ethnically and socially diverse 'multicultural' Britain.

Football – what Walvin famously called 'the people's game'[58] – is associated with the lower classes. Unlike cricket or rugby, which – according to popular belief in England – need the 'proper' expensive equipment and special grounds to play on, all you need to play football is a ball and something to mark the goal posts. Great footballers, in the days before multiple car ownership, tended to claim to have learned to play by kicking a ball around the streets and most still come from working class backgrounds. Their counterparts in cricket and rugby on the other hand generally honed their skills on the fields of the public schools and the ancient universities. However, the history of the institutionalization of the organized game, through the creation of the Football Association in 1863, notes that the middle classes developed the sport. It was at Cambridge University in 1848, and then in the 1860s that an effort was made to formalize the rules of football.[59] In 1863 representatives of Oxford and Cambridge universities, as well as a number of public schools and southern teams, formed the FA, which was effectively an agreement to play each other by the same rules. Football Associations in the other 'home nations' followed in Scotland (1873), Wales (1876) and Ireland (1880). Walvin has argued that football can best be seen as British 'social class in action', with the 'well-to-do in boardrooms' but 'primarily a sporting passion of the urban working class male'.[60]

The FA was dominated by the middle classes from the start, and from the top down imposed rules about playing on Sundays and sanctioning (or not) a women's game. The gulf between those who controlled the game and those who consumed it was huge. The middle classes used sport as a means of conveying their values. The 'games ethic' of the Muscular Christian values of gentlemanly behaviour and fair play was used to 'civilize' the 'outer Empire'.[61] This was also an aim at home, where the working classes were seen as the 'barbarians'. However, the role of Christian morality (no games played on Sundays) and the principle of fair play influenced how the game was played on the pitch. Stoddart[62] has pointed out that this was not a two way process and while the middle class ideals were translated to the working class game, football did not provide a vehicle for the working classes to express their radical ideals and wider political and social concerns in the 1930s.

English football in the 1970s and 1980s was marked by the violence of its fans. Hooliganism and the English became synonymous. The Scottish, Welsh and Northern Irish were not associated with this. Much has already been said on the causes and effects of hooliganism,[63] and I will not elaborate on it here, but the long-term consequences of the violence and the reputation of English and England fans has played a significant role in some of the transformations of the game from the 1990s. One of these transformations is the way in which football became understood as a vehicle for expressing the perceived social concerns of the working classes. It became popular to assume that hooliganism was a response to unemployment and the general decline of Britain's industry and her place in the world 'after Empire'. While sociological and ethnographic investigations discovered that this was a much too simplistic gloss on the situation,[64] the very notion that the working class football supporters were using their game as a vehicle to say something, rather than it being a vehicle to be told something, demonstrates a shift in how class relations where being interpreted in England.

The Hillsborough disaster in 1989, where 96 Liverpool fans died in the crush of an overcrowded terrace, was a tragedy exacerbated by the measures put in place to control fan violence. Locked doors at the exits and cage fencing all round the stand meant that an accidental over-admission lead to tragedy. The introduction of all seater stadia following this disaster changed how the English watched the game. The first consequence was easier monitoring of the stands by the police, and so better control of the violence. It was now considered 'safe' for the middle class supporters to return to the games. Another consequence was increased price of admission, which led to an increasingly affluent spectatorship. Spectators at the games, rather than just in the television watching audiences, became increasingly middle class.

Perhaps as significant as class are the ways in which questions of a newer dimension of Englishness/Britishness have been played out on the football field and terraces. In the second half of the twentieth century England was transformed by the wave of immigration from the former British colonies. Britain 'after Empire' was to be defined by a new group of citizens, who by the 1990s were to become the foundation of 'multicultural Britain'.

In 1978 Viv Anderson was the first black player to play for England. John Barnes, one of the greatest players of the 1980s, endured some of the worst racist attacks when he played for Liverpool. Bill Buford's 1991 account of hooliganism demonstrated that the links between neo-fascism, racism and football were incredibly strong in the 1980s. Managers restricted the fielding of black players until the 1970s, and questions of whether or not there was a place for non-white players on the teams can be seen to be a reflection of the views as to what the place for non-white Britons should be in England. But football, once again, proved to be more than a mirror held up to English society. The increasing presence of black players in English football in the 1980s and 1990s led to parliamentary debates and legislative action on racism. It became a mechanism for change. One of the most radical transformations of the 1990s is the way in which race in football transformed from being a major problem that required an Act of Parliament (1991) to explicitly restrict racism in football, to a moment of national celebration of English multiculturalism. It may have taken until 1978 for the first black England footballer to emerge, but black players now constitute a third of the England squad.[65] Today the role of football in cracking down on wider racism within society is considered incredibly important – even though the FA acknowledge that they could and should have done more to help.

Therefore, one of the greatest anxieties of Englishness lies in where to locate England's growing non-white population within the nation. Borrowing from the American notion of a 'melting-pot' or the Canadian metaphor of a 'mosaic' is difficult when the very definition of nation is posited on ethnicity, rather than the political state. Football provides the most visible means to articulate these concerns, especially for the white community. By embracing black players within *the* symbol of England they become a symbol of Englishness. It provides an aperture into the long process of working out how the English nation can be a multicultural (and specifically multiracial) space.

Claims to Britishness (and rejections of Englishness) within the non-white community demonstrate that there is still a long way to go in achieving this aim. Garland[66] noted that the tabloid press explicitly celebrated England's successes during the FIFA World Cup 2002 as a moment of multiculturalism, where white, black and Asian English men and women celebrated their shared nation. Outside the football context these newspapers were less inclusive, attacking asylum seekers and producing some overtly racist journalism. But what must be noted is that football does seem to provide a space to bring people together. The tensions and conflicts that exist were once scope for extreme racism in English football, but have been more or less worked out. In a football context racism is seen as wholly unacceptable, and international matches become a space to demonstrate just how multicultural and inclusive England now is.

One dimension of multiculturalism that remains hugely problematic is the role of Scotland, Wales and Ireland. As multiculturalism is an ethos that does not just embrace skin colour, but cultural and ethnic diversity too, implicit in this is the inclusion of the other 'home' nations. This is part of the reason why Britishness cannot be wholly divorced from the new configuration of Englishness. The English see themselves as successfully multicultural as demonstrated in their attitudes towards race in and through their football teams, but to be successfully multicultural also requires that they be British, for they cannot deny their shared social and political connections with the Scottish, Welsh and Irish.

Finding a 'middle way' was the early political manifesto of the 1997 Labour government. It should also be noted that the project of multiculturalism is also a project of the middle classes. We have seen that football was utilized by the middle classes from its inception as an organized sport to 'civilize' the masses. It is still a civilizing project, but one that now encompasses the middle class too. To be multicultural is to be 'civilized'. Just as the modernization of the football stadiums, the control of fan violence and the increased ticket prices eradicated the distinctly and exclusively working class dimensions of football, so too did it eradicate much racism. The removal of overt violent racism, often expressed by the National Front (invariably wielding 'Union Jacks' in the 1970s and 1980s), was part of the gentrification process of football. Just as class hierarchies are unacceptable in the new Englishness, so too is racism.

Conclusion – the English anomaly

Football, while once the sport of the urban working classes, is now championed as a symbol of multicultural Britain, shared with the world but not imposed upon it. For football is something of an empty category, celebrated and claimed by nations the world over, retaining nothing distinctly English about it. But this is the value of football. It provides a space for the English to mediate the dilemmas of the England/Britain conflation. Football can distance the English from its imperial past where social hierarchies governed lives at home as much as it did in the 'outer' Empire.

Through devolution the UK state retained its sovereign powers, but drew borders that reinforced the rights of nations and in doing so made the English nation relevant, as a nation, perhaps for the first time. Prior to this it had only been through sport, and especially in the Football Associations, that it had mattered that Scotland, Wales and (Northern) Ireland were not England. This conception of internationalism should now be considered in a new light. England's standing as a nation is in direct reference to its demise as the centre of an Empire. For the English becoming a nation is about loss of power, rather than about gaining it. The most influential works on nation[67] examine post-colonial states for how nation and independence are intimately connected. In these instances recognition as a nation is a moment for celebration and self-realization. Historical analyses of the rise of nationalism in the eighteenth through to the twentieth century have linked it to revolution and the rise of liberalism in non-colonial contexts. In the USA and France this meant the gains of self-determination and sovereignty of the people.[68] These existing models do not provide a useful explanation for the English experience, as for them becoming a nation is a loss of an identity, not a moment of achievement. The English have only begun to value their status as a nation as they have lost their status as an Empire. Football, which was once a location of rigid class structures, extreme violence and overt racism, became by the 1980s *the* expression of the 'problems' of Englishness. Ironically, as England has changed, so too has football. In English football we can see the potential solution to these very problems. Football has been mobilized to mediate the past and the present, as the English try to work out spaces for classlessness and an all-embracing multiculturalism in the one place that is unquestioningly English. The English are something of an anomaly – to move into the future they choose to reject, rather than embrace, tradition, for the past *is* a foreign country.

Acknowledgements

This essay began life as part of a Seminar led by John MacAloon and Boria Majumdar at the University of Chicago in Spring 2005; research which later formed part of my MA thesis. I am particularly grateful to Alex Dent and Anwen Tormey for their advice in the early stages of that project. This essay would never have developed if not for the engaging discussions I have had with my PhD Advisor, John Kelly, who continues to teach me to think critically about nations and nationalism, and with whom it is always a pleasure to talk about sport and the peculiarities of the English. This version developed after Boria Majumdar's kind invitation to first attend, and then participate in, the Conference at SOAS in June 2006. I would like to thank him for that opportunity. In the final write-up William Mazzarella, Jessica Cattelino and Lola Martinez went above and beyond in providing thoughtful and incisive readings. I am just sorry that I was not able to incorporate all of their advice. It is to John MacAloon that I owe my greatest, and ever growing, debts. He introduced me to the anthropology of sport, advised my MA thesis, and continues to be a truly awe-inspiring teacher and friend.

Notes

1. Walvin, *The Only Game*, 16.
2. Technically, this flag should only be flown on Royal Naval vessels, but no flag laws exist in the UK to prevent England fans adopting it as their own.
3. All US states have laws relating to the desecration, burning, defacing and/or abuse of the US Flag: in some it is a misdemeanour, in others a felony. In Chicago in the 1990s an Art student 'Dredd' Scott Tyler, exhibited 'How to display the American Flag?' at the Art Institute, a piece of mixed media art that placed a flag on the ground and seemed to encourage the public to step on it (but by no means forced then to). Angry protests and demonstrations ensued. Thus, writing the name of your football team on a flag, or adding another flag to the corner would not be considered an acceptable display of the American Flag (Becker, *Zones of Contention*, 15; Dubin, *Arresting Images*, 102–24).
4. Buford, *Among the Thugs*, 127.
5. Polley, 'Sport and National Identity in Contemporary England', 10–11; Majumdar, 'Forwards and Backwards', 2004.
6. It is necessary to explain this essay's use of the terms English, British and United Kingdom and the emphasis on England. When I refer to the UK, I am making explicit reference to the political state (not a nation-state) of the United Kingdom of Great Britain and Northern Ireland. Properly, this should be understood as being made up of four nations – England, Scotland, Wales and Northern Ireland. Britain and British I use to refer to shared citizenship of the UK. This political definition does not necessarily reflect the ways in which many people in the UK use 'British', which is often taken to refer to both political and cultural domains, many of which overlap. For the purposes of this essay, I use a stricter political definition than common usage. English is a reference to the people of the country of England who share a common national identity that is distinct from, and contrasted against, the Scottish, Welsh or Northern Irish.
7. See Moorhouse, 'One State, Several Countries', 57.

8. Sahlins, 'Two or Three Things That I Know About Culture'.
9. Ibid., 403.
10. Kelly and Kaplan, *Represented Communities.*
11. Hobsbawm, *Nations and Nationalism since 1780*, 179.
12. See, for example, Chakrabrty, *Habitations of Modernity*; Appadurai, *Modernity at Large*; Comaroff and Comaroff, *Of Revelation and Revolution.*
13. Corrigan and Sayer, *The Great Arch*, 11, 15–16; Kumar, *The Making of English National Identity*, 81–8.
14. Kumar, *The Making of English National Identity*; Davis, *The Age of Conquest.*
15. Kumar, 'Britain, England and Europe', 20–1.
16. Corrigan and Sayer, *The Great Arch*; Colley, *Britons*; Kumar, *The Making of English National Identity.*
17. Kelly and Kaplan, *Represented Communities*, 2.
18. Aslet, *Anyone for England?*
19. Anderson, *Imagined Communities*, 6.
20. Smith, 'The Origins of Nations', 107.
21. Scotland has, and always has had, educational and legal systems that are separate from England and Wales.
22. Renan, 'What is a Nation?'.
23. Kumar, *The Making of English National Identity*, 21–30.
24. Renan, 'What is a Nation?'; Anderson, *Imagined Communities*; Gellner, *Nations and Nationalisms.*
25. Kelly and Kaplan, *Represented Communities.*
26. Ibid., 9.
27. For example, the Trinidad born intellectual C.L.R. James, when writing in 1963, considered himself to be a 'British Intellectual', not a West Indian or a citizen of Trinidad and Tobago (*Beyond a Boundary*, 111). Within a decade, it is unlikely that he could or would still have made this claim.
28. Kelly and Kaplan, *Represented Communities*, 25.
29. Anderson, *Imagined Communities.*
30. MacAloon, 'La Pitada Olímpica', 326.
31. Football is rarely given much consideration by the English media during the Olympic Games. They do not compete because it would have to be a Great Britain team, rather than an England, Scotland or Wales team
32. See Paxman, *The English*; Asle, *Anyone for England?*; and Holt and Mason, *Sport in Britain.*
33. The Falkland Islands, as one of the few remaining British dependencies, places England's relationship with Argentina in a more complex position. However, South America is rarely considered part of the former British Empire despite some influence in this region. England played Trinidad and Tobago in the 2006 World Cup, and potentially could have played Australia and the USA, but they were never considered 'serious' competition.
34. One of the first recorded uses of the term WAG was in *The Guardian*, 3 October 2004, but it became part of the popular vocabulary in 2006. Interest in 'footballers' wives' dates back to the 1960s when Bobby Moore and his wife Tina were portrayed in the press as a 'golden couple'. However, the celebrity status of these women did not develop until the 1990s with Victoria Adams' marriage to David Beckham. A television drama 'Footballers Wives' fictionalized the presumed glamour and drama of this newly developing celebrity status and firmly placed the spouses of footballers in the public eye. Victoria Beckham and Cheryl Cole (wife of Ashley Cole) were both pop stars in their own right prior to marrying, but Wayne Rooney's fiancée Coleen McLoughlin has no other claim to fame. She endorses a line of clothing and has her own column in the women's magazine, *Closer*, solely because she is 'Mrs' Wayne Rooney.
35. Garland, 'The Same Old Story?'.
36. Hill, 'British Sports History', 16.
37. Hobsbawm, *Nations and Nationalism*, 143.
38. Holt and Mason, *Sport in Britain.*
39. Sugden and Tomlinson, *FIFA and the Contest for World Football.*
40. Markovits and Hellerman, *Offside.*
41. For example, Mason, *Association Football and English Society.*
42. Walvin, *The Only Game*, 248; Porter, 'Your boys took one hell of a beating!'.
43. On exporting football, see Mangan, *The Games Ethic and Imperialism*; Sugden and Tomlinson, *FIFA and the Contest for World Football.* Walvin, *The Only Game*, 71–2, has argued that while the British exported a formalized game, the export established itself because it resonated with pre-existing ball games, such as the Florentine game of *calico*; the French *soule*; the Russian *Lapta* and the Inuit game of *kalagut.*

44. Sugden and Tomlinson, *FIFA and the Contest for World Football*, 10, 18–21.
45. Rugby was an Olympic medal sport in 1900, 1908, 1920 and 1924. The IRB became a recognized federation by the International Olympic Committee in 1995 and has been lobbying for reinstatement as a medal sport in the Olympic Games.
46. Sugden and Tomlinson, *FIFA and the Contest for World Football*, 33–6.
47. Mason, *Association Football and English Society*, 148, 150.
48. Smith and Porter, *Sport and National Identity*, 1.
49. Holt and Mason, *Sport in Britain*, 121.
50. Smith and Porter, *Sport and National Identity*, 4.
51. Kelly and Kaplan, *Represented Communities*.
52. The FA can be seen to have asserted the idea that the 'inner Empire' was an expression of English Imperialism when, in 1946, they refused to change their name to the 'English Football Association'; see Holt and Mason, *Sport in Britain*, 25.
53. Aslet, *Anyone for England?*; Paxman, *The English*; and Scruton, *England*.
54. Dunning and Sheard, *Barbarians, Gentlemen and Players*; and Mangan, *The Games Ethic and Imperialism*.
55. Hobsbawm, *Nations and Nationalism*; Mason, *Association Football*; Holt and Mason, *Sport in Britain*; and Walvin, *The People's Game*.
56. Walvin, *The Only Game*, 4.
57. Holt and Mason, *Sport in Britain*, 117; and Beck, 'The Relevance of the "Irrelevant"'.
58. Walvin, *The People's Game*.
59. Mason, *Association football and English society 1863–1915*, 14.
60. Walvin, *The People's Game*, 48.
61. Mangan, *The Games Ethic and Imperialism*.
62. Stoddard, 'Sport, Cultural Politics and International Relations', 390.
63. Dunning et al., *The Roots of Football Hooliganism*.
64. Dunning and Sheard, *Barbarians, Gentlemen and Players*.
65. Racism is a major problem in football across the world. Another perceived example of English superiority against Europe came in November 2004 in a Spain v England match where the Spanish supporters greeted the English team with monkey chants and threw bananas at them. The vitriol in the British press was used to criticize the Spanish and to celebrate how far the English have come since the 1980s when football was considered a national problem rather than the national game. See Walvin, *The Only Game*, 150.
66. Garland, 'The Same Old Story?'.
67. Anderson, *Imagined Communities*; Hobsbawm, *Nations and Nationalism*; and Kelly and Kaplan, *Represented Communities*.
68. Hobsbawm, *Nations and Nationalism*, 39.

References

Anderson, B. *Imagined Communities*. New York: Verso, 1991 [1983].

Appadurai, A. *Modernity at Large*. Minneapolis: University of Minnesota Press, 1996.

Aslet, C. *Anyone for England? A Search for British Identity*. London: Little Brown and Company, 1997.

Beck, P. 'The Relevance of the "Irrelevant": Football as a Missing Dimension in the Study Of British Relations With Germany'. *International Affairs* 79, no.2 (2003): 389–411.

Becker, C. *Zones of Contention: Essays on Art, Institutions, Gender and Anxiety*. Albany: State University of New York Press, 1996.

Buford, B. *Among the Thugs*. New York: Vintage, 1990.

Chakrabarty, D. *Habitations of Modernity: Essays in the Wake of Subaltern Studies*. Chicago, IL: University of Chicago Press, 2002.

Comaroff, J. and J. Comaroff. *Of Revelation and Revolution Vol I: Christianity, Colonialism, and Consciousness in South Africa*. Chicago, IL: University of Chicago Press, 1991.

Colley, L. *Britons: Forging the Nation 1707–1837*. London: Pimlico, 1994.

Corrigan, P. and D. Sayer. *The Great Arch*. Oxford: Basil Blackwell, 1985.

Davis, R.R. *The Age of Conquest: Wales 1063–1415*. Oxford: Oxford University Press, 1987.

Dubin, S. *Arresting Images: Impolitic Art and Uncivil Actions*. New York: Routledge, 1993.

Dunning, E. and K. Sheard. *Barbarians, Gentlemen and Players*. New York: New York University Press, 1979.

Dunning, E., P. Murphy and J. Williams. *The Roots of Football Hooliganism.* New York: Routledge, 1988.
Garland, J. 'The Same Old Story? Englishness, the Tabloid Press and the 2002 Football World Cup'. *Leisure Studies* 23, no.1 (2004): 79–92.
Gellner, E. *Nations and Nationalism.* Ithaca, NY: Cornell University Press, 1983.
Hill, J. 'British Sports History: A Post-Modern Future?' *Journal of Sport History* 23, no.1 (2004): 1–19.
Hobsbawm, E.J. *Nations and Nationalism since 1780.* Cambridge: Cambridge University Press, 1996.
Holt, R. and T. Mason. *Sport in Britain 1945–2000.* Oxford: Blackwell, 2000.
Hornby, N. *Fever Pitch.* New York: Penguin, 1992.
James, C.L.R. *Beyond a Boundary.* Durham, NC: Duke University Press, 1963.
Kelly, J. and M. Kaplan. *Represented Communities.* Chicago, IL: University of Chicago Press, 2001.
Kumar, K. *The Making of English National Identity.* Cambridge: Cambridge University Press, 2003a.
________ 'Britain, England and Europe: Cultures in Contraflow'. *European Journal of Social Theory* 6, no.1 (2003b): 5–23.
MacAloon, J.J. 'La Pitada Olimpíca: Puerto Rico, International Sport, and the Constitution of Politics'. In *Text, Play, and Story: The Construction and Reconstruction of Self and Society,* ed. S. Plattner, 315–55. Washington, DC: American Ethnological Society, 1984.
Majumdar, B. 'Forwards and Backwards: Women's Soccer in Twentieth Century India'. In *Soccer, Women, Sexual Liberation: Kicking off a new era,* ed. Fan Hong and J.A. Mangan. London: Frank Cass, 2004.
Mangan, J.A. *The Games Ethic and Imperialism.* New York: Viking, 1986.
Markovits, A.S. and S. Hellerman. *Offside: Soccer and American Exceptionalism.* Princeton, NJ: Princeton University Press, 2001.
Mason, T. *Association Football and English Society 1863–1915.* Sussex: The Harvester Press, 1980.
Moorhouse, H.J. 'One State, Several Countries: Soccer and Nationality in a "United" Kingdom'. In *Tribal Identities: Nationalism, Europe, Sport,* ed. J.A. Mangan, 55–74. London: Frank Cass, 1996.
Paxman, J. *The English: A Portrait of a People.* London: Michael Joseph, 1998.
Polley, M. 'Sport and National Identity in Contemporary England'. In *Sport and National Identity in the Post-War World,* ed. A. Smith and D. Porter, 1–9. London: Routledge, 2004.
Porter, D. '"Your boys took one hell of a beating!" English Football and British Decline, c.1950–80'. In *Sport and National Identity in the Post-War World,* ed. A. Smith and D. Porter, 10–30. London: Routledge, 2004.
Renan, E. 'What is a Nation?' In *Becoming National: A Reader,* ed. G. Eley and R.G. Suny, 42–56. New York and Oxford: Oxford University Press, 1996 [1882].
Sahlins, M. 'Two or Three Things That I Know About Culture'. *The Journal of the Royal Anthropological Institute* 5, no.3 (1999): 399–421.
Smith, A. 'The Origins of Nations'. In *Becoming National: A Reader,* ed. G. Eley and R.G. Suny, 106–131. New York and Oxford: Oxford University Press, 1996 [1989].
Smith, A. and D. Porter. *Sport and National Identity in the Post-War World.* London: Routledge, 2004.
Stoddart, B. 'Sport, Cultural Politics and International Relations: England versus Germany 1935'. *Paper presented at the Olympic Scientific Congress in Eugene, Oregon,* 1984.
Sugden, J. and A. Tomlinson. *FIFA and the Contest for World Football.* Cambridge: Polity Press, 1998.
Walvin, J. *The People's Game: A Social History of British Football.* London: Allen Lane, 1975.
________ *The Only Game.* London: Longman, 2001.

Soccer in the USA: 'holding out for a hero'?

Dolores P. Martinez

> Where have all the good men gone
> And where are all the gods?
> Where's the street-wise Hercules
> To fight the rising odds?[1]

Introduction

This essay is the result of incidental anthropology, that is, intensive long-term (five years) participant observation without my being aware at the time that I was an observer, just before I became a professional anthropologist. While I did not 'write up' this incidental fieldwork at the time, my analysis of the US soccer scene has taken place in the quarter of a century that I have lived in the UK, mostly as a way of explaining the US attitude to soccer to puzzled Europeans. How can Americans love that often slow-moving, endlessly ritualistic, padded up game *they* call football instead of the fast-paced, highly skilled, brutally beautiful and endlessly enthralling game that is *real* football? And worse, how did rounders, a simplistic version of cricket played by children and girls, become a national sport, baseball, and the source of great amusement with its World Series, an event that shrinks the world to fairly small proportions?[2]

In a brief essay I can only try to offer a general answer, attempting to bring together ideas generated by my teaching on the theories of nations and nationalism, on the construction of heroes in film and by my work in Japan – that *other* nation, also claiming social and cultural uniqueness, where soccer is languishing and baseball reigns supreme in the hearts and minds of most men. As an anthropologist who played women's soccer in the USA, beginning in 1977 – the year when Pelé retired from the New York Cosmos, after two years playing in the North American Soccer League[3] – and who finished my 'career' in 1982 with a major injury, my experience offers but a small window onto the US scene. This ethnographic vignette forms the basis for my argument about national identities, sentiment, the place of women in soccer and a need for heroes – unfortunately with an emphasis on the masculine.[4]

The state of play in 1977

In 1977 I first played on a women's intramural team at the University of Chicago, with some of my fellow fraternity[5] members, women who mostly were at the University of Chicago on sports scholarships for basketball, field hockey and athletics. I was the least experienced athlete in the bunch, but loved playing a game that seemed to suit my inability to coordinate eyes and hands, while allowing me to use my feet, on which I seemed to be surer. Easy victory intramurally led some of my fellow players to wonder if we could play more frequently and with other, tougher, teams. One of the players knew a former captain of the University's men's team, an Argentine named Juan Luco, who seemed willing to coach a group of women. So the club, Quel Bogue (sic, we knew it was bad French), was born. For seven years, until the University finally established its own women's team, Quel Bogue *was* women's soccer at the University of Chicago. During that time, the team included current students, alumni, wives of students and even the occasional Hyde Parker with no connection at all to the University.

Those were interesting years to be involved in soccer in the USA and in women's soccer especially.[6] Told we needed to watch as much 'fútbal' as possible – Juan's English was perfect, but he liked to give the game its 'proper' name – most of us became regular attendants at the Chicago Sting's home matches. We even once played a pre-game women's exhibition match at Soldier Field for them. And so, over the years, we got to watch some of the world's greatest players: Pelé, Franz Beckenbauer, George Best, Jorgen Kristensen (who played for the Sting), Bruce Grobbelaar, Teófilo Cubillas, Hugo Sánchez, Bobby Moore, Johan Cruyff – to name but a few. Some of these internationally known footballers played in the USA during the summer and at home in the winter, others were retired from their home teams and were picking up more play and money in the USA. What was interesting about these matches (aside from the tactical skills we were supposed to be acquiring) was the way in which match attendance, always in the low thousands, varied depending on whom the Sting was playing. If the away team featured a great German player, the German-Americans would be in the stands, waving their flags and cheering the opposing team. If some great Mexican players came with the LA team, the numbers in the stands would swell, Spanish would be the language of the day and only a few souls dared raise their cheers for the home team.[7] This ethnically divided fandom meant that the Sting could rarely count on the support they deserved, since they really had no hometown fan base.[8] These divisions also mirrored the state of play amongst the non-professional leagues.

Since many of the players on Quel Bogue had scholarship obligations to other sports, soccer was a summer sport for them – although many of us did play through the indoor season as well. As a university club rather than team we played few other women's university teams, but seemed to beat them when we did, and so our regular, and more challenging, matches came as a result of joining the Illinois Women's Soccer League,[9] which had both a summer and indoor winter season. In 1977 the IWSL had seven teams and was pleased to take in an eighth; when I left the league in 1982, there were 56 women's teams; and, checking the 2007 website for the league, there are now 133 women's teams. This reveals a great deal about the growth in women's soccer in the USA. What the number and names of these teams do not clearly reveal is their origins. In 1977 the majority of the women's clubs were the 'sister' clubs of the men's non-professional league clubs, the Illinois State Soccer League (ISSL), which was established in 1916.[10] And, in those days of few clubs, both the men's and women's clubs were rarely known by their team names but more often, sadly, by their ethnic affiliation, which generally reflected the neighbourhoods they came from.[11] So we learned, politically incorrectly, of course, to refer to our competitors as the German team, the Mexican team or the Irish team. There was also a clear age difference – except for one suburban women's team, known presciently perhaps, as the 'soccer moms' – the teams we played against were made up of young teenaged girls who tended to give up the sport in their late teens or early 20s. We, on the other hand, were in our early to late 20s and often felt it.

Thus, no matter how well we did on the University circuit where we even took a national championship in 1978, in the IWSL we struggled hard to stay in the middle of the league tables. One year we were consistently at the bottom (our goalie took some months out to have a baby), and another year, the glorious one of 1981, we lost no matches until the playoffs. We had fewer members to call on, so injury, several pregnancies (from our partnered members), and jobs took their toll, as did any University sporting event that conflicted with the IWSL schedule. The fact was, however, that we had no local sponsorship, no real pitch to play on, and no local fan support, in contrast to the other women's teams whom fathers, brothers, neighbours and others would come to watch. In comparison, we often had to argue the West Indian cricket team off the field just to get some practice on a Saturday morning and our 'fans', generally boyfriends or husbands, would rather play soccer themselves than come to watch us. Moreover, the young girls we played against had been watching and playing soccer all their lives – we were only to benefit from such players in the last year or two before the club became a University team, seeing young women coming up who had acquired their soccer skills when young and who outplayed us all. Most importantly, however, despite the many friendships that existed amongst Quel Bogue players, we did not have the fighting spirit of an ethnic identity to drive us.

The ethnic base was also true of many of the men's teams in their league. Several women on Quel Bogue had partners who played for the Jamaican team (the only team near Hyde Park, where we all lived, willing to take in odd players, they had trouble getting 11 Jamaicans together for matches) and they played against the same ethnic mix of teams as we did. In fact, one of my most vivid memories as a spectator of local men's football is of a friend's husband, Paul Buchanan, being called a 'f**king traitor' and then being punched so hard by an opposing player from the Irish team that he was severely concussed. The ethnic divides we saw at Sting matches were based on strongly, even violently, felt distinctions made at the local level that made it impossible for a Chicago team to have a Chicago fan-base.

Soccer, the immigrant's sport

It is difficult to describe the complex and contradictory attitudes that formed the basis of men's participation in soccer in the late 1970s and early 1980s – arguing that there were ethnic divides glosses over the variety of reasons men had for playing and loving football. Looking just at the Hyde Park men, partners of women from the Quel Bogue club, it is possible to demonstrate some of the complexities: from our coach, Juan Luco, an Argentine who had grown up partially in the USA, but had always played soccer and saw it as the only sport; to Paul Buchanan mentioned above, an Irish-American who had grown up in Argentina; to another two former captains of the 'UofC' soccer team, both home-grown mid-western boys, post-graduates, both good athletes at a University that made a point of playing football badly, who took up soccer as a way of playing a team sport that was not considered a joke[12] – everyone had a different reason for their involvement. There was another husband, just recently arrived from Mexico, who could not imagine any other way to spend a Sunday afternoon, as well as two young brothers of Italian descent, sons of academics, who played because it was different and made them feel 'cool' – especially when Italy took the World Cup.

As the sometime 'manager' of Quel Bogue (in our league managers and coaches were not always the same person), I went to IWSL meetings and encountered an older generation of male soccer fanatics. No team was coached by a woman, but all manager-coaches were men, generally some player's father, who frequently spoke English with an accent. This, however, did not mean that all their sentiment was for the old country. Any discussion of changes to the league regulations which required a decision could not occur without one of these men getting up to make a speech in which he pointed out that America was a great country because it was a democracy, that is why they loved it, and why we would have to vote rather than decide by consensus. While playing and coaching soccer spoke to a great passion in these men's lives, as well as to a strong identification with their original 'homes', they were equally devoted to being American. It seemed to be a fact that their sons preferred to play football or baseball, so they supported their sons' participation in these American games while urging their daughters to play the sport they loved best. And, as one of the coaches made a point of telling me, they expected 'their girls' to do everything they knew how to do with a ball. It is this attitude that, I would argue, has helped make women's soccer in the States one of the best leagues in the world – the women have often been coached to a high level of skill. In contrast the men's game, for a long time, was mainly an immigrants' sport, played from nostalgia and by older players who enjoyed the opportunity to speak their native language while practising and playing. Young sons might come along to watch, but when it came to doing sports at school, the choices were both broad – not just football and baseball, but basketball, hockey, swimming, track and field and wrestling – but also better supported by the school as an institution. Soccer was often on offer at schools, but it was seen to be the choice of the less athletically-gifted male. Girls, often opting out of school sports, might well be snapped up by their father or a father's friend for the neighbourhood soccer team.

All that has changed in the last thirty years, of course. Schools support both girls' and boys' soccer teams to a greater extent than in the past, and the term 'soccer moms' no longer refers to a group of women who play soccer themselves. The largely immigrant sport, and thus, by implication, the sport of a working class (although there are examples of soccer having been played at elite schools), has become overwhelmingly middle class. However, a quick glance at the current managers' and team names in the ISSL, reveals a large Hispanic group of teams, as well as an increase in Eastern Europeans. At the men's non-professional level, rather than the primary, high school or college level, soccer is still an immigrants' game. Why is this a point that should be reflected on? For one, there is an important issue to do with styles of play that needs to be understood and examined. That is, while I have noted that it was politically incorrect to call our opponents by their ethnic affiliations, such shorthand also referred to their style of play. The German team was quick and highly skilled, playing their set pieces meticulously; the Mexicans relied on very fast strikers and tough defenders who were not afraid to tackle you even if the ball *might* only be coming in your direction. The Irish team passed more and liked long, wild shots ending in headers and Quel Bogue, trained by an Argentine, worked on ball skills and set pieces, but was perhaps too individualistic. What we all shared in common was the belief that there was no 'American' style of playing soccer and what made watching US professional teams so painful, was that the differing styles of some of the great players of the world never seemed to gel into one team style that would make the game a joy to watch. The 1970s in the USA, then, foreshadowed some of the changes and problems in European soccer that occurred when team membership was opened up to more foreign players.

This lack of cohesiveness, of a local style or technique also reflects the non-US attitude to US players: however good they might be, they just don't have that something that makes a great footballer. Why, after decades of young boys taking to the sport, should this be the case? One possible answer is, of course, that the athletes with the most talent in the USA are drawn to the sports that will gain them the most profit in the long-run.[13] Baseball, football, basketball and hockey[14] stars in the USA make huge amounts of money and have their moments of fame – something that soccer just cannot promise them. US professional soccer teams are still trying to attract the crowds and fans (and sponsorship) that will generate the income that will allow them to attract the big stars. But when the big stars do come, and international stars are invested in the hopes to bolster the reputation of the game, they continue to be big 'foreign' stars, whose stories of struggle to be the best, and their success in the game, are not *local* stories. More to the point, being a middle class kid who is a soccer star at school works against wanting to be a soccer superstar for a career – it is the poor boys of the world who tend to dream of success through sports.

The fact that in the USA most sports stars come through the University system of teams tends to obscure the fact that, for non-US observers, these players are often from the poorest of the working class or from the underclass, just as soccer stars from outside of the USA often are. Upward mobility through sports is one of the mechanisms through which America's egalitarian ideals, the basis for its ideology of exceptionalism,[15] are fostered. The path of underprivileged men through an education system that might support them despite poor academic skills, just because their physical prowess makes them a great team player, highlights the importance of success through sports to Americans. It is another version of the American dream, that egalitarian myth that anyone can make it big in the USA – in short, it is a powerful national narrative, a form of discourse,[16] that both shapes and is shaped by the imagined American community. Moreover, group loyalty, often downplayed in analyses of American individualism, is very important to keep in mind. The success of your High School, and later, College, team can mean everything – and if the institution has to 'buy' the players in, then so be it. Football, basketball, baseball and ice hockey are the sports that *Americans* play and by being bound up in the systems of conspicuous consumption (they cost a lot of money to organize, but can also generate income), excessive display (half-time shows, for example), as well as sporting heroic, legendary names that there are even poems about, such as 'Casey at the Bat' (subtitled 'A Ballad of the Republic'),[17] they symbolize many aspects of what it means to be an American *man*. In short, the players of these sports are bound up in the construction of an idealized national masculinity.[18] How can an immigrant sport now played by middle class suburban white boys, and girls as well, even begin to compete?

Nationalism and sports

I've jumped from women's soccer in Chicago in the late 1970s to a more general argument about the role of ethnicity, class and sport in the USA, solely on the basis of my anthropological understanding of nationalism. These assumptions need to be examined in greater detail.

One often overlooked aspect of Anderson's[19] argument about the development of the nation-state is the role that colonies played early in the process. Key to his argument is an analysis of Latin American Spanish colonies, but Anderson also points to the USA as an important example of a budding nation-state that began to articulate the libertarian principles that were exported to Europe, embraced in the French Revolution, and saw the beginning of the development of European nation-states.[20] The key issue was the distinction between belonging to the state as a matter of right established through place of birth as opposed to belonging as a matter of loyalty to a ruler who embodied the state. For Anderson it was the experience of colonialists born abroad who were seen to be *creole* by fact of birth rather than blood in the Spanish case and were seen as fit only to govern colonies, as well as the experience of British colonists who refused to be taxed without representation, that is, to be treated as a sort of second-class Englishmen, that, combined with the technology of modernity, brought about the nationalist sentiment necessary to the nation-state. Gellner has also noted that nationalist sentiment is often imagined to have long existed – and may have actually occurred in some form[21] – however, the shift to modernity saw the emphasis on this sentiment as *essential* to the construction of the nation-state. Necessary to this process, of course, was the development of the mass media.

As Anderson[22] has famously argued, it was the printing press and early newspapers that allowed for the sharing of nationalistic sentiment. Publishing in larger quantities and publishing in local languages, allowed for the imagined community to see itself as a large group with boundaries beyond that of the city or village. To share a language, was to share a literature, a history, an identity. Thus it should be no surprise that one of the great philosophers of early American independence was Benjamin Franklin, a newspaper owner among his many other accomplishments. Acquiring a sense of shared community through newspaper readership, implies, of course, a system of education open to a majority of a country's citizens. Mass education, especially in relation to promulgating a shared history, is another important component in the development of the imagined national community.

It has been frequently noted that it was initially at the educational institutions of various societies, that team sports were promoted.[23] The USA was no exception: Harvard, established in 1639 and Yale, established in 1701, on the models of Oxford and Cambridge, began playing its famous football matches against each other in 1875, although Rutgers and Princeton had played a first match in 1869.[24] Football in particular was initially the providence of the elites, or of students at elite universities, but through newspaper and later film and television coverage, it became the game of the masses. While in the UK, soccer was promoted to help create a muscular Christianity and to 'subdue' the masses, in the USA, football trickled down through the education system from Universities, to High Schools and, to Junior High Schools, and had a parallel development amongst the factory workers of the Midwest that saw the emergence of professional football at the beginning of the twentieth century. Baseball evolved outside of the college system, but in tandem with football. It was played semi-professionally in the 1860s and the first professional team was established in 1869, and, while less important at the University level, it remains the first team sports many boys encounter while in primary school.[25] When the first US Soccer League was established in 1894, these 'American' sports had already consolidated their place in what Markovits and Hellerman term the hegemonic sports culture of the USA.[26]

This coming together of education and team sports could certainly lead to an analysis of the body, education and governmentality,[27] but more important, it appears to me, is the timing of the development of these sports in the US context. The late 1860s was the era just after the American Civil War, the war that had challenged the concept of the American nation and saw a victory for those who believed that being born in the USA meant all were citizens of the same nation, and that new nations could not be built out of states that belonged to this union. Lincoln's reforms to the government created the modern nation-state that is the USA and it is, as noted by those who wonder if any nation-state fits the ideal type, a fairly singular one.[28] Birth makes you an American, but so does immigration and taking a citizenship test. Few in the country can claim to be of an autochthonous race, and discourses about elitism centre around 'how long' one's family has been in the USA. Ironically, actually being 'native' is not an advantage.

Thus football, baseball and basketball grew up alongside modern American nationalism, increased industrialization, a growing mass media and an expanding education system that not only served the elites, but worked to incorporate the never-ending flow of immigrants into the body politic. As the professional leagues developed into big business in the twentieth century, they found their niche within the mass medium of that era – television. It was here that the games, played locally in schools by children and young adults and in neighbourhood stadia by professionals, fused with big business. These teams serve both to support local identities as their names indicate: the Chicago White Sox, the Boston Red Sox, the Brooklyn Dodgers,[29] the Texas Rangers in baseball, and more generalized identities in football where the teams are less locally named: the Bears, the Colts, the Saints, the Patriots, etc. Given the development of these teams in an era where the USA rarely fought external wars and had made wars between its own states impossible – and I state this in full knowledge that many US states are the size of European countries, which were often at war in the nineteenth and early twentieth centuries – it may well be that these sports became not only the locus of the imagined American community, but also the place within which regional differences could be played out rather than fought out. Symbolic battles over who the local heroes could be (and migration between clubs was possible, of course – how could Americans hate economic migrants?) were fought particularly in the 1950s and 1960s with the emergence of African-American players in all professional sports. In the end sports stars get to be both local and national heroes: for example, despite their identification with a particular team, professional footballers are 'All Americans', great players are incorporated into an 'American Hall of Fame'.

The symbolism of particularly football matches as titanic battles played by heroes and analogous to war is not an original one.[30] Any discussion of the game, during or afterwards, reveals the potency of this imagery: opponents are conquered, smashed or destroyed – to win a game is a victory. The analogy between sports and war should not only be made for American football. The plot of the film *Rollerball*[31] makes the point explicitly through its story about the invented game of rollerball that has replaced war in a future world ruled by corporations rather than nation-states. Attempts to make soccer more popular during the 1980s saw the making of the film *Victory*,[32] in which Sylvester Stallone plays the goalie for a team formed by allied prisoners of war. And sometimes sportsmen themselves make the connection for their fans. During the 2002 World Cup I had to explain Henry V's[33] speech 'Once more unto the breach, dear friends, once more' to my son because David Beckham had quoted it before a match. After I had described the battle of Agincourt as well and the role that English longbows had played in the victory, my son, whose sense of history was not strongly developed at that point, asked the *really* important question: 'Did the French or the English team win?'

National identity has become more and more bound up with national sports, and post-Second World War, it has become far more acceptable to express such nationalist sentiment through sports than through calls to war – although sports have yet to replace war as in *Rollerball*. This fact is obvious to all researchers who write about sports and nationalism, particularly in relation to soccer. For as Hobsbawm has noted, the 'imagined community of millions seems more real as a team of eleven named people'.[34] But the USA, with its large states and local loyalties to local teams, fights such battles through football, baseball, basketball and hockey. That baseball has a World Series, in my experience, doesn't seem odd until you leave the USA, because the series is the accumulation of games played within two separate leagues (with 30 teams in total) – and that is just the professional teams.[35] While FIFA has expanded greatly and more teams participate in the paring down to 16 final teams, early FIFA World Cups did not begin with more than 30 teams either. In short, the USA is large enough to fight such sports battles without needing to go outside its continental boundaries – Canada being one of the few nations that participates in these sporting events.

The argument that nationalist sentiment is supported by the imagined community does not tell us enough about how nationalist sentiment is created as an emotional bond. Symbols acquire meaning not naturally, but through culturally constructed events. For the sociologists Marvin and Ingle, American nationalism requires particular effort to create precisely because the USA is multiethnic and the result of generations of migration.[36] The usual nationalist call, to one people, one language, one set of boundaries could easily flounder on the first two grounds in the USA. The symbols of Americanism, the flag in particular, need to stand for something worth a newcomer's loyalty. For many, as I noted in my discussion of IWSL league meetings, it was the idea of the USA as a land of political freedom and, often unspoken, economic opportunity that made for emotive speeches about belonging. Yet Marvin and Ingle argue that all countries, but especially the USA, need powerful and emotive symbols; and for them it is the heroic war dead, the blood sacrifice made by those who died to protect the country, that cements national sentiment into place.[37] It produces a tautology of 'this country is worth dying for, because people I know or am related to have died for it'. These heroic deaths must be in 'just' wars and since 1945, as Marvin and Ingle note with their discussion of the Vietnam War Memorial, this is a vexed issue.[38]

However, if we look at the playing fields of the USA (or any other country), the just war is fought out locally, nationally and internationally through sports. And, as discussed above, its heroes are also part of that other mythic modern capitalist narrative: the poor boy made good. In sports we have heroes who do spill their blood, literally and metaphorically, by playing their hearts and guts out for their fans' sake. Aside from the occasional scandal – which just shows how human they are – sports heroes can be better than war heroes, because heroism in war, at least in post-modernity, seems to also raise questions of brutality, human rights and the whole problem of gender since women now go to war too. Only on the playing fields, as long as sports teams are single-gendered, do we see heroic masculinity at its pinnacle, with an emphasis on teamwork and group spirit. Movie heroes rely on special effects; professional sport heroes rely on their bodies and skills: they are self-motivated, self-created and 'the best of the best'. Moreover, in the twentieth century the concept of the heroic death has taken a few knocks in popular culture. Western heroes rarely seem to die anymore, but always survive to fight another day. Sports heroes fit into this paradigm quite neatly and thus, as Ellen has recently noted in an article on male soccer fandom, become examples of 'man-love without sex. The deep-rooted desire all men have to be a hero sublimated into excessive admiration for another man.'[39]

Soccer's fit with modern national narratives of identity and sentiment for the 'land of our fathers' just doesn't work for the USA because that conceptual space has been long filled by various 'native' sports as Markovits and Hellerman so persuasively argue.[40] They give the nation heroes known to everyone, beginning in early childhood when children learn of the importance of such heroes as James Thorpe and Jesse Owens at school. Thorpe (1888–1953), partially Native American, one of the few such sporting heroes, was both a football and a baseball legend, as well as winning Olympic medals in Pentathlon and Decathlon. Jesse Owens (1903–80) an African-American, winner in the 1936 Berlin Olympics, created problems for Hitler's ideology of the superiority of the Aryan race, or so American schoolchildren are taught. More important, however, is the mythic and powerful narrative about the talented poor boy who becomes a sports superstar – decades before European soccer began to pay outrageous salaries to, and transfer fees for, its players, the American sports heroes were heroes who made money.

Conclusion: holding out for a hero

If national sports provide national heroes, then the USA has a long history of such sports and such heroic legends going right back to the consolidation of the nation-state in the nineteenth century: Red Grange (1903–91), known as the Galloping Ghost; The Gipper (1895–1920), immortalized on film by Ronald Reagan of all people; O.J. Simpson (b.1947), now more infamous than famous; Babe Ruth (1895–1948), who has a candy bar named after him; Lou Gehrig (1903–41), who has a disease named after him; Ty Cobb (1886–1961) who had a recent film made of his life; and Ernie Banks (b.1931), the first African-American to play for the Chicago Cubs – this is a brief list compiled partly from memory based on my childhood as a-disinterested-in-football-and-baseball-girl in the USA. Moreover they are masculine narratives about what it means to be a gifted man who is willing to sacrifice much for one's team, team-mates, fans and, it is implied, one's country. It was not accidental plotting that made Rocky (aka Sylvester Stallone) the goalkeeper in the Second World War film *Victory*. The overlapping of various narrative strands that aimed to appeal to a US audience – the working class man made heroic through sport, the American learning to be great at soccer and outwitting the Nazis to boot while somehow contributing to winning the war – do not require much skill to unravel.

That such narratives appear to *have* to be about men in order to have real emotive power reveals much about the patriarchal nature of the nation-state. Heroic male suffering and 'sacrifice' remain symbolically central to the imagined national community. While there are national heroines, it is the cult of the male hero that appears to matter the most in every nation-state. There is no space here to pursue the possible reasons for this, but I find Marvin and Ingle's argument, focused on the example of the USA, persuasive. They use Jay's theory that blood 'sacrifice' makes kinship among men, who form the core of all patriarchal religions, to show how this sense of 'kinship' is created in the nation-state through the cult of war heroes.[41] In the light of my 1970s–80s experience in which daughters were encouraged to play soccer, a sport that spoke to an ethnic, non-American and, possibly shifting identity (i.e., support for soccer teams can famously and seamlessly move between local and national teams); while sons were expected to play 'American' sports in which loyalty is invariably to one local professional team, says much about the construction of gender in the USA.[42] Women may be needed in order to biologically reproduce the nation, but they are seen to lack the sort of gung-ho and unquestioning single-minded loyalty that defines masculine American identity.

The lives of heroic players are key defining narratives in this construction of a national masculinity: they tell tales of triumph in the face of adversity, of suffering and stoicism, tragic death, or racism overcome as well as cautionary tales about the price of fame. They live in the national consciousness and it is not necessary, as noted above, to be male or sports mad to know something about these heroes. In contrast, when in 1969 a friend asked me who Pelé was because she had to write a report on him for her Spanish class, neither she nor I – long term residents of a predominantly middle class Jewish neighbourhood – had the faintest idea.

The continued spread of soccer in the USA in the last thirty years would make such ignorance less likely in the twenty-first century. My point, however, is that whatever tales of heroic triumph exist concerning US soccer, they belong more to the women's league, who have been hugely successful; or to foreign male players bought in to bolster US teams. They are not *home-grown* narratives about being an American man – fighting, loving, drinking too much, failing and succeeding in the end – 'making good' and becoming great.

Without recognizable American elements to their stories, it becomes difficult for young boys to identify with these foreign heroes. Lacking a powerful narrative history, soccer in the USA remains both the sport of middle-aged immigrant men and of middle class boys who don't need to succeed in sports in order to survive whatever adversity life has to throw at them. Issues of both class and ethnicity combine to undermine the symbolic value of male participation in soccer. It has become a sport in which 'less able' boys, who want to play it safe, or older men, who pine for the 'old country', participate. Thus, men's soccer remains somehow un-American. In contrast, American women's professional soccer has transcended its early affiliation with ethnicity and class, and has succeeded at a global level. Unfortunately, the success of women could well be the final nail in the coffin of male soccer participation – if women can triumph in the sport, it really must not be tough enough to qualify as a true test of *American* masculinity.

Yet the USA's ire at its lack of success in modernity's only truly global sport, its desire to win the symbolic war between nations, combined with increasing US business investment in foreign soccer teams, means that we shouldn't think it is all over yet. Bringing David Beckham to the US looks like the beginning of a new era. Will Beckham succeed where Pelé and others before him have failed? It is difficult to play the prophet at such a point. On the one hand, he already has filmic fame in *Bend it Like Beckham* and so will be familiar to Americans; on the other, he has never led his national team to World Cup glory and his last few years have been plagued by injury.[43] He may well be seen, glamorous metrosexual that he might be, to fall into that category of failing foreign superstar trying to make it big in the USA. Ticket sales in LA have already increased and may stay strong for a time; away games will probably see the English in America come out to cheer him on, but will it change the place that soccer holds in the American consciousness? I doubt it.

What *might* achieve such a change would be for an ordinary kid, preferably from a city and possibly poor, to be so brilliant at soccer that he is headhunted to play for one of the great foreign clubs (that being said, it must be a club that Americans recognize). Perhaps in an unconscious imitation of the 'if you build it, they will come' mantra from the film *Field of Dreams*,[44] such a FIFA-approved narrative already has been made into a film, *Goal!*[45] I would add, however, that for true success, the hero would have to choose, at the height of his skills and foreign fame – and he would have to achieve fame, not just be a good team player – to come home to play for his local and national teams: *that* would have great symbolic meaning. Giving up the glory of playing for Manchester United, A.C. Milan or Real Madrid and the lure of foreign life (and women?), for the greatness that is America, that would be the stuff of a new national narrative – and these ideas already form the plots imagined by fans of the released straight to DVD *Goal 2* and not-yet-made *Goal 3*.[46] It would help if this as-yet-to-exist hero's style of play also had changed the way the foreign club played, that is, if America offered something to the world of soccer technique. An American soccer hero in this mould, a home-grown talent who achieves international fame, could change the face of the game in the USA. This is the hero that US soccer is holding out for.

> He's gotta be strong and he's gotta be fast
>
> And he's gotta be fresh from the fight.
>
> I need a hero. I'm holding out for a hero 'til the morning light.
>
> He's gotta be sure
>
> and it's gotta be soon
>
> And he's gotta be larger than life.[47]

Acknowledgements

I must thank Projit Mukharji who asked for my help in organizing the conference this volume is based on and then encouraged me to write this piece. Paul Buchanan and Beth Wachter confirmed and corrected my memories about Quel Bogue; while Judith Maclean of the IWSL provided me with additional help. I also must thank my husband, David Gellner, fellow football fanatic, for discussing the ideas in this essay with me and his careful proofreading, as always. Of course, any errors or inaccuracies are entirely my own. This essay is dedicated to the memory of Juan Luco (1950–2000) who coached the women's team Quel Bogue from 1977–84 and the University of Women's Soccer team from 1987–90.

Notes

1. Steinman and Pitchford, *Holding out for a hero*.
2. Markovits and Hellerman begin their book on soccer and US exceptionalism by asking similar questions (*Offside*, 4–5).
3. The National American Soccer League (NASL) was first formed in 1967, and amalgamated with the FIFA-recognized United Soccer Association in 1968; it was the professional league in the USA until it was suspended in 1984. It was eventually succeeded by Major League Soccer (MLS) in 1993. Giulianotti and Williams (*Game without Frontiers*, 3–4) give a more detailed overview of soccer in the USA beginning in the nineteenth century.
4. See the Robinson article in this collection.
5. The fraternity we belonged to was the only co-ed fraternity on campus; there were no sororities at the University of Chicago at that time. Our fraternity liked to claim it was the model for the film *Animal House* (Landis, 1978) and was the only Chicago fraternity that was not associated with any particular team sports until the women starting playing soccer.
6. See Markovits and Hellerman, 'Women's Soccer in the United States', 14–29, for an overview of the development of women's football in the USA. They note that the early 1980s saw a massive increase in the number of women's teams.
7. Price and Whitworth, 'Soccer and Latino Cultural Space', 167, note that this was still a problem in 2001, with an example of how a USA versus Honduras match saw half of the home crowd supporting the Honduran team.
8. Except for the female fans who came especially for Kristensen.
9. Their website can be found on http://www.iwsl.com/.
10. More information on them can be found at http://www.illinoissoccer.org/main.htm.
11. In this sense, Mangan's concept of 'tribal' identities, referring to the nation as a tribe, breaks down further and maps onto 'ethnic' identity within multi-ethnic US society (Mangan's, *Tribal Identities*). Price and Whithouse, 'Soccer and Latino Cultural Space', again provide a good example of this with their analysis of the Latino Soccer League in Washington, DC.

12. This was in contrast to the general case in US colleges, where, as Markovits and Hellerman argue (*Offside*, 123), it is the *weaker* male athletes who play soccer. In the late 1970s, the UofC clung to its image of a college that was too intellectual to do sports well, despite a strong men's rugby team and several nationally successful women's teams. It should be said, then, that it was the mainstream sports that the University's men disdained.
13. See Note 12 above.
14. Or the 'Big Three and one-Half' as Markovits and Hellerman (*Offside*, 52) term these sports.
15. It is not just in its lack of soccer success and support of less international sports that makes the USA exceptional, but its political ideology which fosters a notion of difference from the rest of the world; cf. Lipset, *American Exceptionalism*.
16. I am using the term discourse here in the full Foucaultian sense of that which defines and produces knowledge (*The Archaeology of Knowledge*). Americans *know* that their sports are better than anyone else's, because of the mythic tales about their heroic sports stars, that hold out the promise of achieving the same sort of fame, power and money to others. I discuss this is more detail in the rest of the essay.
17. Thayer, 'Casey at the Bat, A Ballad of the Republic'.
18. Many scholars have noted the strong identification of sports with masculinity, despite the fact of women's increasingly involvement. See especially Mangan, 'Duty unto Death, 10–38 on masculinity and militarism; and MacClancy, 'Sport, Identity and Ethnicity', 16 on how this seems to occur across societies.
19. Anderson, *Imagined Communities*.
20. Although the philosophical basis for some of the ideas, *pace* Thomas Paine for example, originated in Europe.
21. Gellner, *Nations and Nationalism*.
22. Anderson, *Imagined Communities*.
23. See Sage, 'Sport in American Society', 4–14; Betts, 'The Technological Revolution and the Rise of Sport, 1850-1900', 58–80; and Spring, 'Mass Culture and School Sports', 81–96, who together provide a fairly comprehensive overview of the history of sports and education in the USA.
24. Gardner, *The Simplest Game*.
25. Sage's edited volume, *Sport and American Society*, on sports in US society, provides a fairly thorough overview of the history and evolution of sports in the USA.
26. Markovits and Hellerman, *Offside*, 7–51.
27. Foucault, *The History of Sexuality Vol. 2* and *The History of Sexuality Vol. 3*.
28. Lipset, *American Exceptionalism*.
29. Although they, of course, made the very post-modern move and became the Los Angeles Dodgers in 1958.
30. Both Mangan, 'Duty unto Death', 10–38, and Holt, 'Contrasting Nationalisms', 39–54, examine various aspects of this in relation to militarism and concepts of masculinity in the UK and France.
31. Jewison, *Rollerball*.
32. Huston, *Victory*.
33. Shakespeare, 'King Henry V', 717.
34. Hobsbawm, *Nations and Nationalism*, 143.
35. See Klein's article in this issue, which analyses the hubris of the 'World' Series.
36. Marvin and Ingle, *Blood Sacrifice and the Nation*. An earlier version of their argument was published in 1996 in 'Blood Sacrifice and the Nation: Revisiting Civil Religion'. Ehrenreich makes similar points in her *Blood Rites*.
37. Marvin and Ingle, *Blood Sacrifice and the Nation*.
38. Ibid., 182.
39. Ellen, 'Glossy hair, hard tackles, impressive ball control', 5.
40. Markovits and Hellerman, *Offside*, 52–98.
41. Jay, *Throughout your Generations Forever*.
42. See Klein's article in this collection, which makes this point about the problem of shifting loyalties among soccer supporters; this point helped me formulate this last strand to my argument.
43. Chadha, *Bend it Like Beckham*.
44. Robinson, *Field of Dreams*.
45. Cannon, *Goal! The Dream Begins*.
46. See the discussion boards at www.imdb.com./Goal!
47. Steinman and Pitchford, *Holding out for a hero*.

References

Anderson, Benedict. *Imagined Communities: Reflections on the Origin and Spread of Nationalism.* New York: Verso, 1991 rev. edn.

Betts, John Rickards. 'The Technological Revolution and the Rise of Sport, 1850–1900'. In *Sport and American Society, Selected Readings,* ed. George H. Sage, 58–80. London: Addison-Wesley Publishing Company, 1980.

Cannon, Danny (director). *Goal! The Dream Begins.* Milkshake Films, 2005.

Chadha, Gurinder (director). *Bend it Like Beckham.* Kintop Pictures, 2002.

Ehrenreich, Barbara. *Blood Rites, Origins and History of the Passions of War.* London: Virago Press, 1998.

Ellen, Barbara. 'Glossy hair, hard tackles, impressive ball control … Footballers are a bunch of herosexuals'. *Observer Magazine* (6 May 2007): 5.

Foucault, M. *The Archaeology of Knowledge,* trans. A.M. Sheridan Smith. London: Tavistock Publications, 1972.

________ *The History of Sexuality Vol. 2: The Use of Pleasure,* trans. Robert Hurley. New York: Random House, 1985.

________ *The History of Sexuality Vol. 3: The Care of the Self,* trans. Robert Hurley. New York: Vintage Books, 1988.

Gardner, Paul. *The Simplest Game, The Intelligent Fan's Guide to the World of Soccer.* London: Macmillan, 1996.

Gellner, Ernest. *Nations and Nationalism.* Ithaca, NY: Cornell University Press, 1983.

Giulianotti, Richard and John Williams. *Game without Frontiers, Football, Identity and Modernity.* Brookfield, VT: Ashgate Publishing Company, 1994.

Hobsbawm, Eric. *Nations and Nationalism since 1780: Programme, Myth, Reality.* Cambridge: Cambridge University Press, 1990.

Holt, Richard. 'Contrasting Nationalisms: Sport, Militarism and the Unitary State in Britain and France before 1914'. In *Tribal Identities, Nationalism, Europe, Sport,* ed. J.A. Mangan, 39–54. London: Frank Cass & Co, 1996.

Huston, John (director). *Victory.* Lorimar Film Entertainment, 1981.

Jay, Nancy. *Throughout your Generations Forever: Sacrifice, Religion, and Paternity.* Cambridge: Cambridge University Press, 1992.

Jewison, Norman (director). *Rollerball.* Algonquin, 1975.

Landis, John (director). *Animal House.* Universal Pictures, 1978.

Lipset, Seymour Martin. *American Exceptionalism; a Double-Edged Sword.* New York: W.W. Norton & Company, 1996.

MacClancy, Jeremy. 'Sport, Identity and Ethnicity'. In *Sport, Identity and Ethnicity,* ed. Jeremy MacClancy, 1–20. Oxford: Berg, 1996.

Mangan, J.A. 'Introduction'. In *Tribal Identities, Nationalism, Europe, Sport,* ed. J.A. Mangan, 1–9. London: Frank Cass & Co, 1996.

________ 'Duty unto Death: English Masculinity and Militarism in the Age of New Imperialism'. In *Tribal Identities, Nationalism, Europe, Sport,* ed. J.A. Mangan, 10–38. London: Frank Cass & Co, 1996.

Markovits, Andrei S. and Steven L. Hellerman. *Offside, Soccer and American Exceptionalism.* Princeton, NJ: Princeton University Press, 2001.

________ 'Women's Soccer in the United States: Yet Another American "Exceptionalism"'. In *Soccer, Women, Sexual Liberation, Kicking Off a New Era,* ed. Fan Hong and J.A Mangan, 14–29. London: Frank Cass, 2004.

Marvin, Caroline and David W. Ingle. 'Blood Sacrifice and the Nation: Revisiting Civil Religion'. *Journal of the American Academy of Religion LXIV,* no.4 (1996): 767–80.

________ *Blood Sacrifice and the Nation, Totem Rituals and the American Flag.* Cambridge: Cambridge University Press, 1999.

Price, Marie and Courtney Whitworth. 'Soccer and Latino Cultural Space, Metropolitan Washington *Fútbal* Leagues'. In *Hispanic Spaces, Latino Places: Community and Cultural Diversity in Contemporary America,* ed. Daniel D. Arreola, 167–186, Austin. TX: University of Texas Press, 2004.

Robinson, Phil Alden (director). *Field of Dreams.* Gordon Company, 1989.

Sage, George H. ed. *Sport and American Society, Selected Readings.* London: Addison-Wesley Publishing Company, 1980.

________ 'Sport in American Society: Its Pervasiveness and Its Study'. In *Sport and American Society, Selected Readings,* ed. George H. Sage, 4–14. London: Addison-Wesley Publishing Company, 1980.

Shakespeare, William. 'King Henry V'. In the *Complete Works of William Shakespeare.* Edinburgh: William P. Nimmo, n.d. [vol.1]: 701–47.
Spring, Joel H. 'Mass Culture and School Sports'. In *Sport and American Society, Selected Readings,* ed. George H. Sage, 81–96. London: Addison-Wesley Publishing Company, 1980.
Steinman, Jim and Pitchford, Dean. *Holding out for a hero.* ©1984.
Thayer, Ernest. 'Casey at the Bat, A Ballad of the Republic'. In *The Annotated Casey at the Bat: A Collection of Ballads about the Mighty Casey,* ed. Martin Gardiner. Chicago, IL: University of Chicago Press, 1984 [1888] rev. edn.

Football in the reconstruction of the gender order in Japan

Wolfram Manzenreiter

Introduction: the future of football is female ... and in Asia

'The future of football is feminine', promised FIFA President Blatter after the final curtain had fallen at the USA Women's World Cup in 1999. Four years later, when the International Olympic Committee bestowed the special award for 'Women and Sport' upon the 2003 World Cup finals, he renewed the pledge. A year later, when the Asian Football Confederation celebrated its 50th anniversary, the courteous chief representative of the world football federation claimed that the future of football was in Asia. Whether the future prospects of the people's game now actually will be with women or in Asia, both phrases allude to the expansionary will of football's control body into regions, markets and consumer segments that have been so far largely excluded from the 'house of football', another bright catchphrase coming from the Blatter presidency of FIFA. As with the conventional phrase of the 'people's game', the house of football wantonly conceals the indisputable fact of the marginalization of close to half the people of the world. In most parts of the globe, gender discrimination is the most evident rupture in the ideology of the people's game. Gender inequality in football is particularly noticeable in those societies where football has emerged as the preferred leisure activity of the male working and middle classes.

As feminist interventions have shown, the consumption and experience of football continue to provide one of the last reserves of patriarchy in late modernity, notwithstanding broader economic, political, legal and social developments in society. Burton Nelson explained the burgeoning popularity of American football as an escapist response to the progress of women in many social fields: 'The stronger women get, the more men love football'.[1] Adapted to an East Asian context, this hypothesis would require understanding the recent establishment of professional leagues throughout the region as a conservative backlash against East Asian women's progress in social and public life, particularly if overwhelming male support for the game can be proved.

Yet without the historical ballast of traditional sporting rivalries, turf wars and violent fan behaviour, the cultural implant of football could have equally acquired a unique set of symbolic meanings for gender relations in East Asia. To understand the junction or disjunction between football and masculinity in Japan, we have to explore both the vernacular lines which form the images of masculinity and the way football has been appropriated by society on a practical and symbolic level. The next sections will show that football in Japan is far from being an exclusively male domain, but nonetheless provides a fallback position for some men to experience and perform their idea of masculinity. This contradictory design and development, I will argue, is related both to the crisis of hegemonic masculinity, and to the nature of the commodity form, which also is in Japanese football the precondition for the reproduction of a global gender order.

The quantitative face of women's football in Japan and East Asia

First, we have to consider the representation of both sexes in football.[2] Taking into account the lack of competition with men's football, the US 'soccer exceptionalism' hypothesis[3] explains the comparatively huge popularity of women's football in the USA where two out of three officially registered players are female. In nearly all other countries however, the proportion of women players is much lower, if it is recorded at all. FIFA's Big Count on the global state of football in 2000 listed particularly low percentage rates for the member states of the continental football federations in Africa and Asia. In Japan, where the semi-professional L-League (the 'Japan Ladies' Soccer League', now called the Nadeshiko League) was launched some years ahead of the men's full professional J. League, the Big Count revealed about 20,000 women out of a total of 3.3 million players and 1,120 male professionals, who were all registered with the Japan Football Association. Slightly less than half of the 20,000 was comprised of female youth players. If these figures, which were based on data provided by the national football association, are assessed in relation to population statistics, the under-representation of women in football becomes even clearer. Country-specific participation rates can best be demonstrated by using a per capita index model that correlates the athletic production of a nation with the population base of the country.[4]

Thus in terms of continental output, in 2000, Europe produced approximately 2.5 times more football players than the world norm, whereas Asia spawned slightly less than half of the norm. In a global perspective, the only East Asian country that outperforms the world average is Japan with an index of 1.30. In contrast, all the 'Chinas' (including the People's Republic, Hong Kong, Macao, Chinese Taipei and Singapore), Mongolia and the two Koreas are underachievers in the generation of football players. Measured against the continental average, Japan is joined by South Korea, Macao and Singapore as the four countries in East Asia that exceed the continental average; all others are well below it. The output of football players, however, is highly gendered, as total output tables and the indices reveal. In absolute numbers, FIFA counted ten times more male players among its member associations than female players. Thus countries all over the world tend to produce much higher numbers of male athletes, as the medium variant of the sex distribution ratio is otherwise just 101.3 males per 100 females (and not 10 males per 1 female). In terms of female players, an exceptionally high output is generated by the USA, where the per capita index for female players is more than five times higher than the index for men. The first Women's World Cup winners, Norway, also record a double-digit output of 11.21. Other examples, where the output of female athletes is significantly higher than the production of male footballers, include Canada (7.68/1.60), Norway's Scandinavian neighbours Sweden (6.55/2.91) and Denmark (6.64/3.31), and the 2003 Women's World Cup winners Germany (4.98/3.74). In Asia, all countries produced many fewer female players than male footballers. The poor condition of women's football is a common feature in all of these countries that have indices of less than 0.10. Compared to the all-Asian per capita index of 0.03, the position of women's football in Japan (0.08) and Korea (0.06) seems to be slightly better.

Table 1. National variations of football player output in East Asia and other selected areas

	total	*male*	*female*
	1.00	1.00	1.00
World			
Asia	0.46	0.50	0.03
China	0.28	0.30	0.02
Japan	1.30	1.47	0.08
South Korea	0.55	0.60	0.06
North Korea	0.25	0.27	—*
Hong Kong	0.18	0.20	0.03
Macao	0.70	0.82	0.01
Singapore	0.71	0.78	0.04
Taipei	0.19	0.20	0.03
Mongolia	0.23	0.25	0.01
Europe	2.46	2.71	1.13
England	3.28	3.64	0.58
Germany	3.77	3.74	4.98
Brazil	2.03	2.28	0.11
USA	3.09	2.12	12.31

* No figures available for female players from North Korea.
Sources: Own calculations derived from the following: Data on players according to FIFA's Big Count (2000), population size according to Population Division of the Department of Economic and Social Affairs of the United Nations Secretariat, World Population Prospects: The 2002 Revision and World Urbanization Prospects: The 2001 Revision, http://esa.un.org/unpp (accessed 1 November 2003); population data for England according to National Census 2001.

Intra-continental variations become more pronounced when the single country data are computed against the continental norm (that is, all Asia = 1.0, see Table 2). In these cases, the output numbers of female football players appear to be more buoyant for at least two of the three football powerhouses of the East Asian region. Japan is the continental leader in the field of women's football with an index of 3.12, followed by South Korea with 2.22, Singapore (1.52), Chinese Taipei (1.19) and Hong Kong (1.07). The per capita index level indicates that most of East Asia, with the exception of the 1999 world championship runners-up China PR (0.72), Macao and Mongolia, outperform the remainder of Asia, including the Middle East and other Islamic societies in South East Asia. It is interesting to note that in most East Asian countries the per capita index of female footballers is higher than the per capita index of male football players if measured against the continental norm. In Singapore, both indices are on the same level, whereas Macao and Mongolia are the only countries with a significantly higher per capita index of male footballers.

A simple market explanation of men's and women's football alone – as rival suppliers of the same commodity competing against each other for income from the turnstiles, corporate sponsorship and broadcast revenues – is not particularly helpful in explaining the quantitative characteristics of women's participation in football. Such a model would include success on the pitch as a crucial variable and determinant of economic viability. Yet a comparison of female and male national team rankings reveals the flaws of such an assumption: all female national teams are placed higher in the ranks than the male teams. In May 2006, five teams from East Asia were placed twenty-fifth or better, with two even among the top ten (see Table 3). For the male teams,

Table 2. National variations of football player output in East Asia (inc. Singapore)

	total	***male***	***female***
	1.00	1.00	1.00
Asia			
China	0.61	0.60	0.72
Japan	2.80	2.92	3.12
South Korea	1.19	1.20	2.22
North Korea	0.53	0.54	—*
Hong Kong	0.38	0.39	1.07
Macao	1.51	1.63	0.43
Singapore	1.53	1.55	1.52
Taipei	0.40	0.40	1.19
Mongolia	0.49	0.50	0.24

*No figures available for female players from North Korea.
Sources: Own calculations derived from the same data sources as Table 1. Population size for Chinese Taipei according to the July 2000 estimate of the Yahoo! References, World Fact Book.

the highest position was held by Japan (18), followed by South Korea at number 29 and China PR already well down at number 68 (Singapore: 92, Hong Kong: 116; Taipei: 156, Mongolia: 179). North Korea's men were ranked 88th, but the female national team of the Democratic Republic of Korea was placed seventh, and China's women's team was at number eight (Japan: 13, South Korea: 23, Taipei: 25; Hong Kong: 67; Singapore: 92, Mongolia not listed).

The inroad of women into football and their success at international tournaments threaten to disrupt culturally bound ideas of self, gender and nation in places where the collective imagination stereotypically identifies football as a male domain and where images of national power and status are thus related to the achievement of the men's national team.[5] But how does Japanese society conceptualize the ideals of female and male, particularly with reference to sport, and what kind of body practices are 'naturally' associated with the respective images of the sexes? To understand the gender-specific representative role of football in Japan thus requires a double strategy of, on the one hand, looking at the cultural meaning of being a man and the respective

Table 3. World ranking of women's and men's national teams in 2006

Team	Women	Men
Korea DPR	7	88
China PR	8	68
Japan	13	18
Korea Republic	23	29
Chinese Taipei	25	156
Hong Kong	67	116
Singapore	92	92
Mongolia	-*	181
Macao	-*	185

*Mongolia and Macao are not listed among the 129 teams in FIFA Women's Football Rankings.
Source: Rankings derived from FIFA statistics (www.fifa.org).

gender norms and roles in Japan, and on the other hand, it is necessary to reflect upon gender-specific functions and expectations attached to football, and sport in general, in this society.

The gendered order of Japanese sports

In recent years, motivated by the desire to produce greater fan support and increase revenues, football leagues and teams around the world have started to target women as a new component of their potential fan base. With the imperative of extending the reach for customers wherever they can be found, marketing specialists have attempted to inverse the traditional relationship between the female body and the male gaze. Whereas football has traditionally been performed by men for a male spectatorship, the feminization of the audience has challenged established concepts of maleness in the stadia, and probably more among male spectators than the athletes.

Opening new spaces of consumption for new consumer groups was one of the most cogent explanations for the commercial success of the J. League in the mid-1990s. In order to maximize popular support, the J-League devised the home town principle that rooted a football team within its home region, and marketed football as a respectable, clean and safe leisure activity for the entire family. A meticulously styled corporate identity for almost all of the teams, consisting of uniforms, cute mascots, team songs, slogans and cool merchandise goods, was a deliberate attempt to attract Japan's most important consumer group of the 1990s, young females, who had repeatedly shown their power to move entire leisure markets, even in such dubious cases as horse-racing. The marketing strategy worked out well. Huge numbers of young women flocked into the football stadia, enthusiastically buying the accompanying merchandise goods which turned into the most important revenue source of the first two years.[6] The importance of the female fans to the new football league was symbolically acknowledged by the editorial staff of the *Gendai Yōgo no Kisō Chishiki*, a reference book on recent changes of the Japanese vocabulary, when it nominated *sapōtā* (supporter) as trendy word of the year in 1993 and invited Shitara Risako, a well known TV starlet and wife of the best known player of the time, Miura Kazuyoshi, to receive the award.

Rather than supporting a team, many of these female fans felt attracted by singular players such as Miura or Nakata, in later years.[7] Magazines that address a large and exclusively female readership featured cover spreads and articles on Japanese and international football stars during the 1990s and at the time of the 2002 World Cup.[8] The visual attraction of the J. Leaguers as a new breed of sport athletes set apart from the normative standard of baseball players, as well as the later 'Beckham-Boom',[9] underline the particular phenomenon of turning the male players into a commodity for consumption by, amongst others, a young and wealthy female audience. Even after the novelty of the J. League and the World Cup boom had faded, women made up a large proportion of the crowds in the stands. According to a J. League spectatorship survey, 42.3% of football supporters on any given match day during the 2005 season were female.

The large share of women in the stadia only partially conflicts with the notion of football as a male domain. Rather the phenomenon corresponds with the gender-specific role division of bourgeois society: men appear as actors on the pitch, in the back office or in the media, whereas women fulfil supporting roles in the stands or behind the scenes. Looking at Japan's junior and senior high schools where football has come to be the most or second-to-most popular sport amongst students, no girls' football team is registered with the High School Sport Federation. For younger girls, football was only officially acknowledged in 2001; hence there is only one girl for every 109 boys playing football. But female students have often been granted the role of 'managers' of school teams, where their duties primarily consist of serving food and drinks to the players, washing the kit, cleaning up and keeping the score.[10] This gendered separation of roles is quite common among other school sports clubs in Japan and plays an 'important role in reproducing and naturalising a masculinist gender ideology which places men in public places of performance and women in private, behind-the-scenes support roles'.[11]

Sociological interventions have shown the mechanisms and dynamics by which gender in sport is socially constructed in various ways. The physicality embodied in sport renders it a prominent site for the experience and reinforcement of traditional gender roles and relations between the sexes.[12] Gender socialization is considered as a lifelong process, with the family, the school and the media as prime sites of transmitting and reaffirming traditional gender roles. Families are the focal group in which young children develop a sense of self; they also strongly influence preferences of taste and style that a person develops. Schools, which are also the most important channel for recognizing and nurturing sports talent, promote the officially sanctified versions of femininity and masculinity; and the mass media enhance the differences as well as play a leading role in reproducing gender divisions, particularly in their sport sections.

With regard to football, essentialized categories of 'male' and 'female' and appropriate gender behaviour hamper women's progress in Japan as elsewhere,[13] where the male/female dichotomy in sports is most openly expressed in the national game of football.[14] The anthropologist Edwards noted that women's involvement in Japanese football was constrained by an inherently comparative logic, and the firm belief 'that the world of competitive sport is naturally and irreversibly first and foremost the domain of male and natural masculinity'.[15] The discourse on sportswomen's mental, emotional and physical inferiority in Japan originates from an antiquated deterministic assertion of sexual difference and a related focus on women's reproductive capabilities. In many respects the female body seems to have been reduced to its uterus – in scientific literature, training manuals for coaches and in such training routines that require players to record their menstrual cycle. While this discourse has lost some of its authority over the past few decades, female athletes' choices continue to be framed by a comparative (with the male norm) scientific approach that reflects male hegemony as the broader cultural ideology.

Men in general benefit much more than women from a cultural reading of sport that values speed and power, because men are on average taller, have more muscle mass, larger hearts and greater lung capacities. These and other physiological factors enable male (top) athletes to be more powerful, to run faster, jump higher and throw further than their female counterparts. The biological approach usually is accompanied by specific moral discourses. The muscular body of a football player and a certain degree of aggressiveness, for example, are considered desirable for men, but less so for women. The acquisition of such qualities enforces male solidarity, while women who equally celebrate competitiveness, stamina, strength and aggression endanger the core of male identity. Hence the biological gap explains only some performance differences and not the whole picture, as the borderline between the sexes is the re-emphasis of an oversimplified dichotomy. This argument neither pays attention to international or intra-national differences in sports participation, nor does it respect the rich variety of concepts and ways of living of women and men, particularly as differences *within* a sex are much greater than *between* the sexes. Solely emphasizing the physiological issue directs attention away from other causes of gender stereotyping in sport, which include gender norms and values that shape the popular vision of men's and women's position in society, and the functions officially assigned to sport by dominant forces in society.

Many researchers perceive the gendered media representation as part of a vicious circle relegating women to the fringe of active sport participation. Negligence means a drop in public awareness, spectator turn out, sponsorship income and new blood in the sport. Access is granted to women without dispute only at the sidelines, on the stands, in front of the TV screen or in the ad section of the sports paper pages. As Whannel observed, 'sport characteristically provides a space for the eradication, marginalisation and symbolic annihilation of the feminine'.[16] In Japan, as in general, men figure much more than women as media-sport professionals, sport writers and academics in all sport-related fields. Among the 46 Japanese newspaper journalists who covered the Sydney Olympics 2000, Iida identified only three women, who contributed a mere 4.1% of 635 articles and not a single photo to the print media display of the Olympics.[17] While the coverage of women's and men's sport in three national dailies was quite evenly balanced in quantitative terms, it differed considerably in qualitative terms, that is, the kind of sport featured and contextualization strategies. Women were often reported on either in disciplines that had gained social acceptance long ago, such as track and field or swimming, or in 'typically' feminine sports, such as synchronized swimming and beach volleyball.[18] The women's beach volleyball team did not advance very far in the tournament, yet its photo shots were, together with the synchronized swimmer teams, most often displayed on the sport pages. Hence the observable gains women made in the media representation of sports were not always good news, if the increase was primarily based on the permissive (or compelled) disclosure of the female body to the male gaze. As Bernstein has commented, the sexualization of female athletes trivializes their achievements and in fact robs them of athletic legitimacy, thus preserving hegemonic masculinity.[19]

Research on the role of the sport media in the reproduction of gender stereotypes has found the coverage to be often framed within stereotypes which emphasize social expectations toward the athlete as a woman rather than athletic skill.[20] According to Hirakawa's analysis of sport-related TV commercials,[21] women were clearly underrepresented (comprising 14.4% of images) and staged in comparatively passive or over-determined roles that were easily connected with the dominant normative destination of female existence: as wife and mother. In contrast male athletes were typically shown in action, in actual competition, or in the limelight of fans and admirers. Women hardly appeared as active performers, and if they were, then in domesticated contexts, such as running with the dog, or playing with children. Masculinity was valorized by the celebration of the sport hero in very condensed heroic situations, whereas the sport heroines were deprived of all of their heroic features. It seems that the success of the female athlete causes alarm or a sense of crisis in the world of masculine domination. In order to mitigate the arising tensions, sport heroines consequently have to be demystified and redefined as 'normal' girls and archetypal women. Iida also found that female athletes were often called by pet names and endearing terms stressing their cuteness and 'lovely' dependence on men.[22] As male athletes are referred to in a much more detached and honourable way, the verbal annexation of the female athlete is a linguistic practice that reinforces gender-based status differences. The gender biased language use, as in Zen Nihon Sakkā Senshuken (All Japan football championship) as opposed to Zen Nihon Joshi Sakkā Senshuken (All Japan *women's* football championship), is a universally recognizable phenomenon.

The crisis of masculinity

Many accounts of the relationship of the sexes in Japan tend to attribute gender inequality to the preponderance of Confucian values. Country-specific versions of Confucianism differ considerably, yet the overall picture includes the notion of predominance of man over woman, the separate domains of men and women, and clear-cut gendered standards for bodily action and behaviour. Cultural orientations and habituated practices, as well as legal codifications, support the maintenance of a gendered order in which men are placed in superior positions to women, and women are regarded as weak, passive, subordinate and dependent. The underlying principle is the reduction of women to their primary roles in family reproduction and housekeeping. The household registration system that once incorporated male dominance in Japan continues to work at the cultural level of commonly shared perceptions and informal orientations against the legally enforced notion of gender equality.[23]

While undeniably there is some truth in relating women's discrimination to Confucian traditions, relying on the cultural argument in a reductionist way is, more than anything else, ahistorical and socially blind. Neither does it explain intra-regional differences nor the way in which traditions themselves are edified. As a conceptualization of a general principle that resists the pressure of the social environment to change, the argument ignores the ways in which power relations between men and women, and between the individual, state and society, are constructed.

The introduction of modern sport in Japan, among many other Western institutions, took place at a time of vast social turmoil. Threatened by Western military supremacy, the Japanese state was forced to modernize in line with requests and models set by the colonizing powers of the nineteenth century. The pressure to change was most clearly exerted upon the male elite. In former times, the samurai differed from the commoners not only in physical terms by their right to wear arms and their skill in warfare (*bu*), but also by their literary and intellectual education (*bun*).[24] This composite ideal of masculinity dissolved when the former warriors turned into the teachers and bureaucrats of the new Meiji State. The disembodied notion of masculinity was partially substituted by the willing acceptance of western styles of masculinity. Photos depicting representatives of the male elite posing in the public present very little visible difference from Caucasian males, but displayed a deliberate self-distancing from the presentation of male bodies and postures in East Asian cultures.[25] The Western bourgeois idea of masculinity with its specific form of gender relations turned into the new role model, and the patriarchal status of the household head was codified by the civic code.[26]

Japan's rapid modernization and geopolitical changes at the turn of the century revived the traditional Japanese notion of masculinity. Victories on the battle field against China (1895) and Russia (1905) strengthened the physical component of the *bunbu* ideal. The body was also instrumentalized as an expressive medium of maleness when modern sports found a new institutional homeland within the educational system. Particularly at the boarding schools of higher education, the future male elite students were educated in the spirit of 'muscular spiritualism',[27] a Japanese variant of muscular Christianity, which was tainted by neo-Confucianism, modern pedagogy and male cardinal virtues such as self-discipline, leadership qualities and group loyalty.

How important political power differences were for the collective imagination of maleness was revealed in the commentary of a French observer who tried to discredit Japan's military advances by characterizing the Japanese as 'an essentially female people'.[28] The rivalry between the West and Japan continued to mark the most important poles for the oscillating spectrum of Japanese maleness until defeat at the end of the Pacific War in 1945 led to the abandonment of the legitimacy of the warrior ideal. Again the *bun*-element came to the fore, when the salary-man (*sarariiman*), whose career chances were based on his educational merits, emerged as the new hegemonic model of masculinity.[29] The figure of the loyal and self-sacrificing corporate warrior (*kigyō senshi*) embodied individual hopes of social mobility as well as the state's aspirations of gaining influence as a civilian, and civilized, trading nation. Promising status gains by way of membership to a respected organization and social power over family members due to the sole breadwinner role, the *sarariiman* developed into a normative model for the entire male generation born after the war. But the subordinated man, a 'non-man that sacrificed his hedonist and escapist inclinations in favour of a higher organisation',[30] hardly qualified as an inspiring ideal of virtue. The lack of masculine appeal and male self-esteem was partly obscured by the manifold services of an entertainment industry tailored to the needs of covering the internal fissures and ruptures of the *sarariiman* image.[31]

The cultural industries also subversively undermined hegemonic masculinity since they found a never-ceasing source of revenue in the tense relations between modern, de-masculinized and traditional manful ideas of masculinity. Innumerable movies, ballads and *manga* were indebted to a rather conservative idea of maleness, which especially appeals to the physically stronger, but economically weaker working class. This working class ideal is based on traditional moral virtues such as courage, bravery, independence, honour, truthfulness and the willingness to defend all these values against the pressure of society, even, if necessary, through physical means. Popular culture immortalized this ideal in the figures of the *kōha*, the hard man, and the smart vagabond; genres like the Yakuza film or the popular Tora-san serials have been dedicated to the archetypes of heroic maleness.[32] The popular interest in these productions encompasses all social classes and indicates the missing charisma and moral attractiveness of the hegemonic *sarariiman*.

It's a male world: fandom and hyper-masculinity in Japanese football

The launch of professional football during the early 1990s coincided with the bursting of the bubble-economy and the rise of the largest crisis of Japan's post-war economy. The huge devaluation of stock and real estate assets initiated waves of unemployment and bankruptcy in previously unknown dimensions. The crisis eroded the financial system and weakened the consumption power of private and public households, which run into the largest debt rates among all OECD countries. During the 'lost decade', as the 1990s were coined by the media in view of crises, the lack of social reforms and political leadership, the traditional employment system came to an end making employment and job security increasingly precarious. The Victorian compromise between capitalism and patriarchy, which assigned men the breadwinner role in public and women the unpaid support role in the private domain, had been known in Japan since the end of the nineteenth century, but had become mandatory only in the course of the socio-economic transformations after the Pacific War. The formerly unknown shortage of employment opportunities equally concerned men and women, but it threatened more seriously the male self-understanding as the family breadwinner. While decades of feminist interventions had gradually increased the spectrum of roles for women in public and working life, Japan's society of labour denied men the opportunity to develop alternatives to the hegemonic idea of masculinity.

The crisis of hegemonic masculinity bore new forms of male behaviour that refused to follow the conventional rites of passage: getting a job and setting up a family. If both primary and secondary social groups are losing currency for purposes of integration and identity construction, the meaning of tertiary groups, such as fan clubs or spontaneous 'emotional communities' are gaining importance. Hence it can be said that football as a spectator sport met a certain kind of social demand at this time. 'Starting from zero', spectators in the stadia were faced with the task of creating a fan culture of their own. For that purpose, the images of a global football fan culture were studied and adapted to the local needs.[33] Since then, colourful clouds of smoke (made from dry ice, since explosives were banned from stadia), posters of Che Guevara, samba rhythms and Japanized versions of *You'll Never Walk Alone* also belong to the stock images of Japanese football support.

Fan clubs were often initiated under the guidance of local elites who were in charge of linking the football project with the regional economy and bureaucracy.[34] Event manager Yamamoto Yoshiharu was mandated by AS Yokohama Flügels to found the fan club of the Yokohama Jets; the musician Mario Yamaguchi was invited to set up a samba group as a core element for the fan club of Verdy Kawasaki – named after the fan club of Sport Club Corinthians Paulista – the *Camiza Doze* (Twelfth Shirt) numbered at times up to 16,000 members, including 10,000 women. Satō Hiroshi, football-loving employee of the Mitsubishi Corporation and manager of the company's former club Urawa Red Diamonds, explicitly modelled the fan club according to that of Manchester United and other European clubs. In order to stir up sentiments in a way known from video-taped matches in Europe or South America, club members as well as non-affiliated visitors were encouraged to participate in the songs and battle calls orchestrated by fan club leaders and their sub-leaders. CDs and flyers were used as educational material to teach the audience the art of cheering.

Group management techniques in Japan usually guarantee that the performance and display of the official fan clubs comply with the family leisure policy of the J. League. After an unscheduled pitch invasion by dissatisfied Urawa Red fans, Satō produced a match day flyer showing an Urawa player together with a young supporter. The accompanying text expressed the hope: 'You and me, let's see about great football'. The lower part of the flyer noted acknowledgements of gratitude for the atmosphere created by the spectators, some basic rules including no fireworks, no smoke-bombs, no pitch invasions, and the call to sing along with the Reds supporters' song during the halftime break: 'For the lyrics, please turn to the back page.'

This kind of controlled fan behaviour did not find unanimous support. Some spectators fancied a more spontaneous and uncompromised support style they knew from first hand encounters in the homelands of football or from video-taped matches. Yet, support for a club without a past or historical sets of rivalry, afforded an artificial accentuation of emotions, hostilities and antagonisms. Implementing a mixture of punk, rock, sex and provocations, a rougher alternative to the official fan clubs gradually emerged in the stands. Local youths at Urawa established the Crazy Calls who coloured the Komaba stadium red with showers of confetti or by hanging huge banners saying things like 'Red or Dead'. Long before kick-off they set out to sing themselves into the right mood. The Elvis-song *I can't help falling in love* expressed their undying devotion to a rather unsuccessful team. A localized version of epitomized English patriotism, *Land of hope and glory*, was heard on the rare occasion of victory. The trade mark of the Crazy Calls was the 'warrior', a battle cry taken from the Slade-hit *We'll bring the house down* from 1981, which roared through the stadium at the beginning of the match and welcomed the players onto the pitch.[35]

Delinquency, rebellion and machismo are key terms of *The Red Book: The Twelfth Player of Fighting Urawa Reds* which explains the making of the Crazy Calls:

> In the Fifties, there were Elvis Presley and James Dean, and in the Sixties, the Beatles and The Rolling Stones represented the 'Counter Culture'. The Punk movement took over in the '70s with The Sex Pistols and The Clash. The theme 'delinquency' always came up when I thought about what young people were enthusiastic about over the century. Of course, from an adult's point of view, the very word 'delinquent' does not sound very good, but I think young people use the word to describe something cool. Crazy Calls focused on those people who wanted to be cool, and they stimulated people into realizing that soccer is an exciting and great sport. (*The Red Book*)[36]

Women were not considered to be cool and were banned from the core area behind the goal posts. 'We don't mind women, but we didn't want our image to sissify', said Crazy Call leader Yoshizawa Kōichi. Another member remembered:

> I am not saying that women are not good enough, but the people you can rely on in case of an emergency are either young people or men in their 20s and 30s. In such cases, physical strength is needed and this is connected to fighting power, although I do not want to think that way too much... As society is becoming less macho, there is more desire to be macho.[37]

This playful attitude towards a macho identity is related to the apparent contradiction between performances of self in public settings and in the stadium. Usually, behaviour in the public is regulated by bowing to common conventions and the cultural norm of restraint. However, within the confines of the stadium, aggressiveness, hostility and exaltedness are expected to fuel into an appropriate bedlam mood. The spatial segregation of sections for the different supporter groups was introduced not to mitigate tensions, but for the purpose of heightening tension in the stadium, and it was initiated by the fans themselves. As Kawazu Tōru, leader of the Kashima Antlers fan club, In.Fight, wrote in fanzine columns, free riders enjoying the party mood without contributing were not welcome behind the goal. In.Fight was set up by members from a former punk band that had lived together in Tokyo during the live-house boom of the early 1990s. 'None of us were interested in football – we just liked standing up and making noise. The Japanese in general don't like football. So we decided to make it fun', remembered Kawazu. It took some time to convince the local residents of the fun, but after the first year thousands of stadium visitors were willing to join the In.Fight chants.[38]

In Kashiwa, the football-only stadium became famous for having one of the noisiest stands in the league, thanks to the Yellow Monkeys who regularly climbed the net in front of the terrace. Their most famous contribution to Japan's football support culture was the *buriifu tai* (briefs corps), a group of fans who lined up to salute the players before matches wearing just white underpants. The public display of the naked upper part of the body is a global aspect of ritualized expressions of masculinity, but in Japan it is sometimes more than that. At the beginning of a Kashiwa Reysol match, two completely nude fans appeared when the passage of a giant Kashiwa flag through the terraces came to an end. One danced a can-can kicking up his left leg – whenever the leg came down he used a club flag to cover his private parts; the other wore just a peaked hat and stood motionless, with the arms folded over his breast. 'They said this kind of behaviour is bad for children', said fan club leader Yamamoto Yōichi. 'But I like being accused of behaving badly. That's more fun.'[39] When the Yellow Monkeys carry an inflatable sex-doll into the net and taunt players from away teams '*Okusan to yatte yaru*' (I'm going to do it to your wife), they perform an act of ritualized hyper-masculinity, yet still remain within the strict confines of acceptable behaviour. However, the borderlines between pseudo-hostility, testosterone-induced insulting, play-like aggression and symbolic violence are often blurred.

Usually, the Japanese are well acquainted with techniques of crowd auto control. Membership in a group does not just induce the individual to perform in a very extroverted fashion, but reflections on the social context also prevent him or her from actions that may harm the group or representative group members. Yet since the mood in the stadium may sometimes invite over-excessive behaviour, fans and fan club leaders are expected to take responsibility for both individual action and the social face of the group. This is one of the reasons why the dirty face of hooliganism is close to non-existent in Japan. Kashiwa supporter Yamamoto, who once stopped a young member from invading the away fan section, said: 'I don't mind confrontations, as long as no violence is involved and no one gets hurt. This line may not be stepped over.' When the line is transgressed, someone must step in to shoulder responsibility. When a member from the Kaizoku (Pirates), a group of Yokohama Marinos supporters, threw a coin at a former Marinos player who had gone over to the city rival Flügels, the group leader Miyazaki Kazuyoshi accepted a personal ban from the stadium for the rest of the season. Taking the blame for the fan who had thrown the coin, Miyazaki clearly indicated the seriousness of the incident to the group and prevented officials from implementing harder crowd control measures.[40]

Conclusion

Observations from the terraces of Japanese stadia show that football in Japan has been appropriated by both men and women, albeit in quite different ways. Despite girls' and women's undeniable advances both on the pitch and in the stands, football continues to be primarily a man's world. As the case studies and their historical contexts suggest, football became a last resort of masculinity precisely because it met a certain kind of social demand during the 1990s. In terms of active participation, girls are largely excluded from playing the game, while the women's teams are struggling with their subordinate position vis-à-vis the unquestioned standard of the men's game. The low status of women's football is questioned by their relatively high success on the international pitch. However, these achievements do not suggest that a progressive gender policy is pursued in Japanese sport since in many other countries football is much more exclusively male. As Hargreaves observed: 'The longer men practically and ideologically have appropriated an activity, the more difficult it is for women to get inside'.[41] While the male appropriation of football is not so deeply rooted in history and collective memories of Japan as in Europe, it nevertheless seems that on Japanese grounds as well it is not a woman's place to represent the nation.

Football certainly has had a lasting impact on society in the realm of consumption, lifestyles and popular culture. While women are widely excluded from the opportunity to exercise the power of definition as producers, they can do so as consumers. As Iida has noted, the feminization of masculinity, or the increasing awareness of style, fashion and cosmetics, has been an outstanding phenomenon of the past decade in Japanese society.[42] Women increasingly are in a position to act upon the definition of dominant concepts of masculinity and to impose role models on their male contemporaries. But the same trend also provoked a reactionary backlash among some men who preferred to cling to established ideas of dominant masculinity. Many men openly expressed their deep discomfort with the feminine style of football support, discrediting female fans as *miha* (immature, unknowing faction). As in many other countries, empiricism served as the ultimate argument to exclude women from their terrain: 'In order to know football and to talk about football, you have to have played the game'. Within the subculture of highly committed football fandom, dominant images of masculinity were shaped according to models from western fan culture as well as autochthonous traditions. Traditional images and ideas of masculinity based on physical attributes (strength, courage) and social qualities (responsibility, leadership) had survived through the years within the canonized artefacts of popular culture, even though sometimes exaggerated, over-idealized, parodied or distorted by a nostalgic longing for the past. But they remained particularly valued by the working classes and those men who saw their social position endangered by the transformations of globalization.

The appropriation of football in Japan cannot be completely explained by reference to traditional cultural values, the economy or the political system alone, but requires a contextualized study of gender power relations. Female subordination and male superiority are performed in everyday life, codified at political and administrative levels, exploited in economic relations and symbolically reproduced in popular cultural forms. But gender relations are far from being static, and football serves as one battle field for the reconstruction of the gender order in Japanese society.

Notes

1. Burton Nelson, *The Stronger Women Get.*
2. Manzenreiter, 'Her Place in the "House of Football"'.
3. Markovits and Hellermann, *Offside.*
4. The model used is derived from John Rooney's per capita index introduced in his path-breaking study *A Geography of American Sport* and since then reapplied for numerous purposes (see, for example, the sport geographic survey of regional distribution patterns of Kenyan world class runners by Bale and Sang, *Kenyan, Running.*). The application of the general formula $I = (N/P) \times (A/1)$, where N is the number of players and P the total population of this country, and A the number of people per athlete in the overall field, presents national differences measured against the overall output figure calculated as 1.0. To produce results for male and female players, P becomes the population share of the respective sex (see Table 1).
5. Precisely for that reason, in the West women's inroads into sport has generally been facilitated in fields that have emphasized an aestheticized version of feminine physicality – such as gymnastics, figure skating, or synchronized swimming – over overt 'masculinity sports rituals' associated with strength, exhaustion and violent physical contact (Iida, 'Media supōtsu to feminizumu', 73). Looking at participation rates in East Asian societies, similar patterns of gendered sports emerge with high participation rates in 'female sports' and low rates in 'male sports'.
6. Schütte with Ciarlante, *Consumer Behaviour in Asia*, 229.
7. Esashi and Kisanuki, *Supōtsu fan ni miru jendā*.
8. Tanaka, 'The Positioning and Practices of the "Feminized Fan"'.
9. Shimizu, 'Football, Nationalism and Celebrity Culture'.
10. Nogawa and Maeda, 'The Japanese Dream', 227.

11. Blackwood, 'The Reproduction and Naturalisation of Sex-based Separate Spheres in Japanese High Schools', 22.
12. Horne, Tomlinson and Whannel, *Understanding Sport*, 111.
13. Nogawa and Maeda, 'The Japanese Dream', 227.
14. Duke and Crolley, *Football, Nationality and the State*; Fasting, 'Sexual Stereotypes in Sport'; Caudwell, 'Women's Football in the United Kingdom'.
15. Edwards, 'Gender Lessons on the Field'.
16. Whannel, *Media Sport Stars*, 45.
17. Iida, 'Media supōtsu to feminizumu', 81–3.
18. Ibid., 79.
19. Bernstein, 'Women in Sports Media'.
20. Iida, 'Shinbun hōdō ni okeru josei kyōgisha no jendā-ka'.
21. Hirakawa, 'Supōtsu, jendā, media imēji'.
22. Iida, 'Shinbun hōdō ni okeru josei kyōgisha no jendā-ka', 10–11.
23. Sugimoto, *An Introduction to Japanese Society*, 136–42.
24. Roden, 'Toward Remaking Manliness', 133.
25. Low, 'The Emperor's Sons go to War', 82–8.
26. Schad-Seifert, 'Männlichkeit und Gesellschaft im Modernen Japan', 283–5.
27. Kiku, 'Kindai no puro supotsu no seiritsu ni kansuru rekishi shakaigakuteki kōsatsu', 10.
28. 'Ce people [...] et surtout un peuple femme', quoted in Schad-Seifert, 'Männlichkeit und Gesellschaft im Modernen Japan', 282.
29. Dasgupta, 'The "Salaryman" and masculinity in Japan'.
30. Schad-Seifert, 'Männlichkeit und Gesellschaft im Modernen Japan', 286.
31. Allison, *Nightwork.*
32. Buruma, *A Japanese Mirror.*
33. Takahashi, 'Soccer Spectators and Fans in Japan'.
34. Manzenreiter, 'Japan und der Fußball im Zeitalter der technischen Reproduzierbarkeit'; and 'Sport zwischen Markt und öffentlicher Dienstleistung'.
35. Shimizu, 'Japanese Soccer Fans'; Moffet, *Japanese Rules*, 75.
36. Quoted in ibid., 138.
37. Ibid., 139.
38. Moffet, *Japanese Rules*, 79.
39. Ibid., 84.
40. Ibid., 83.
41. Hargreaves, *Sporting Females*, 279.
42. Iida, 'Beyond the "feminization of masculinity"'.

References

Allison, Anne. *Nightwork: Sexuality, Pleasure and Corporate Masculinity in a Tokyo Hostess Club.* Chicago, IL: University of Chicago Press, 1994.

Bale, John and Joe Sang Kenyan. *Running. Movement Culture, Geography and Global Change.* London: Frank Cass, 1996.

Bernstein, Alina. 'Women in Sports Media: Time for a Victory Lap?' Paper presented to the 3rd Play-The-Game Conference, Denmark, 10–12 November 2002. Available online at www.play-the-game-org. Accessed 20 October 2003.

Blackwood, Thomas. 'The Reproduction and Naturalisation of Sex-Based Separate Spheres in Japanese High Schools: The Role of Female "Managers" of High School Baseball Teams'. *Social Science Japan 25* (2003): 22–6.

Burton Nelson, Mariah. *The Stronger Women get, the More Men Love Football. Sexism and the American Culture of Sports.* New York: Avon Books, 1996.

Buruma, Ian. *A Japanese Mirror. Heroes and Villains of Japanese Culture.* London: Penguin Books, 1984.

Caudwell, Jayne. 'Women's Football in the United Kingdom: Theorizing Gender and Unpacking the Butch Lesbian Image'. *Journal of Sport & Social Issues* 23, no.4 (1999): 390–402.

Dasgupta, Roman. 'The "Salaryman" and Masculinity in Japan'. In *Asian Masculinities. The Meaning And Practice Of Manhood In China And Japan,* ed. Kam Louie and Morris Low, 118–34. London and New York: Routledge, 2003.

Duke, Vic and Liz Crolley. *Football, Nationality and the State.* Essex: Longman. 1996.

Edwards, Elise M. 'Gender Lessons on the Field: the Philosophy and Practice of Coaching the Female Athlete in Contemporary Japan'. Paper presented to the International Conference 'Sports and Body Culture in Japan', Yale University, New Haven, CT, 31 March–1 April 2000.

Esashi, Shōgo and Hisayo Kisanuki. 'Supōtsu fan ni miru jendā. Sekushuariti no gōraku' [Gender as seen among Sport Fans. Pleasures of Sexuality]. In *Supōtsu fan no shakaigaku* [Sociology of Sport Fans], ed. Sugimoto Atsuo, 111–28. Kyōto: Sekai Shisōsha, 1997.

Fasting, Kari. 'Sexual Stereotypes in Sport – Experiences of Female Soccer Players'. Paper presented to the international press seminar on 'Sport, Media and Civil Society', Vingsted, Denmark, 18–22 June 1997. Online available at www.play-the-game-org. Accessed 20 October 2003.

Hargreaves, Jennifer. *Sporting Females, Critical Issues in the History and Sociology of Women's Sports.* London: Routledge, 1994.

Hirakawa, Sumiko. 'Supōtsu, jendā, media imēji. Supōtsu CF ni egakareru jendā' [Sport, Gender, Media Image. Gender Depictions in Sport TV Commercials]. In *Gendai Media Supōtsu Ron* [Contemporary Media Sport Debates], ed. Hashimoto Junichi. Kyōto, 91–115. Kyōto: Sekai Shisō Sha, 2002.

Horne, John, Alan Tomlinson and Garry Whannel. *Understanding Sport. An Introduction to the Sociological and Cultural Analysis of Sport.* New York: E&FN Spon, 1999.

Iida, Takako. 'Media supōtsu to feminizumu' [Media Sport and Feminism]. In *Gendai Media Supōtsu Ron* [Contemporary Media Sport Discourses], ed. Hashimoto Junichi, 71–90. Kyōto: Sekai Shisōsha, 2002.

________ 'Shinbun hōdō ni okeru josei kyōgisha no jendā-ka. Sugawara Kyōko kara Narazaki Noriko e' [The Gendering of Female Athletes in Newspaper Coverage. From Mrs Noriko Sugawara to Ms Noriko Narazaki]. *Journal of Sport and Gender Studies 1* (2003): 4–14.

Iida, Yumiko. 'Beyond the "Feminization of Masculinity": Transforming Patriarchy with the "Feminine" in Contemporary Japanese Youth Culture'. *Inter-Asia Cultural Studies* 6, no.1 (2005): 56–74.

Kiku, Kōichi. 'Kindai no puro supotsu no seiritsu ni kansuru rekishi shakaigakuteki kōsatsu. Wa ga kuni ni okeru senzen no puro yakyū o chūshin ni'. [Socio-Historical Study of the Development of Professional Sports in Japan. Baseball in Pre-War Years]. *Taiiku Supōtsu Shakaigaku Kenkyū 3* (1984): 1–26.

Low, Morris. 'The Emperor's Sons go to War, Competing Masculinities in Modern Japan'. In *Asian Masculinities. The Meaning and Practice of Manhood in China and Japan,* ed. Kam Louie and Morris Low, 81–99. London and New York: Routledge, 2003.

Manzenreiter, Wolfram. 'Japan und der Fußball im Zeitalter der technischen Reproduzierbarkeit: Die J. League zwischen Lokalpolitik und Globalkultur' [Japan and Football in the Age of Technical Reproductivity: The J-League between Local Politics and Global Culture]. In *Global Players. Kultur, Ökonomie und Politik des Fußballs,* ed. Michael Fanizadeh, Gerald Hödl and Wolfram Manzenreiter, 133–58. Frankfurt and Wien: Brandes & Apsel/Südwind, 2002.

________ 'Her place in the "House of Football": Globalization, Sexism and Women's Football in East Asian Societies'. In *Football Goes East. Business, Culture and the People's Game in East Asia,* ed. Wolfram Manzenreiter and John Horne, 197–221. London and New York: Routledge, 2004.

________ 'Sport zwischen Markt und öffentlicher Dienstleistung. Zur Zukunft des Breitensports in Japan' [Sport between Market and Public Good. The Future of Mass Sports in Japan]. In *SWS-Rundschau (Journal für Sozialforschung)* 44, no.2 (2004): 227–51.

Markovits, Andrei S. and Steven L. Hellermann. *Offside. Soccer and American Exceptionalism.* Princeton, NJ: Princeton University Press, 2001.

Moffet, Sebastian. *Japanese Rules. Why the Japanese needed Football and How they got it.* London: Yellow Jersey Press, 2002.

Nogawa, Haruo and Hiroko Maeda. 'The Japanese Dream: Soccer Culture towards the New Millennium'. In *Football Cultures and Identities,* ed. Gary Armstrong and Richard Giulianotti, 223–33. London: Macmillan, 1999.

Roden, Donald. 'Toward Remaking Manliness'. In *Nitobe Inazō: Japan's Bridge Across The Pacific,* ed. John F. Howes, 133–56. Boulder, CO: Westview Press, 1995.

Schad-Seifert, Annette. 'Männlichkeit Und Gesellschaft Im Modernen Japan' [Masculinity and Society in Contemporary Japan]. In *11. Deutschsprachiger Japanologentag in Trier 1999. Band 1: Geschichte, Geistesgeschichte/Religionen, Gesellschaft, Politik, Recht, Wirtschaft,* ed. Hilaria Gössmann and Andreas Mrugalla, 279–90. Münster: LitVerlag, 2001.

Schütte, Hellmut with Deanna Ciarlante. *Consumer Behaviour in Asia.* New York: New York University Press, 1998.

Shimizu, Satoshi. 'Japanese Soccer Fans. Following the Local and the National Team'. In *Japan, Korea and the 2002 Football World Cup,* ed. John Horne and Wolfram Manzenreiter, 133–46. London and New York: Routledge, 2002.

________ 'Football, Nationalism and Celebrity Culture – Reflections on the Impact of Different Discourses on Japanese Identity since the 2002 World Cup'. In *Football Goes East. Business, Culture and The People's Game in East Asia,* ed. Wolfram Manzenreiter and John Horne, 180–94. London and New York: Routledge, 2004.

Sugimoto, Yoshio. *An Introduction to Japanese Society.* Cambridge: Cambridge University Press, 1997.

Takahashi, Yoshio. 'Soccer Spectators and Fans in Japan'. In *Fighting Fans: Football Hooliganism as a World Phenomenon,* ed. Eric Dunning, 190–200. Dublin: University College Dublin Press, 2002.

Tanaka, Toko. 'The Positioning and Practices of the "Feminized Fan" in Japanese Soccer Culture through the Experience of the FIFA World Cup Korea/Japan 2002'. *Inter-Asia Cultural Studies* 5, no.1 (2004): 52–62.

Whannel, Garry. *Media Sport Stars. Masculinities and Moralities.* London: Routledge, 2002.

Stanley Rous's 'own goal': football politics, South Africa and the Contest for the FIFA presidency in 1974

Paul Darby

Introduction

This essay assesses one of the most significant events in the history of the Fédération Internationale de Football Association (FIFA). The election for the FIFA Presidency in 1974 at which the Brazilian João Havelange replaced the Englishman, Sir Stanley Rous, as head of the world body was important in three main respects. Firstly, in heralding the emergence of Havelange as FIFA President, it transformed the world body from a Eurocentric, conservative organization into one that pursued a policy direction characterized by a commitment to globalize, democratize and commercialize the game. Secondly, it demonstrated the growing political power of FIFA's under-developed constituencies and their ability to effect meaningful change in the governance of the game. Finally, and most importantly for the purpose of this essay, it also revealed the significance of South Africa's status within FIFA in the politics of world football at that time. This study focuses on this latter issue by drawing on primary source material such as personal correspondence, written at the time, between Stanley Rous and members of the South African football authorities and the Confédération Africaine de Football (CAF), as well as minutes of FIFA and CAF Congress and Executive Committee meetings and those of CAF. In particular, it juxtaposes Rous's stance over South Africa's membership of FIFA with that of João Havelange's and argues that this was one of the most significant factors in determining the outcome of the election. Before turning to this specific issue it is important to provide some context. Thus, the essay begins by assessing the political climate in world football, particularly the relationship between FIFA's core European constituencies and the world body's emergent members from Africa, prior to 1974.

Africa and FIFA pre-1974: a fractious relationship

For the first 50 years of its existence, FIFA played little or no role in the dissemination of football to Africa. This was simply a consequence of the fact that until the shedding of colonial rule in the late 1950s and early 1960s, FIFA contained only four African affiliates (South Africa, Egypt, Ethiopia and Sudan). This is not to say that the reach of the game was not evident elsewhere on the continent. Although football had been introduced by Europeans for their own recreational and ideological ends and had originally developed in an elitist fashion, the game soon assumed widespread popularity.[1] Football's position amongst indigenous populations in colonial African society extended beyond that of simply providing opportunities for sport and leisure. In the decade and a half leading up to the collapse of colonial authority, the game increasingly came to represent an invaluable cultural and political resource for Africans and was used to harness resentment against the colonial order and express aspirations for emancipation.[2]

With independence secured, many newly independent countries saw football as an inexpensive but potentially potent medium for registering their presence in the international community of nation states. Thus, they formed national football federations, joined the CAF, established in 1957, and affiliated to FIFA, fully expecting to benefit from the opportunities of being part of the international football 'family'. However, FIFA at this time was an organization that was run almost exclusively in the interests of its European and South American constituencies. Indeed, rather than embrace the dramatic globalization of its membership that had accompanied decolonization and use it as an opportunity to fulfil its self-stated objective of developing the game throughout the world, FIFA's European-dominated hierarchy looked inwards and sought to preserve their own interests.

As a consequence of this approach, Africa was regarded largely as an irrelevance and the world body simply refused to countenance the aspirations of a growing lobby that sought the opening up of the game's institutional and competition structures. For example, attempts to procure a place on FIFA's Executive Committee and organize a continental confederation for the African game in the first half of the 1950s were frustrated by the world body's Eurocentric bias.[3] Such an approach was becoming increasingly intolerable to FIFA's African constituency that, by the mid 1960s numbered over 30 nations. With the world body's electoral franchise at Congress operating on the pseudo-democratic principle of one nation one vote, it might have been expected that African aspirations for fulfilment in the world game were realizable. However, the world body's European hierarchy continued to refuse to sanction any significant democratization of the world game. For example, Africa's calls for a more equitable distribution of World Cup places were met with stiff opposition from FIFA's established European constituencies and it took a boycott of the qualifying rounds of the 1966 World Cup by the International Federation's African members to secure the continent a guaranteed berth at the finals of the competition.[4] The approach of those Europeans who held the position of FIFA President in this period did little to encourage the world body to adopt a more progressive and inclusive approach towards the game's emerging constituencies. For example, Jules Rimet, President of the International Federation between 1921–54, had a conception of the world body which followed a paternal and neo-colonial view of global development in which economic and cultural hegemony radiated from a 'modern' European centre to a 'pre-modern' third world periphery. Indeed, this continued to be the basis upon which FIFA expanded under the stewardship of the Belgian Rudolfe Seeldrayers (1954–56) and the Englishmen Arthur Drewry (1956–61).

Under Rous, who took over the FIFA Presidency in 1961 after a long career as Secretary of the English Football Association stretching from 1934–62, the world body did take its responsibility to globalize the game more seriously. However, Rous's ability to throw himself fully into the task of making FIFA an organization that was representative of all of its members was undermined by a contradiction that characterized much of his presidency. On the one hand, Rous could demonstrate himself to be an adventurous modernizer within FIFA affairs. For example, as FIFA vice-president he was a key player in the lobby to decentralize the world body, administratively, in the mid-to-late 1950s. On the other hand though, Rous could also be a conservative traditionalist, as evidenced by his questioning of the political power that emergent nations were beginning to wield at FIFA congresses vis-à-vis the game's established European members in the 1960s.[5] This tension was particularly visible in his dealings with FIFA's African constituencies. Thus, while he was a frequent visitor to the African continent and initiated a programme of coaching and refereeing courses there, he described it as the beginning of the 'general missionary work'.[6] This, almost colonial mindset, did not go down well with sections of FIFA's African membership and some spoke out against what they saw as his continuation of a policy direction within the world body characterized by the marginalization of African football and European protectionism. CAF officials, most notably Ydnekatchew Tessema, the confederation's President at the time, increasingly gave voice to their frustrations and indignation and Africa's relationship with Rous's FIFA grew steadily fractious. Beyond the broader concerns over inequality and lack of opportunity within world football, the status of South Africa within the world body between the late 1950s and early 1970s came to represent a central dynamic around which African acrimony towards FIFA cohered and it is to this issue that this essay now turns.

South Africa, apartheid and football in the pre-Rous period

At the time of Sir Stanley Rous's election as FIFA President in 1961, South African sport was structured according to the same system of apartheid which characterized the organization of the rest of the country's social, political and economic institutions. Although a system of segregation had long been in existence, it was not until 1956 that the government formally incorporated its racist policies into sport. The government's sports policy, outlined in late June by the Minister of the Interior, Dr Dönges, stated that whites and non-whites had to organize their sports separately; prohibited any form of mixed sport within South Africa; prevented mixed teams from competing abroad and required international teams competing in South Africa to send an all-white team. In addition, the policy insisted that non-white sports federations seeking recognition within international governing bodies could only do so by affiliating to white organizations.[7] Conscious of the fact that this policy would be highly contentious amongst the non-white South African population and could lead to problems in terms of South Africa's status within international sport, Dönges added that the government would 'severely discourage' and withhold passports for those seeking to pressurize international federations into excluding South Africa from international competition.[8]

Whilst this policy statement formalized racial segregation in sports, football in South Africa had long operated according to the government imposed principle of multi-racialism. Thus, there existed associations for white, African, coloured and Indian branches of the game. The all-white, European-controlled South African Football Association (SAFA), established in 1892 by British and Dutch settlers, was the most powerful body in the South African game and in 1952, it was recognized within FIFA as the country's controlling federation. Although non-white associations could and did affiliate to it for a time, no playing contact between the different racial and ethnic groups was permitted. Alongside this white association there existed a governing body, the South African Soccer Federation (SASF), formed in September 1951, which had responsibility for African, coloured and Indian football and operated without racial barriers.[9] Despite the fact that SASF represented over 80% of South Africa's population,[10] SAFA's affiliation to FIFA meant that the interests of the majority of football activity were not represented within the world body. Eager to address this state of affairs SASF attempted on a number of occasions, between 1952–54, to negotiate a merger with SAFA and hence the establishment of a unified national body that would ensure that South African football was represented by a racially inclusive federation within FIFA. SAFA's response was that it would consider a merger if SASF accepted a constitution that would deny them any voting rights on the national committee, a position that was, of course, totally unacceptable to SASF.[11]

The racially exclusive nature of football and the lack of representation within FIFA was clearly a source of much discontent within non-white football circles. Thus, in 1954, SASF formally sought recognition from FIFA as *the* governing body for football in South Africa. Unwilling to become embroiled in the issue, FIFA was reluctant to consider SASF's application for membership and instead encouraged them to continue their internal negotiations with SAFA, despite the fact that this body maintained its resolute stance on preventing mixed football. Continued lobbying on the part of SASF kept the issue on the world body's agenda and a modicum of success was achieved when a FIFA Emergency Committee meeting, convened on 8 May 1955, concluded that SAFA did not control all football activity in South Africa and as such did not conform to the International Federation's statutory definition of a 'real' national association.[12]

In an attempt to seek out a resolution that would satisfy both parties, FIFA sent an investigative commission to South Africa. Conscious of being viewed in an unfavourable light, SAFA responded to FIFA's visit by removing from its constitution reference to its racial exclusivity and changing its name to the Football Association of South Africa (FASA), thus, according to Alegi, seeking 'to create the perception of substantive change'.[13] This move was indeed about perception because, at the same time as making these changes to its constitution, FASA insisted that it would continue to abide by the customs of South Africa and in doing so, made clear its intention to leave intact the system of apartheid that underpinned the organization and administration of football in the country. Despite this 'subterfuge',[14] FIFA was satisfied that FASA did not ban mixed football, and at its Congress in Lisbon in 1956, this body was confirmed, in FIFA's eyes at least, as the officially recognized governing body for football in the country.[15]

With its policy of multi-racialism effectively sanctioned by the game's International Federation, FASA felt sufficiently confident about its status within the world game to seek to participate in international competition on its own terms. Within Africa though, the politicization and symbolism of football, in a period of African history marked by a strong movement for pan-Africanism and self-autonomy, was such that a governing body that functioned according to the principles of racial segregation was never going to be accepted in that continent. Thus, FASA's insistence on sending either an all-white or an all-black team to the Sudanese capital Khartoum to contest the first African Cup of Nations (1957), was an anathema not only to the other contesting nations (Egypt, Ethiopia and Sudan), but also to all those colonies throughout the continent that were on the verge of achieving their independence. South Africa was duly expelled from the tournament. It was also subsequently excluded from the 1959 edition for the same reason and, prior to the 1961 tournament in Ethiopia, CAF took the decision to bar South Africa from all future African championships while apartheid continued to be replicated in the sporting domain.

Opposition to the South African government's segregationist policies and their direct application to the sports domain extended beyond football. The non-racial Table Tennis Board had already been granted recognition within the International Table Tennis Federation,[16] whilst the non-racial rugby, cricket and weightlifting federations had also agitated for membership of their respective international federations. Perhaps most significant though was the formation of the South African Sports Association (SASA) established in a London hotel in October 1958 by Dennis Brutus. SASA immediately adopted a coordinated approach to the promotion of non-racial sport by encouraging the formation of inclusive sporting bodies and by urging international sporting federations to withdraw recognition for their South African (White) affiliates.[17] The political and ideological significance of SASA's strategy is succinctly outlined by Jarvie: 'By providing a source of unification in purely sporting terms, SASA permitted black sporting culture to support the broader struggle against apartheid… SASA remained one of the few avenues for protest against apartheid during the 1960s.'[18]

Whilst SASA's primary target for agitation was the Olympic movement which included a non-racial clause within its rule book, football, which constituted 50,000 of the organization's

70,000 members and provided a number of influential officials on its executive committee,[19] became a focus for SASA's lobbying efforts. Reinvigorated by the formation of this association, SASF submitted another formal application for membership of FIFA at the world body's 1958 Congress in Stockholm. The real significance of SASF's application lay in the fact that, if it was accepted into the FIFA fold, then FASA would be expelled on the basis that only one association from each country was eligible for membership of the parent federation. However, further cosmetic moves by FASA in the period between 1956 and 1958 which included the offer of associate status and access to playing facilities to a number of non-white associations, swayed the FIFA Congress and SASF's application was rejected.[20]

Despite this setback, SASF, buoyed by the formation of SASA and angered by the establishment of FASA's all-white National Professional Football League (NPFL), redoubled its efforts to tackle FASA's separatist approach and its membership of FIFA. At FIFA's 1960 Congress in Rome, SASF made a third formal application for FIFA membership and lodged a request that FASA be expelled. The outcome of lengthy deliberations on the matter at the Congress was an anti-discriminatory resolution, later incorporated into FIFA's constitution, which stated that 'a National Association must be open to all who practise football in that country whether amateur, "non-amateur" or professional and without any racial, religious or political discrimination'.[21] FIFA's Executive Committee also established a one year time limit within which FASA had to conform to this almost unanimously accepted resolution.[22]

The SASF was content that international attention had been brought to bear on FASA's segregationist approach and the Rome resolution, as it came to be known, represented a significant milestone in the struggle against the application of apartheid to sport. At an Extraordinary Congress the following year, SASF's anti-racist campaigning came to fruition when FIFA's Executive Committee decided that FASA had been unable to fulfil the principles which inspired the Rome resolution. The Committee's decision in view of FASA's failure to operate as a non-racial association, reads as follows;

(1) To suspend the Football Association of Southern Africa from its membership with FIFA.
(2) To put the question on the Agenda of the Ordinary Congress of FIFA to be held at Santiago de Chile in 1962, so that, if necessary, further disciplinary measures be adopted and ratified.[23]

Sir Stanley Rous and the anti-apartheid football lobby

The preceding narrative highlights the centrality of football in the anti-apartheid sports movement and illustrates the depth of resolve on the part of both FASA and SASF to be recognized as South Africa's true representative in international football affairs. FIFA's brokerage of the dispute between these bodies emphasized, in the main, the conservative nature of the world body and its propensity to favour the status quo. However, the Rome resolution and the subsequent decision to suspend FASA demonstrated a growing awareness of, and sensitivity to, the segregated nature of football in South Africa. On the eve of the 1962 FIFA Congress in Santiago, SASF was confident that FASA's suspension would lead to their expulsion. However, in the interim, Stanley Rous had emerged as FIFA President and almost from the outset he adopted a sympathetic approach to the all-white association which eventually led to its re-admittance into the world body's fold.

On taking up his position at the helm of world football, Rous, almost immediately, began to correspond personally with Fred Fell, the President of FASA, Dave Marais, the Chairman of the all-white National Proffesional Football League (NPFL) and Vivian Granger, General Manager of the NPFL. In a move aimed at garnering support from the new FIFA President, these representatives of white football submitted a report to FIFA's Executive Committee which argued that they had made considerable moves on the issue of racial segregation, despite the fact that a system of apartheid continued to dominate their stance on the organization of football in South Africa. The thrust of FASA's argument was that it was not responsible for clubs and associations remaining outside its remit and therefore it refuted the allegation that it practised active discrimination on the grounds of race. The association also insisted that in implementing a system of sporting apartheid it was merely abiding by the laws and customs of the Republic of South Africa. Furthermore, with South Africa's position in the international game seriously compromised, there was a broad consensus amongst FASA's administrators and the white population in general that international and domestic criticism of its operations was tantamount to political interference.[24] In response to this allegation, those who represented non-white sportsmen took an altogether different view, arguing that it was the whites who had introduced racial and political discrimination into the sports arena.

Given his proclaimed philosophical aversion to the intrusion of politics into the sports domain, Rous allied himself to FASA's cause, arguing that the non-white lobby did not have the interest of sport at heart, but rather sought to abuse sport to further their own political ends.[25] The weight of FASA's report within FIFA's Executive, combined with Rous's sympathetic relationship with leading figures within South Africa's white football administration, resulted in a decision, taken at the world body's 1962 Congress, to set up a second investigative commission to assess the organization of football in the country. When the composition of the commission became known, particularly Rous's presence at the head of the FIFA delegation, it provoked considerable outrage amongst the non-white soccer federation. The view within SASF was that Rous lacked the necessary impartiality in light of his previous statements of support for FASA's reinstatement into the International Federation's ranks. In a cable to both the FIFA President and the FIFA General Secretary, SASF forcefully expressed the depth of its aversion to Rous's involvement in the commission:

> South African Soccer Federation most urgently request recusal of yourself from proposed FIFA Commission to South Africa on grounds that you are deeply committed by FASA's statements to lifting FASA suspension STOP Also perturbed by FIFA ignoring our repeated requests for information regarding Commission STOP Strong protest being lodged with FIFA STOP Letter follows.[26]

In the letter that followed, SASF outlined in detail some of the FASA statements which indicated Rous's support for the cause of the white association. For example, at FASA's 1962 Annual General Meeting, it was revealed that not only had Rous been in correspondence with FASA, but that he had congratulated the association for the able way in which it had presented its case at FIFA's Santiago Congress. More significantly, it was reported that Dave Marais, speaking at FASA's AGM, had indicated that 'he [Sir Stanley] repeatedly told delegates at Chile that FIFA was not going to be used as a political football, that they were not interested in a country's politics but merely in their soccer administration'.[27] SASF presented Rous and FIFA with an ultimatum which was to have damaging ramifications in terms of the respect and standing of both the President and the world body within the whole African continent:

> If Sir Stanley insists on coming out as a commissioner the non-white soccerites in this country represented in the big majority by our federation will have lost faith and confidence in the commission even before it starts work and we contend that the confidence which the non-whites in this country have reposed in FIFA for their emancipation from racial oppression will be shattered.[28]

Much to the annoyance of the country's non-white football administrators their appeals to have Rous removed from the commission fell on deaf ears. Thus, on 5 January 1963, the FIFA President, accompanied by Jimmy Maguire, secretary of the United States Soccer Federation and Executive Committee member set out to attempt to resolve the matter once and for all. During their two week visit, representatives from FASA, SASF as well as a range of other sporting organizations and providers were interviewed by the FIFA delegation. The outcome of these deliberations was complete backing for the all-white association. The conclusions of Rous's and Maguire's report to the FIFA Executive Committee are worth quoting at some length:

> There is no wilful discrimination on the part of FASA in respect of any organization in South Africa, and there is no obstacle placed in the way of anyone becoming affiliated to FASA, if they so desire. If the suspension of FASA is not lifted, the progress of the game in the Republic of South Africa will be retarded, to a point of possibly no recovery. FIFA must not interfere with the internal affairs of any country. In the present regime in South Africa, soccer enjoys being one of the major sports in the country... The curtailment of the co-operation of the Government and Municipal Authorities would be disastrous... There is no other body which can take the place of the FASA. The members of the dissident Federation (SASF) whom we interviewed, would in our opinion, be quite unsuitable to represent association football in South Africa. Their attitude was one of destruction and not construction in any way. We found that they desired to hinder and to act contrary to Government Policy, which clearly indicates their inability to foster and propagate the game of soccer in that country ... FIFA cannot be used as a weapon to force a government to change its internal sports policy. To do so, would wreck the true purpose of FIFA. We unreservedly recommend that the suspension be lifted and that the offer of FASA to make progress reports periodically, if requested to do so, be accepted.[29]

Acrimonious discussions ensued within FIFA's Executive Committee between supporters of FASA and what Rous described in a letter to FASA official, Aleck Jaffe, as a 'left wing' bloc.[30] The weight of Rous's report and his representations on behalf of the white association ultimately 'won the day'[31] at this meeting and FASA was readmitted back into the FIFA fold in January 1963. As a caveat, Rous announced that an African team would be sent to South Africa to test the plausibility of FASA's claims of racial inclusivity. The decision to revoke FASA's suspension left the majority of Africa's football playing nations dumbfounded. An Extraordinary General Assembly of the African confederation was convened in Cairo shortly after FIFA's decision. Despite Rous's presence at the meeting and repeated overtures to the delegates to accept his findings, the African nations were totally unanimous in their opposition. CAF refused to accept that FASA was anything other than a racist organization and Rous's dogged insistence in supporting its re-entry into the FIFA fold was perceived in African quarters as a direct insult to pan-Africanism. As a consequence, CAF's general secretary at the time, Mustapha Fahmy, stated the African confederation would now regard South Africa 'as if she belonged to another continent' and duly refused to send an African team to the country.[32]

The condemnation and anger that emanated from CAF manifested itself most visibly in the form of a resolution, passed at the Cairo Extraordinary General Assembly which stated that

> (1) The African Football Confederation shall have nothing to do with the FASA until such time that its obnoxious apartheid policy is *totally* eliminated from its set-up, and operation and that
> (2) Our objection and dissatisfaction be conveyed to the Executive Committee of FIFA with the *warning* that the AFC proposes to table a substantive motion for the complete expulsion of the South African Football Association from FIFA at the next Congress to be held in Tokyo in 1964, if by that time the damnable apartheid policy was still practiced by the South African Football Association.[33]

CAF's reaction to the world body's stance on the South African issue sounded a stern warning to Sir Stanley Rous's FIFA on the vigour of African unity on this issue. Nonetheless, FIFA, through its actions and words, continued to ignore pan-African sensibilities leading to suggestions within the continent that FIFA and its President were not only condoning racial discrimination in football,[34] but were sympathetic to the South African government's apartheid policies.[35] CAF's resolve to oppose FIFA in respect of South Africa was hardened further when it received a letter from Dr Kaeser, FIFA's General Secretary, which accused the African confederation of not only taking decisions in an emotional and sentimental way, but of following a policy line which carried with it 'a germ of despotism and dictatorship'.[36]

FIFA's and Rous's stance on FASA's expulsion was not only intensely unpopular within Africa but was also out of kilter with developments elsewhere in international sport. The IOC for example, had adopted a tough stance on South Africa's segregated approach to Olympic sport. Indeed, at an IOC meeting in Baden-Baden in June 1962, the white South African Olympic and National Games Association (SAONGA) were given a year to demonstrate racial inclusivity or face expulsion from the 1964 Olympics in Tokyo. The Baden-Baden resolution, as it came to be known, was more than an idle threat and when SAONGA failed to convince the IOC that it would provide adequate opportunities for non-white sportsmen and women to represent South Africa, it was expelled from the Games. Encouraged by these developments Africa's footballing nations maintained the pressure on FIFA and kept their campaign against sporting apartheid in South Africa firmly on the world body's agenda. Thus, in May 1964, the Football Federation of the United Arab Emirates (UAE) wrote to Dr Kaeser requesting that its proposal regarding the expulsion of FASA from FIFA be placed on the agenda of the forthcoming FIFA Congress.[37] Crucially, the African nations sought to galvanize international support for their cause and prior to the Tokyo Congress SASF sent a memo to all of FIFA's affiliated members detailing examples of racial discrimination in football that had occurred under FASA's remit and which therefore merited its expulsion from the world body.[38]

At the Tokyo Congress the South African issue was debated in the most acrimonious of circumstances. For example, Rous accused some of the African agitators of attempting to manipulate the situation for political and nationalistic purposes and he recalled with some alarm an occasion when a president of an African football association, who also happened to be a politician, approached him with the following request, '"for goodness sake suspend these people because if you don't, my country being against apartheid, I shall lose votes in my party"'.[39] Ohine Djan, the Ghanaian FIFA Executive Committee member, countered Rous's suggestions by stating that opposition to FASA was not politically motivated and that CAF's protests against the sporting apartheid which had persisted in South African football under FASA had not been used to 'propel the cause of nationalism on the continent of Africa'.[40] During the course of the deliberations the UAE Football Federation were persuaded to modify their proposal to seek the suspension as opposed to the complete expulsion of FASA and in the vote which closed the discussions, the proposal was carried by 48 votes to 15.[41]

In the years immediately following the suspension, any hopes that this sanction would serve to dissuade FASA from continuing to organize football according to the government's apartheid system were quickly shattered. Indeed, if anything, the discrimination against non-white soccer players and associations became more extreme. For example, in a memo to CAF, the South African Non-Racial Olympic Committee (SANROC) detailed incidents of racial discrimination ranging from the banning of non-white spectators from games involving all-white teams to the refusal of the municipal authorities to allow non-white associations to use their playing facilities.[42] SASF and CAF endeavoured, through a series of memos to FIFA members, to ensure that these developments were communicated to the world body.[43] Despite clear evidence relating to discriminatory practices by FASA, Rous continued to back that Association, both through his personal correspondence with prominent FASA officials and in open declarations of support at FIFA Executive Committee meetings.

The FIFA President's views were not only the source of increasing animosity on the part of African sporting organizations, but continued to run counter to growing international pressure for an end to sporting segregation in South Africa. As noted earlier, this pressure was particularly evident within the Olympic movement which had expelled South Africa from the 1964 Games. This expulsion was lifted at the IOC's 1968 session in Greenoble, after it gained assurances from

South Africa's white Olympic body that it would send a multi-racial South African team to the Games in Mexico City. However, when it was revealed that there was only one black African among the 71 members of the team, over 40 National Olympic Committees (NOCs) primarily from Africa, Asia and the Americas, as well as the Eastern bloc countries, threatened to boycott the Mexico Games.[44] The IOC was left with no option but to exclude South Africa's Olympic team from the Games, thus consigning the country to Olympic isolation until the demise of the apartheid regime in 1992.

Rous, South Africa and FIFA politics

Rous was undoubtedly aware of the chain of events that had led to South Africa's exclusion from Olympic sport and his appraisal of the circumstances surrounding the threatened boycott of the 1968 Games increased his awareness of the growing international lobby that was demanding South Africa's sporting seclusion. Perhaps more significantly, he also recognized that his stance on South Africa not only left him increasingly isolated within FIFA's executive, but was also likely to have serious repercussions in respect of his future within FIFA. Regardless of the weight of international opinion and the views of those with whom he worked most closely, Rous continued to endorse FASA. For example, in a letter to a FASA official he bemoaned the refusal of FIFA's executive to permit a British or European team to take part in FASA's 75th anniversary celebration in the following terms:

> I was extremely disappointed ... but most of the people on the Executive Committee are now influenced by their government in this matter of South African support and although I have done my utmost to break it down I am still being accused by many of them of being pro South Africa and one member from Africa even said that my position as president would be in jeopardy if I continue to support South Africa. This matter doesn't worry me in the slightest.[45]

The strength of Rous's resolve in this matter was further highlighted by his encouragement of FASA to bring to FIFA's attention alleged instances of discriminatory practices on the part of other African football associations as a way of encouraging a sympathetic outlook to their problems.[46] Perhaps Rous's gravest error in respect of his support of FASA was the fact that on a number of occasions during the late 1960s and early 1970s, he aired his controversial views to CAF's General Assembly. By doing so, FIFA's figurehead was condemning the position adopted not only by the African national associations, but also by a significant proportion of international opinion. Furthermore, rather than contributing to a softening in the outlook towards South Africa within CAF, Rous's overtures served only to reinforce Africa's resolve to oppose FASA's re-admittance into world football and further hardened African resentment against FIFA's leader. In a response to Rous's declaration of support for FASA and a strongly worded attack on the South African Non Racial Olympic Committee (SANROC) at the 1968 CAF General Assembly, the Kenyan delegate gave vent to the disdain which much of African football was feeling towards Sir Stanley at that time;

> I stand with him [the Guinean delegate] in condemning the unwarranted attack of Sir Stanley Rous against the General Secretary and the AFC [African Football Confederation]. In his declaration, we saw the manifestation of old and dying colonialism. It is of no avail of him to say that the Football Association of South Africa has committed no crime because it is the government which is responsible of the Apartheid policy. It is the government which controls the affairs of the FASA. We in Kenya wish to see that all means possible are used to bring about a change in South Africa so that our brothers there may enjoy the freedom of sports we have.[47]

Detailed analysis of Rous's personal correspondence on the South African question reveals that throughout his presidency he remained immovable and resolute in the face of considerable pressure from a significant section of FIFA's constituency. Even during his final term of office

Rous maintained his commitment to FASA, despite recognition of the fact that his position was likely to have a potentially inauspicious bearing on the outcome of election for the FIFA Presidency in 1974. As he approached his last term of office the strain of heading the largest international sports federation and dealing with the many disputes therein, particularly the case of South Africa, was beginning to tell. In a private letter to Fred Fell, the President of FASA, Rous conceded that, 'I am not sure that I am being wise in accepting another four year period as President… at seventy five one begins to have a smaller appetite for hard work and problems'.[48] Despite his reservations about leading the world body for a further four years and the level of antagonism which had emanated from the African continent over his handling of FASA, Rous, elected unopposed at FIFA's 1970 Congress, faced up to the challenges of leading FIFA in an ever-changing environment with renewed vigour and commitment.

Rous versus Havelange and the significance of South Africa

João Havelange, who had launched his bid for the FIFA Presidency in 1971, was an interested observer in the developing relations between FIFA, FASA and CAF during Stanley Rous's tenure of office. His canvassing campaign throughout the third world and exposure to the sentiments of SANROC, in his capacity as a member of the IOC, had given Havelange an understanding of the centrality of South Africa's continued sporting isolation in the psyche of African politicians, sports administrators and its general population. As the 1974 election grew closer, so the bearing of South Africa's status on world football politics increased. In 1972 FASA had once again utilized its links with Rous in order to secure special dispensation from FIFA's Executive Committee to allow them to invite amateur select teams from England, Brazil and West Germany to take part in, what FASA described as, a 'multi-racial' sports festival in March of the following year.

Rous had hoped that the festival would 'achieve a general relaxation of the existing governmental policies in respect of sport'.[49] However, as Ramsamy has correctly observed, initiatives of this type were merely aimed at appeasing international opinion and actually represented a major outlet for the 'aggrandizement of white supremacy'.[50] Indeed, when it became known that the festival would not include a racially mixed South African team, the FIFA Executive Committee's decision to grant the authorization for the tournament to go ahead provoked strong protests not only from the traditional supporters of FASA's suspension who claimed that the International Federation had acted unconstitutionally in allowing the tournament to go ahead,[51] but also from the governments of those countries which had agreed to send a representative team. FIFA's Executive was forced into a climb down and the English and West German FA's quickly withdrew their entries, closely followed by Brazil. Whilst the foreign offices of both England and West Germany played a central role in procuring the withdrawal of their respective teams, Brazil's retreat was orchestrated by Havelange who, in his position as President of the Brazilian Football Federation, was ultimately responsible for sanctioning such actions.

Havelange's role in the withdrawal of the Brazilian team from the South African multinational sports festival provides an enlightening insight into the nature of his political campaign in Africa. It not only illustrates that he was sympathetic to CAF's outlook on South Africa, but also reveals that he possessed the political acumen to exploit Rous's problems with Africa's national associations in order to increase his political support. Stanley Rous was in no doubt as to Havelange's influence in the withdrawal of Brazil and the motivation which underpinned his backing for CAF's anti-South Africa campaign:

> The Brazilians withdrew, I am told on good authority, because Tessema, the President of the African Confederation threatened that Mr. Havelange would lose the support of the African associations in his fight against me for the presidency of FIFA.[52]

The fact that Tessema was in a position to threaten the withdrawal of African support for Havelange's presidential challenge illustrates that CAF not only had the confidence to assert itself within world football politics but also recognized the potential that its voting powers offered the African continent. Indeed, it is clear from African accounts of the 1974 FIFA Congress,[53] that the African nations did not see themselves merely as pawns in a power struggle for the control of FIFA. Instead, they saw Havelange as the means through which to achieve a realignment of the distribution of power and privilege within world football in ways that would more adequately reflect their interests. Nonetheless, Havelange clearly sought to harness Africa's growing confidence as well as the antipathy between CAF and Stanley Rous over the South African issue in order to increase his appeal to FIFA's African constituents. Oroc Oyo, the first secretary of the independent Nigerian Football Association, explains how Havelange weaved the status of FASA into the fabric of his political campaign:

> I remember the 1974 elections very vividly. There was this struggle [between Rous and Havelange] and I was in the centre of it. Dr. Havelange mounted his campaign in 1971 and he produced a brochure on himself that was circulated around the world... At that time Africa had a Supreme Council for Sport in Africa, and the secretary general was Jean Claude Ganga. The plank of Havelange's campaign was to ostracize South Africa, because this was the clarion call of African football. This was the carrot which Dr. Havelange brandished before Africa. So Ganga mustered Africa.[54]

Havelange's attempt to elevate the South African question to the status of a major voting issue was facilitated by the fact that right up until the vote in Frankfurt, just prior to the 1974 World Cup Finals in West Germany, Rous maintained his desire to see FASA re-admitted into FIFA and stood squarely against SASF's continued attempts to see the all-white body's suspension upgraded to a full expulsion.[55] In doing so, FIFA's president further alienated himself from a growing constituency within FIFA that supported South Africa's continued exclusion from world football and also demonstrated just how out of touch he had become with international opinion on the apartheid regime.[56] The Brazilian, on the other hand, made his intentions for South Africa explicitly clear, professing that 'so long as I am in charge and apartheid still exists, South Africa will never come into FIFA'.[57] Indeed, Havelange's promise to exclude FASA from the world body was realized two years after he replaced Rous as FIFA President, when the Executive Committee, on the new President's prompting, expelled South Africa from its ranks until such time as 'racial discrimination (apartheid) had ceased to exist in their club matches'.[58]

Conclusion

This essay clearly demonstrates the significance of South Africa in the transformation of world football that was heralded by the election of João Havelange as FIFA President. Although Stanley Rous's position going into FIFA's 1974 Congress was undermined by his stance on a number of other political crises involving China and Taiwan and the former Soviet Union and Chile,[59] his position on the FASA-SASF dispute clearly did most to swing the election Havelange's way. As highlighted earlier, Rous was patently aware of the potential repercussions of his support for FASA for his candidacy for a job that he clearly loved and wanted to keep. So how do we make sense of his actions in relation to South Africa? There are two interpretations in this regard, both of which are supported to varying degrees by the narrative above. The first, and certainly more benign of the two, is that Rous, in his dealings with FASA and SASF, was motivated solely by a principled but naive aversion to the intrusion of politics into sport. If this was the case then Rous was always going to be predisposed to the association that could demonstrate, on the surface at least, that it was the least interested in matters of a 'political' nature. In their representations to Rous, FASA consistently stressed that they were not politically motivated, but rather were acting in accordance with their country's customs and traditions. SASF's campaign to have FASA removed from FIFA, as part of the broader anti-apartheid movement in sport, was much more visibly and recognizably political and while the non-white football federation would not have denied this, it pointed to the fact that it was the association that had, through their application of segregation into football, been guilty of bringing politics into sport in the first instance. This polemic, which was played out across the spectrum of sports in South Africa in this era, is well described by Leo Kuper:

> Generally in sport, a strong, though not absolute colour bar is raised between white and non-white. White sports administrators tend to regard this as non-political, simply one of the customs of the country, and they often characterise attempts to remove the colour bar as the intrusion of politics into sport. The more militant non-white sportsmen see apartheid in sport, and the monopoly of national colours by whites, as obviously political, and part of systematic political discrimination.[60]

If Rous sided with the white association solely because he accepted their argument that they were merely following the laws of South Africa and not acting in a political manner, then he was displaying a considerable naiveté about the complex manner in which sport and politics interact.

The second interpretation is that Rous's insistence that sport and politics were two distinct spheres of activity and therefore should not have been allowed to intermingle may have actually disguised his own political outlook, one that was characterized by a leaning towards right-of-centre politics and an aversion to positions that were located on the political left. This view is supported by recognizing that in a number of political disputes which bedevilled the latter years of his leadership of FIFA,[61] including the case of South Africa, Rous's personal stance, which he claimed was taken according to a strict adherence to FIFA's statutes, ultimately reflected this position. This interpretation is supported by Lapchick's contention that those international sports governing bodies which chose to allow or at least support South African participation in international competition did so for their own political and/or economic reasons:

> The decisions of these bodies in general, and of individual nations in particular, at times have seemingly been motivated by means other than strictly sports criteria. In fact, these decisions, as well as internal sports decisions in South Africa, often seem motivated by racial, economic, and political factors as by sports factors.[62]

In this sense, it is feasible to argue that Rous's support for the white South African football administration was reflective of his own right-of-centre political tendencies and also revealed his tendency to work against organizations which were in any way resonant of leftist politics. Writing in his autobiography, published four years after the election, Rous described his defeat to Havelange as being reflective of 'changing attitudes and standards' in world football and that his desire 'to avoid politics becoming a dominant influence in football', may have seemed 'outdated and amateurish'.[63] If one accepts this second interpretation of his stance over South Africa, then Rous's comments fail to disguise the possibility that, at a time when politics was encroaching on the sporting domain, his own approach had become increasingly politicized. Indeed, rather than opting to avoid the inevitable overlap between sport and politics, Rous's biggest mistake in respect of South Africa, as it impacted on his tenure of the FIFA presidency, was that his own politics left him at odds with the majority of the those whose votes determined the outcome of the Frankfurt election.

Notes

1. Darby, *Africa, Football and FIFA*; Darby, 'Football, Colonial Doctrine and Indigenous Resistance'.
2. Darby, 'Football, Colonial Doctrine and Indigenous Resistance'.
3. FIFA Minutes, 14–15 November 1953; FIFA Minutes, 21 June 1954.
4. Darby, 'Africa and the *World* Cup'.
5. Rous, *Football Worlds*.
6. Goldman, 'My Life and Times in World Football – Sir Stanley Rous'.

7. Lapchick, *The Politics of Race and International Sport.*
8. Cited in Guelke, 'The Politicisation of South African Sport'.
9. Alegi, *Laduma!.*
10. SASF, *Memo Presented to FIFA's South Africa Commission*, January 1963.
11. Lapchick, *The Politics of Race and International Sport.*
12. SASF Memorandum to FIFA, 8 May 1955.
13. Alegi, *Laduma!*, 113.
14. Ibid.
15. It should also be noted here that SASF's ability to counter FASA's claims regarding the racial basis of football in South Africa was precluded by the government's refusal to grant passports to SASF delegates wishing to attend the 1956 FIFA Congress.
16. Jarvie and Reid, 'Sport in South Africa'.
17. Guelke, 'The Politicisation of South African Sport', 122.
18. Jarvie, *Class, Race and Sport in South Africa's Political Economy*, 65–7.
19. Alegi, *Laduma!*, 116.
20. FIFA, *Minutes of the XXXIst Ordinary Congress*, Stockholm, 5 June 1958.
21. FIFA, *Minutes of the XXXIInd Ordinary Congress*, Rome, 22 August 1960.
22. Ibid.
23. FIFA, *Minutes of the IIIrd Extraordinary Congress,* London, 28–29 September 1961.
24. V. Granger, *Personal Letter to Stanley Rous*, 27 August 1962.
25. Hill, *Olympic Politics*, 207.
26. SASF, *Cable Telegram to Dr. Helmut Kaeser, FIFA General Secretary*, December 1962.
27. SASF, *Letter to Dr. Helmut Kaeser, FIFA General Secretary,* 20 December 1962.
28. Ibid.
29. FIFA, *Report of the Visit of Sir Stanley Rous and Mr. J. Maguire to South Africa*, 5–19 January 1963.
30. S. Rous, *Letter to Aleck Jaffe*, 1 February 1963.
31. Ibid.
32. Cited in Lapchick, *The Politics of Race and International Sport*, 58.
33. CAF, *Minutes of Extraordinary General Assembly*, Cairo, 24 January 1963.
34. Mourad Fahmy (General Secretary, AFC), *Letter to FIFA*, 15 November 1963.
35. United Arab Emirates Football Federation, *Letter to Dr. Helmut Kaeser*, 5 May 1964.
36. H. Kaeser, *Letter to CAF from FIFA General Secretary*, 15 November 1963.
37. United Arab Emirates Football Federation, *Letter to Dr. Helmut Kaeser.*
38. SASF, *Memorandum to all FIFA Members on racial discrimination in South Africa Soccer and relating to (1) Expulsion/Suspension of FASA and (2) Our application for membership in FIFA*, July 1964.
39. FIFA, *Minutes of the XXXIVth Ordinary Congress*, Tokyo, 8 October 1964.
40. Ibid.
41. Ibid.
42. SANROC, *Memorandum to CAF*, 1 November 1967. Lapchick, *The Politics of Race and International Sport*, described the actions of the white football authorities in systematically denying facilities for non-white football as going to 'war'. See also Alegi, *Laduma!* for further detail on the discriminatory way that FASA dealt with non-white football in this period.
43. SASF, *Memorandum to FIFA Members on the latest developments appertaining to football in South Africa*, May 1966.
44. Ibid., 212–13.
45. S. Rous, *Letter to Mr. Pat Murray (FASA Official)*, 11 February 1967.
46. Ibid.
47. CAF, *Minutes of VIIIth Ordinary Congress*, Addis Ababa, 10 January 1968.
48. S. Rous, *Letter to Fred Fell, President of FASA*, 23 April 1970.
49. S. Rous, *Letter to Dave Marais, President of FASA*, 26 January 1973.
50. S. Ramsamy, 'Keep South African Sports in Isolation', *New York Times*, 11 December 1988.
51. Chris de Broglio (on behalf of the SANROC Executive), *Letter to Stanley Rous*, 3 February 1973; Ydnekatchew Tessema, *Letter to Stanley Rous,* 5 February 1973.
52. S. Rous, *Letter to Denis McIldowie*, 1 May 1973.
53. See, Darby, Africa, the FIFA Presidency 2003, and Darby, *Africa, Football and FIFA.*
54. Interview with O. Oyo cited in Darby, Sugden and Tomlinson, 'Who Rules the People's Game?', 18.
55. SASF, *Brief Memorandum in support of the SASF's application for the expulsion of FASA and for membership of FIFA*, 30 January 1974.

56. Rous's last declarations of support for South Africa's white football administrators as FIFA President came just three years prior to the Gleneagles Agreement through which all Commonwealth heads of government unanimously accepted that contact or competition with teams from South Africa should be discouraged.
57. Interview with M. Wade, cited in Darby, Sugden and Tomlinson, 'Who Rules the People's Game?', 19.
58. FIFA, *Minutes of the XLth Ordinary Congress*, Montreal, 16 July 1976.
59. See Darby, *Africa, Football and FIFA*, 68–71.
60. Cited in Guelke, 'The Politicisation of South African Sport', 119.
61. For a discussion of Rous's stance over disputes between the former USSR and Chile and China and Taiwan which revealed a tendency to work against leftist political positions see Darby, *Africa, Football and FIFA* and Sugden and Tomlinson, *FIFA and the Contest for World Football.*
62. Lapchick, *The Politics of Race and International Sport*, xxi.
63. Rous, *Football Worlds*, 203.

References

Alegi, P. *Laduma! Soccer, Politics and Society in South Africa.* Scottsville, South Africa: University of KwaZulu-Natal Press, 2004.

Darby, P. 'Football, Colonial Doctrine and Indigenous Resistance: Mapping the Political Persona of FIFA's African Constituency'. *Culture, Sport, Society* 3, no.1 (2000): 61–87.

________ *Africa, Football and FIFA: Politics, Colonialism and* Resistance. London and Portland, OR: Frank Cass, 2002.

________ 'Africa, the FIFA Presidency and the Governance of World Football: 1974, 1998 and 2002', *Africa Today* 50, no.1 (2003): 3–24.

________ 'Africa and the *World* Cup: Politics, Eurocentrism and Resistance'. *International Journal of the History of Sport* 22, no.5 (2005): 883–905.

Darby, P., J. Sugden and A. Tomlinson. 'Who Rules the People's Game? FIFA Versus UEFA in the Struggle for the Control of World Football'. Paper presented at *Fanatics! Football and Popular Culture in Europe*, Manchester Metropolitan University, 11–13 June 1996.

Goldman, K. 'My Life and Times in World Football – Sir Stanley Rous', *World Soccer,* September (1986): 12–14.

Guelke, A. 'The Politicisation of South African Sport'. In *The Politics of Sport,* ed. L. Allison, 118–148. Manchester and New York: Manchester University Press, 1986.

Hill, C.R. *Olympic Politics: Athens to Atlanta 1896–1996.* Manchester and New York: Manchester University Press, 1996.

Jarvie, G. *Class, Race and Sport in South Africa's Political* Economy. London and Boston, MA: Routledge and Keegan Paul, 1985.

Jarvie, G. and I. Reid. 'Sport in South Africa'. In *The International Politics of Sport,* ed. J. Rioradan and A. Krüger, 234–45. London and New York: E & FN Spon, 1999.

Lapchick, R. *The Politics of Race and International Sport: The Case of South Africa.* Westport, CN and London: Greenwood Press, 1975.

Rous, S. *Football Worlds: A Lifetime in Sport.* London: Faber, 1978.

Sugden, J. and A. Tomlinson. *FIFA and the Contest for World Football: Who Rules the Peoples' Game?* London: Polity Press, 1998.

'Feeble Bengalis' and 'big Africans': African players in Bengali club football

Projit Bihari Mukharji

With the rise of postcolonial and cultural studies, the history of sports has emerged from its natal home in the West. An increasing number of quality monographs are today available on the role, impact and development of modern sports in non-western societies. Necessarily these studies have also highlighted, in a number of ways, the various networks of capital, commerce and media that position these societies vis-à-vis the dominance of the West. In the case of football studies this has often led to poignant explorations of complex circuits of capital, race and global power politics that inform international player transfers from the talented, but poverty stricken, nations of Africa and Latin America to the exploitative premiere leagues of Europe and to a limited extent Japan. Yet what remains relatively under-researched are the various flows and networks that connect the non-western world without any putative mediation of the West.

This oversight is partly due to the way globalization has been equated with the neo-imperialism of the West. While there is no denying that the two are intimately related, globalization is a much broader and many faceted process, or as some would like to say, itself a symptom of a deeper process of the movement of capital.[1] After all, the global reach of the Stop the War movement is also a result of the same globalization that aids and abets the new western imperial project. Amin has rightly pointed out that the space of the management of capital accumulation no longer coincides with the management of the social and political dimensions.[2] As Latour has been at pains to point out, the 'global' does not erase the 'local', but rather creates a complex economy of signs, within which to re-imagine the networks that connect the local within the global.[3] Pieterse has argued that while there is a greater synchronization of networks, brought out by economic, technological and cultural flows, there is no single global world.[4] Thus instead of *modernization* we must speak of *modernizations*; *westernization* as a unidirectional movement now needs to be understood as a complex process of *global melange.* Globalization has thus created a 'mosaic of differentiated sites of potential investment'.[5]

The only two explorations of the process of globalization on Indian football have both tended to focus principally on the impact of the international media on the game. While noting the use of foreign footballers, somewhat in passing, both comment that by flooding the market with sub-standard and highly paid expatriate players, globalization has had an overwhelmingly negative impact on the game.[6] This negative evaluation of the presence of foreign players on Calcutta's football has also been re-iterated time and again by a host of ex-players and by many football enthusiasts in the city. Whilst this evaluation indubitably has its merits, it is only part of the picture. The aporia is partly the result of the sources which historians use. Dependant principally upon textual sources and using interviews and oral narratives only to corroborate the textual material, these approaches fail to adequately explore the informal structures which do not often produce textual traces. Following in the tradition inaugurated in South Asian history by Cohn, I seek to use an approach that combines both historical and anthropological methods to situate formal structures of Calcutta's football (which produce adequate textual traces) within an overall context that accounts also for the informal structures (which can be retrieved only through conversations and interviews).[7] Methodologically, structured interviews have been used only seldom, depending in turn on a number of informal conversations. The world of the Maidan – the large open space in the centre of the city where most clubs have their tents and the more important ones even have their small stadiums – is the hub of football in Calcutta. Since professional management of the clubs is still a distant dream, paperwork is often partial and fragmentary and much more is to be gained by talking to the many old hands who have made the Maidan their second home. Being informally run, Maidan administration is often a rough business.[8] This in turn makes regulars at the Maidan hesitant to speak on record and very little is to be gained from formal interviews, whereas informal conversations are startlingly revealing.

What emerges from these conversations is a complex picture of the effects of the process of globalization on modern sport. An intricate informal economy involving illegal immigrants, cross-border smuggling, 'informal' football tournaments called *khep khela* etc. are all held together by ideas about racial prejudice and privilege. Racial difference is not so much a matter of 'institutional discrimination', as King pointed out in his study of English football coaching procedures.[9] Rather, developing Goffman's insights, it is how roles are played out or performed in the day-to-day lives of people and the structural consequences of these performances, where racially differentiated and discriminatory modes of behaviour are to be discerned.[10] It underwrites and naturalizes a number of networks of movement, relationships and structures by creating a commonsensical mode of thinking which, almost reflexively, uses racial difference as a structuring principle. St Louis has shown that 'racial athleticism' or the stereotyping of athletic styles by racial identities, is not simply a matter of prejudice or ignorance. St Louis contends that it is 'common-sense' for most people and therefore infiltrate and inhabit a host of different discursive practices. Merely showing contrary examples, therefore, argues St Louis is not enough to challenge this racialized imagination; instead he calls for a thorough-going 'ethical critique' that goes beyond 'social constructionism of embodied difference'.[11]

Foreign Players

Though none of the South Asian countries have made their mark in international football, there remain old, entrenched and passionate football cultures in several parts of South Asia. Kerala, Goa and Bengal are the principal regions where passionate footballing cultures thrive. Of these, Bengal perhaps has the oldest and most conspicuous following. Traditionally some of the most successful and oldest clubs are based in Calcutta and its fan cultures are perhaps the most intricate.[12]

Foreign players in Calcutta club football are nothing new. The Burmese striker Pagasley achieved superstardom in 1940s Calcutta. A member of the 1942 East Bengal side that lifted the IFA Shield (the premiere Indian championship), Pagasley went on to become the highest scorer in the 1945 season. In the process, playing for Bengal in a Santosh Trophy encounter with Rajputana, he pumped in seven goals in a single match. Similarly in the 1950s, Pakistani greats Musa and Fakri set the Calcutta turf alight with their brilliance. This trend of talented international recruits from the neighbouring countries donning the colours of the Calcutta clubs continued into the 1980s and 1990s with players coming from Nepal (C.B. Thapa, Dev Narayan Chaudhury and Hari Khadkader), Bangladesh (Rumi and Munna), Sri Lanka (Roshan Periera), Thailand (Dushit Chalersman) etc.

The first African player to play in Calcutta was the Nigerian David Williams who moved to East Bengal in 1979 after having played in Tamil Nadu. The same year also saw the introduction of the first Iranian players. Although the Iranians Sanjari and Khabazi achieved conspicuous success and even directly facilitated the introduction of other Iranians such as the talented Majid Baskar and Jamshed Nassiri, the 1980s clearly saw the emergence of the trend towards the recruitment of big-bodied Africans. In 1985, Chima Okorie, a Nigerian student of architecture who had been playing for his University team in Vishakhapatnam, moved to Calcutta. Okorie, or Okerie, as he came to be called in the Calcutta press, had a huge impact on the city's football. Playing for nearly two decades, the robust Nigerian played for all three major Calcutta clubs during his career and scored a whopping 280 goals in 400 matches. Soon fellow Nigerians Emeka Ezeugo, Chibuzor and Christopher added muscle and speed to Calcutta football. Of these Ezeugo went on to greener pastures in Bangladesh and Europe before finally representing Nigeria in the World Cup.[13]

Traditionally the Bengali football season coincides with the South Asian monsoons – a season of torrential late-afternoon downpours. Played thus on slushy pitches and often through blinding rain, special skills are required. Lacking often in speed or passing, it is dependent mostly on great individual ball-control, deception and tackling. The Iranians too continued this trend of deft touches and dribbling skills, but the big-bodied Nigerians depended more on bludgeoning power. Often taking hold of the ball on the fringes of the midfield, players like Chima then used their superior build and stamina to literally bulldoze through the defences before unleashing a powerful shot to the back of the net.

By the 1990s, as football began to lose out its appeal and audience to the ever-increasing popularity of cricket, and the talent pool began to dry up, the clubs started seeking easy success by loading the team with powerful muscular men. There emerged a notion that 'power football' was the way ahead. In 1993 when Chima, then nearly 30 and well past his prime, moved to Mohun Bagan, one of the oldest clubs in the country and one that had until then held out against the urge to include foreigners on its teams, this signalled the final acceptance of the mantra of 'power football'. It was believed that even as a dead weight, Chima was to be preferred to the scantily built local lads.

It is this imagination of physical difference, that is, of slightly built Bengalis and muscular big-bodied Africans, that has animated much of the drive to recruit African players. Irrespective of their skills, not only Super Division teams, but even Second Division teams started digging deep into their coffers to hire African players, while they remained hesitant to fund youth training programmes in their own backyards. An official of the Khidderpore Club was reported as saying in 2005, while playing the Nigerian James Agbo on their team, that, 'We don't care whether they are drivers, lawyers or beggars in Africa. At least they have the power to put one pile driver at the back of the net. And their size terrifies the locals.'[14] Another official, Bibhash Manna of the lowly ranked Janbajar FC tried to justify playing a string of big Nigerians in 2003 by saying, 'The Calcutta League is played at the height of the rains. The pitches are very muddy and slippery. On these pitches the superior build, strength and stamina of African footballers, apart from other advantages, allows them distinct advantages in charging, tackling or merely staying on their feet when tackled.'[15] That none of these advantages are in themselves enough was comprehensively shown in 2003 when Manna's Janbajar, despite his Nigerians, was trounced 4-1 by an un-fancied Goralgachha team comprised solely of local players.

As hinted above, Africans are by no means the only group of foreign players in Calcutta. Apart from other Asian and African countries, there have also been players from Europe. Over the years there have been at least a dozen British players, for example. John Divine and Peter Macguire have been the better known of these. Unquestionably though, the single largest group after the Africans are the Brazilian recruits. The star Brazilian is the Mohun Bagan striker Jose Ramirez Barreto. The Brazilian's popularity is such that in 2003 when, following internal squabbles, the club failed to raise the money required to retain their star striker, one of the club's loyal supporters wrote to the administrators offering to sell his ancestral house in order to raise the sum required.[16] Significantly not all foreign players are associated with the same stereotypes: while Africans are consistently thought of as powerhouses, the Brazilians are, for example, seen to be skilled ball players. Most Calcutta football fans would agree with the 65-year-old Sisir Lal Banerjee that, 'Brazilians are artists, they are so skilful'.[17]

It is not my intention here to argue for or against the use of foreign players by Bengali clubs; instead it is the complex role that globalization has had in generating, circulating and sustaining ideas about racial difference and the ways in which these ideas have affected and changed the football played in Calcutta, that I am trying to highlight.

Table 1. African players in Super Division at Calcutta

Year of First Appearance	First Club	Name	Country of Origin
1979	East Bengal	David Williams	Nigeria
1985	Mohammedan S C	Chima Okorie	Nigeria
1986	East Bengal	Emeka Ezeugo	Nigeria
1985	East Bengal	Chibuzor	Nigeria
1985	East Bengal	Christopher	Nigeria
1995	Eveready	Felix Celeatine	Nigeria
1997	East Bengal	Sammy Omollo	Kenya
1998	East Bengal	Jackson Egupong	Ghana
1998	East Bengal	Suleh Musah	Ghana
1998	East Bengal	Emmanuel Opoku	Ghana
1998	East Bengal	Mohammed Salissu	Ghana
1998	Mohun Bagan AC	Friday Elaho	Nigeria
1998	Mohun Bagan AC	Emeka Achilefu	Nigeria
1998	Mohammedan SC	Bernard Rodriguez	Nigeria
1999	East Bengal	Abu Idrisu	Ghana
1999	East Bengal	Kennedy Ofosuhene Amponsh	Ghana
1999	East Bengal	Willie Brown	Ghana
2000	East Bengal	Siva Mumuni	Ghana
2000	East Bengal	Omoloja Olalekan	Nigeria
2000	Tollygunge Agragami	Abdul Wastu Saliu	Nigeria
2001	East Bengal	Ally Mayaytembele	Tanzania
2001	Mohun Bagan AC	Ezch Colly Barnes	
2002	East Bengal	Isa Musa Eroje	Nigeria

Table 1. *(continued)*

Year of First Appearance	First Club	Name	Country of Origin
2002	East Bengal	Mike Okoro	Nigeria
2002	Mohun Bagán AC	George Ekah	Nigeria
2002	Mohun Bagan	Yakubu Rasiu Mallam	
2002	Mohammedan SC	Christian Okolonko	Nigeria
2003	Mohun Bagan AC	Chukuwama Olusegun Akunito	Nigeria
2003	Tollygunge Agragami	Ebi Bar Bar	Nigeria
2003	Mohammedan SC	Edeh Chidi	Nigerian
2003	Mohammedan SC	Godwin Abu Baker	Liberia
2003	Mohammedan SC	Eugene Gray	Nigeria
2004	East Bengal	Louis Aniwata	Nigeria
2004	East Bengal	Ernest Jeremiah	Nigeria
2004	Mohun Bagan AC	Suleiman Hamid	Nigeria
2004	Mohun Bagan AC	James Agbo Ugwo	Nigeria
2004	Mohun Bagan AC	Noel Tafadzwa Kaseka	Zimbabwe
2004	Mohammedan SC	Michael Ajayi	Uganda
2004	Eveready	Emmanuel	Nigeria
2004	Eveready	Theodor Swrobeh	Nigeria
2004	Eveready	Francis Chukura	Nigeria
2005	East Bengal	Lisa N'Duti	South Africa
2005	East Bengal	Sydney Bonginkosi Nakalanga	South Africa
2005	East Bengal	Ngassa Ewane Gyu Mertial	Cameroon
2005	East Bengal	Ndem Gwy Kiyeck Herve	Cameroon
2005	Mohun Bagan AC	Akeem Abul Alem	Nigeria
2005	Mohun Bagan AC	Glay Yao Rodriguez	Togo
2005	Mohun Bagan AC	Coffi Edem Agbessi	Benin
2005	Mohun Bagan AC	Awudu Ibrahim	Nigeria
2005	Mohun Bagan AC	Ajibade Babalade	Nigeria
2005	Mohammedan SC	Okonji Onyelo Patrick D'Souza	Nigeria
2005	Mohammedan SC	David Mkandawire	Zimbabwe
2005	Mohammedan SC	Henry Chukwukei	Nigeria
2006	East Bengal	Bonifa Ngairah Ambani	Kenya
2006	Mohammedan SC	Eric Bolwe Mputu	Nigeria

Systems of recruitment

Like Chima, the early African recruits were almost all recruited from amongst students who were in India to pursue tertiary education. Lucrative contracts were used to lure these students away from their studies and into club football. This changed once it became established that the only way to easy success was to enrol powerful players. As demand far out-stripped supply, clubs sought other ways to find big African players. At the same time the prospect of easy money and the success of players such as Chima, Emeka and Musah were also reported back to the countries of their origin and enticed many to seek their fortune in Calcutta, irrespective of their football skills.

The flows of men, money and information thus converged to create a complex network of recruitment. Some players came through their fathers or uncles who used to visit the city to tend to business interests. Edeh Chidi, who played for Mohammedan SC, for instance, came to the city with his brother, who used to visit in connection with his business. Others paid hefty commissions to dubious scouts and spotters. Some were also introduced by earlier players who had played in the city. Occasionally, it was said, some even turned up unannounced and asked to be given a trial.[18] Recently the Mohun Bagan coach Carlos complained in exasperation at a press conference, 'Everyday one or two foreign players turn up for trials. Am I to look at them or at the team?'[19]

Just as their footballing skills varied, so too did the pay cheques they could draw. While the big clubs like Mohun Bagan and East Bengal dug deep into their pockets to pay their African recruits handsomely, the minor clubs had neither the resources nor the sponsors to raise as much money. Players such as Flacis or Godwin Abu Baker of Peerless or Saidi and Kunley who played for Muslim Institute were among several players who managed to stay in Calcutta, at least initially, at their own expense. They bought their own gear and kept trying out at these minor clubs in the hope of eventually getting a contract with one of the big ones.

In order to understand the recruitment and payment structure of the majority of the African players it is important to have some idea of the general condition of Africans in Calcutta. There are a significant number of African expatriates in Calcutta who are part of a precarious and dangerous informal economy. Most of them live in the filthy and dilapidated Mess Houses in the Sudder Street, Free School Street, Kyd Street region of central Calcutta. The facilities at these Mess Houses are very basic. Between eight to ten people are crammed into a single, long, unfurnished room with bedding on the floor. The houses themselves are in a dilapidated condition with roofs that often leak during the torrential Calcutta rains. Many of the expatriates come to the city with as little as a thousand Indian rupees (approximately £12). A good many of them are recruited by cross-border smuggling rackets and help bring in a variety of goods across the border from the neighbouring countries. They are usually known to peddle clothes and electronic goods. A few also act as guides to the City's many western tourists. These latter are often said to hâve understandings with local shops and get small commissions from them in lieu of bringing the tourists to these shops during the course of their visits. Some of them, especially the better built ones, often work in the Burra Bazar, Calcutta's largest wholesale market. Here they combine the roles of labour supervisor with that of a muscleman. Some are also involved in the drug rackets of the city. Predictably, many do not even have valid visas and hence their numbers are difficult to determine. Worse still, being illegal immigrants involved in such hazardous, illegal trades they often fall foul of the local police.[20]

It is from this pool of large Africans that many of the players who played in the lower divisions were recruited. The recruits were at times paid as little as Rs 31 for a match (about 40 pence), given lunch, loaned a pair of boots and a jersey to play the match. A good many of these lower division teams are grossly mismanaged and often do not even have 11 players to turn up on the day of the match. Walkovers are a regular feature at the lower levels of Calcutta football. These clubs have capitalized by using these powerfully built Africans to win a few occasional matches in order to fight off relegation. Such clubs had neither the interest nor the wherewithal to employ these players on a regular basis. Paid thus on a match-to-match basis, most of these players earned around Rs 50 per match along with the free lunch and boots for the day. The lunch usually comprised of a few slices of bread and a translucent liquid passed off variously as 'soup' or 'stew'. Only the top bracket of players could earn a monthly salary of around a couple of thousand rupees.

The careers of Louis Ola or Balwoa are typical of the trajectory followed by many of these players. These two were involved in a drug-related police case some three or four years ago. Released on bail, they were both broke and were playing small football tournaments organized by small-scale local clubs. On one such occasion, playing a match on the Rangers' Ground in the Maidan, Balwoa was spotted by City AC and recruited for one of their fixtures. He was paid Rs 31, given lunch and loaned a pair of boots for the day. After he scored a couple of goals and ensured City's victory, they hired him on a permanent basis for the princely salary of Rs 50 per match along with lunch. Ola similarly landed up with the Garifa Students Union. David of Shyamnagar Jyoti Sangha and Baba from Tollygunge Agragami similarly were arrested and cautioned after a street brawl before eventually landing full-time assignments with their respective clubs.[21]

For the Super Division teams the system is slightly different. While they continue to scout for locally available Africans, a majority are nowadays recruited from the African countries themselves. The system of recruitment though is as random and haphazard as that followed by the lower level clubs. There are three possible avenues through which an African player may be drafted onto one of the major Calcutta clubs.

First there are the club's local scouts who are on the look out for African players playing for other teams in the country. Before the introduction of the Token System, this avenue of player recruitment, or transfer to be more precise, was the source of much intrigue. Describing the system, noted sports journalist Novy Kapadia wrote:

> The transfer season in Calcutta lasts for 15 days, either in April or in May, just before the new season commences ... Star players were often smuggled to safe hideouts, secluded bungalows or resorts outside Calcutta or in some remote area in the City and protected by henchmen. There were occasions when a player did not want to sign for the club that had kidnapped or protected him. Subtle psychological pressure was then applied to cajole the player to sign. In some cases, players were given bodyguards, who stayed with them day and night and prevented emissaries from other clubs from approaching them.[22]

From 1993–94 the Indian Football Association (IFA) introduced the Token System of player transfers. In this system, players receive a token which they can hand over to the club they wish to move to. The club can then fill out the necessary forms at the IFA offices showing the token without the player having to be present. The clubs too have agreed to the system since it has helped reduce the price wars that clever players stoked by playing one club off against another.

The second mode of recruitment is by one of the club's officials actually travelling to their African country of choice and recruiting players there. The decision on which country to visit is often determined by international performance. There are no fixed decision making processes, nor are international recruiting and scouting agencies used. Recently a renowned FIFA-recognized German recruiting agency had forwarded details of some of its players to the leading Calcutta clubs. The agency revealed that the Calcutta clubs did not even bother to acknowledge receipt. Moreover those who make the choice abroad are seldom players or coaches. Instead club officials are the ones to go on these recruiting trips. The official, who returns home usually along with the players, gets a hefty commission on the recruitment as an agent's fees. It is this commission as well as the adoration of the fanatical supporters if the players perform well, that motivates the strange system of sending officials rather than coaches on recruitment drives. East Bengal club official Swapan Bal's visit to Ghana in 1999 after their former foreign players failed to perform, was typical of such trips.[23]

Finally, the last mode of recruitment is through past African players who have played in Calcutta. The Nigerian Sammy Omollo is reported to be the man behind many of the Africans such as Ambani who are currently playing in Calcutta.[24] The rumour mill has it that none other than Chima has now submitted a list of players to the Mohun Bagan officials for recruitment. These players usually do not get paid directly by the clubs. Instead part of their reward lies in being able to head an international patron-client chain through which they enjoy substantial power and status at home. The ability to get their friends and acquaintances at home plush contracts in Calcutta undoubtedly contributes towards bolstering their social prestige and clout in Nigeria. These players also take a percentage of the fees from the recruited players themselves, once the fees have been paid. Though dependable figures for the money paid by the big clubs to their international recruits are difficult to find, since audit sheets are unavailable, according to sources within the clubs, these 'recruiting commissions' could sometimes be as high as 50% of what is given to the players.

Making ends meet

Most of the African players who play in the lower levels at Calcutta make ends meet by what is known in Maidan lingo as *khep khela* (roughly meaning 'playing by turns'). This comprises of playing in a range of tournaments organized by various small local clubs. The tournaments range from being a one day affair to being a massive seven day fest. Organized usually between various localities (called 'paras') within the city or outside the city between various village clubs, these tournaments are keenly contested as they help articulate the sharp rivalries that may exist between neighbouring localities or villages. There are also a few small Maidan clubs which are regulars at these tournaments. The better known amongst these are the Barasat Naba Palli Samiti Tournament, the Mahadeb Sen Smriti Challenge Shield, the Mega Football (Ashok Nagar), the Gupti Para Football Club Knockout Shield and the Dum Dum Cantonment Noishalok Football. Most of the *khep* tournaments are held between September/October and January/ February.

There are no fixed rules for the *khep khela* tournaments. Each tournament comes up with its own rules according to its playing conditions. Most of these are not played with 11-member sides and nor are they usually played over 90 minutes. Normally, they are either 7-a-side or 9-a-side affairs. This means that several matches are squeezed into the schedule. Moreover the attempt to get their money's worth often means that schedules are made up in such a way as to have the African players playing in most of the matches.

This day-long strenuous work usually earns a player about Rs 4,000 to Rs 6,000. Furthermore the players normally end up bagging the small prizes for the 'highest goal scorer' or 'best player' etc. All things put together thus, the players end up making around Rs 7,000 to Rs 8,000 (approximately £100) for playing one such tournament. The usual pay structure is about Rs 1,500 to Rs 2,000 per match and a small percentage of the winner's prize money, to be divided equally amongst the foreign players. From this a small commission is also often charged by the men who recruit these players. When a club decides to field foreign players to contest a particular *khep* tournament, they usually get in touch with men known in Maidan circles for arranging such recruitments. Raghu Nandy (simultaneously the coach of nearly 14 to 15 lower division clubs in the Maidan, including the once famed George Telegraph AC) or Subol Das (involved with the lowly Avenue Sammilani), are well-known for being able to arrange foreign recruits to play in the *khep* tournaments.

After the banning of foreign players from the lower leagues in January 2005, many of these African players have taken to playing *khep* tournaments in the neighbouring provinces of Bihar, Orissa, Tripura etc. The more popular tournaments in the neighbouring provinces that draw Calcutta-based African players include the Sijua All Colliery Football Tournament in Bokaro (Jharkhand) and the Brahmoni Cup in Bandamunda (Orissa). In the case of these tournaments in the neighbouring provinces, since its relatively difficult to hire the foreign players, many tournaments with even smaller budgets are synchronized with these larger tournaments, so that the players, once in the province, can then be taken to tournaments in neighbouring areas for relatively smaller fees. Therefore once a player attends one of these better known *khep* tournaments in the neighbouring provinces, he is likely to be in the province for a month or so, travelling to other, smaller events in the vicinity. The more successful and regular contestants in these tournaments include the Garifa Students Union, the Shyamnagar Jyoti Sangha, the Itina Memorial Club along with lower division clubs from the Calcutta League such as Kumartuli SC, City AC, Mohammadan AC, Aryans AC etc. The most successful amongst these is the Allama Iqbal. Allama Iqbal usually has 10 to 15 different teams which it fields depending on the quality of the tournament and the likely opposition. Among these, its first squad is almost solely comprised of Nigerians.[25]

Unfortunately, like most pipe dreams, the stories of these African footballers frequently end in tragedy. Seeking an escape from the poverty at home, they often fall prey to the same poverty made worse by the distance from home. The death of Enyilord Lawrence brought the tragic plight of these poorly paid footballers to the public's attention. Lawrence, who had sought to escape grinding poverty at home, had been unable to find a permanent place in any of the big City clubs since the late 1990s and had instead taken to playing club football in the neighbouring state of Tripura by 2003–04, while still being based in Calcutta. He had been ill for sometime, but could not afford to miss his matches, since his illness had already further impoverished his already precarious finances. He tried to supplement his income by giving English tuition to the children of the neighbourhood. By all accounts that surfaced after his death, he was a kind-hearted man and it was not clear if he always paid for his teaching. In any case he had been reduced to utter poverty by the time of his death. Moreover, it was alleged that his visa had long run out and technically he was an illegal alien in the country.

His father was a poor farmer in a remote village in Nigeria and unable to pay for his son's corpse to be flown back to Nigeria; neither was he able to afford the charges of the Calcutta morgue where his son lay. For 14 days no one knew what was to be done with the body of the poor footballer and the morgue authorities were running out of patience. The Nigerian High Commission in Delhi refused to intervene as the dead player was an illegal alien. Finally fellow Nigerian players came forward, as did the Chief Minister of West Bengal, after reading about the unclaimed body in the newspapers. The fees were cleared, the necessary certificates obtained including a clearance from Lawrence's parents allowing the burial to proceed in Calcutta. His parents merely requested a video cassette of the funeral of their dear boy. Fellow Nigerian players and a throng of local mourners attended an emotionally charged funeral procession in the City wearing T-shirts with the dead player's face on it. Mike Okoro, a Nigerian striker with East Bengal even wore the T-Shirt under his jersey in the next match and dedicated his next goal to Lawrence. Yet at the end, despite all efforts, his friends had failed to raise the money to send his body back to the family or to pay for the family to travel to India.[26]

The Lawrence tragedy was just waiting to happen. Poorly fed and continually engaged in what is one of the most physically demanding climates to play football, these hapless African players who do not make it to the big club teams have the toughest of lives. Another Nigerian, Aiibade Olaniran Babalade, had sometime earlier collapsed on the pitch out of sheer exhaustion. It was learnt later that he was hiding serious injuries and jaundice in order to be on the pitch. While Babalade's antics on the pitch drew the mockery of the crowd and the ire of the sports press, the human suffering that compelled him to play to the point where he collapsed, passed without comment.[27]

The plight of these players was often made worse still by the cultural and social exclusion they faced. Contrary to images of third world camaraderie, these players often found it difficult to gain social acceptance. While the bigger stars like Chima were undoubtedly adored, the lesser known African players often had a tough time living in Calcutta. During the festival of Holi in 2003, for example, three African players of Tollygunge Agragami were beaten up by a crowd after protesting against being smeared by colours as is the norm at the festival.[28]

Following the Lawrence tragedy once again there were calls to ban foreign players from the Calcutta League and the IFA Shield tournaments. Though the move was eventually scuttled and the Vice-President of the All India Football Federation called its rejection a 'great decision for Bengal', it led to changes in the law regarding foreign players. The stringent criteria which laid down that players would now have to furnish extensive proof of their previous background, performance and fitness before recruitment, was said to be aimed at ridding Calcutta football of 'painfully mediocre talent'.[29]

Foreign footballers were finally banned from the lower levels of the Calcutta League in January 2005. The move was represented both by the officials and the media as a step aimed at lifting the standards of the Calcutta game. Critics note a very different set of motivations for the move. Some IFA insiders point out that the IFA is controlled, quite ironically, not by representatives of the big

Super Division clubs, but rather by representatives of lower division clubs, including some from clubs chronically stuck in the fifth division. For the bosses of these poorly managed outfits, the power to give young enthusiasts a chance to play club football was, and remains, an important source of local clout and prestige. It is this patronage chain that underwrites much of the social power wielded by these men in their local areas. The presence of African players on some of the teams forced the others to do the same in order to fight off relegation. This helped put an end to the ability of these clubs to play sub-standard players from the boss' own constituency. Contrary to popular wisdom then, at this level, however ironically, the presence of the African players may well have been actually ensuring a minimum standard. Though the Africans themselves were nothing great, their presence in the fray destroyed the patron-client chain by which sub-standard players were and are drafted into the lower division clubs.

The political economy of feebleness

The flip side of the argument about big Africans is that Bengalis are by nature feeble and small. By representing the difference in the statures of African and Bengali players as a matter of racial difference, what is ignored is that Bengali footballers today come from the poorest of backgrounds. Their lack of proper nutrition is reflected largely in their poor physiques. The acceptance of the racialized imaginations of bodily difference pre-empt any critique of the political economy that results in the physical diminution of Bengali players.

That physical frailty was a consequence of poor nutritional intake was painfully shown when a study found that once young players left the Tata Football Academy, where nutrition is monitored, the players became physically much weaker, even losing out on muscle power indices. Moreover most schools today ignore the importance of physical culture and athleticism which had been part of the Bengali project of modernity since the late nineteenth and early twentieth centuries.[30]

It will come as no surprise to those who follow Calcutta football that the class backgrounds of footballers in the city have changed dramatically in the post-Independence era. Especially since the 1980s, when cricket's popularity soared, the middle-class urban youth that formed the backbone of the Bengali footballing talent seemed to give way to the youth of struggling rural backgrounds. Shashti Duley, East Bengal's talented midfielder, whose career floundered after getting mixed up with the under-world, is a classic example of the contemporary Bengali footballer. Having quit school in his early teens, Duley worked as an agricultural wage labourer before rising to football stardom.[31] Another Bengali striker for Mohun Bagan grew up in a shack made of plastic sheets and bamboo splinters far away from Calcutta.[32] One of Mohun Bagan's current defenders, Sumon Dutta, comes from utter poverty; his father, who was a mill worker, was left without a job almost a decade ago when the mill closed down. Bhaskar Adhikary, of Milon Bithi, who died last year, similarly had been the sole breadwinner in his family, barely able to make ends meet. His father had died in penury and his mother and sister had been living with an uncle, before the factory in which the uncle worked also closed down, eventually leading to the death of the uncle.[33] Though Adhikary's death was said to have been caused principally by maltreatment and medical negligence at a government hospital, the fact that his condition had been worsened by strenuous exercise coupled with a lack of proper nutrition is unquestionable. Moreover his inability to be able to afford proper medical care, despite being one of the most promising young goalkeepers in the country, also points to the straightened circumstances under which India's young footballing talents labour.[34] Boria Majumdar and Kaushik Bandopadhyay wrote with ample justice that: 'Native footballers in India still come from lower-middle class backgrounds and try their hand at the game because they have few other livelihood options. Financial crises continue to threaten the longevity of their careers.'[35]

Moreover many of these players, finding themselves famous and thrust into relative plenty after enduring years of utter penury and without any professional management structure, fall victim to profligate lifestyles. In the absence of a professional management, the proverbial 'wine, women and song' have laid low many a promising young Bengali player. Apart from the Shashti Duley affair, which included another East Bengal player as well, there have been others such as Abid Hussain (Muhammadan Sporting) or Abhijit Roy Choudhury (who represented all the big three clubs at one time or the other), who have been linked to the underworld. Another player to have played for all of the three big clubs was Tapan Das, who was later arrested on charges of cheating and forgery. The litany of players such as the hugely promising Falguni Dutta, who played for East Bengal and Muhammadan Sporting and sacrificed his career at the altar of alcoholism after rising out of utter and crushing poverty, is even larger than the underworld related scandals. Another talented Mohun Bagan striker finished his career early after hitting the bottle.[36] In the absence of professional management structures, the clubs are often managed by a number of non-technical, non-playing people who are both incapable, and unaware, of imposing any kind of strict professional discipline. Majumdar and Bandopadhyay have called this 'tendentious amateurism'.[37] Club administration, in such a context, is dominated by factional politics and as long as a player is seen to be performing well, there is no one who can discipline him. Coaches seldom have enough authority to be able to control star players and even renowned coaches often owe their jobs to the whims of amateur club officials, who tend to side with star players. All this leads inexorably to a general lack of fitness amongst the players even after they have pulled themselves out of the crippling poverty of their youth.

When the racial difference between the big and strong Africans and the feeble Bengalis are presented as a natural and immutable law, it is this political economy of the feebleness that is glossed over.

A related issue is the so-called decline of Calcutta football, which is often used as a rationale for the use, or indeed to oppose the use, of foreign players. To judge whether Calcutta football had enjoyed a higher standard vis-à-vis other international leagues in the past, is bound to be fraught with a certain degree of guesswork and anachronism. But if we speak of the fans following the game, the 'decline' is largely exaggerated. Considering that a Mohun Bagan-East Bengal derby can still at times draw crowds of over 100,000, it is surely untrue to say that the game has 'declined' in popularity.[38] Yet what has undoubtedly happened is that the predominantly urban, educated, middle-class fan base of the game has, especially since the 1970s, been replaced by a more rural, less educated and relatively under-privileged fan base.[39] This shift has, if not inaugurated, definitely exaggerated the problems of malnutrition at the beginning of players' careers and their prodigal profligacy at a later stage, both of which have adversely affected the fitness and stamina of the Bengali players. By framing this complex sociological phenomenon in terms of natural, biological and racial difference between big bodied Africans and feeble bodied Bengalis a multifaceted process is obscured. In this process many flows and counter-flows reinforce a situation in which a series of unequal and exploitative relationships are maintained and depicted as being natural through a corresponding economy of signs and stereotypes. This multifaceted process whereby diverse flows of goods and people on an international scale are legitimized and naturalized through corresponding flows of globally mapped ideas about identity and difference is globalization.

Conclusion

In studying the use, employment, lives and representations of African footballers in Calcutta football, I seek to show that the story of globalization can be revisited without reproducing the currently accepted discourses about the hegemonic position of the West. The processes of globalization can also be studied through an engagement with multiple cross-cutting networks between non-western countries. Tropes such as those of 'race' then become unpinned from its usual Black and White chromatism, revealing in the process a complex armature of difference. It generates a matrix of meanings and commonsense in which feeble Bengalis and sturdy Africans complement and mutually define each other, along with artful Brazilians, deft Iranians, persevering Britons etc.

In this complex network, movements of goods, information and people are held together by ideas of racial difference which in turn informs and underwrites a number of relationships and institutional structures. While this network naturalizes a number of exploitative relationships, it also opens up the scope to a certain limited degree of social mobility for a select few. Globalization is the sum total of all these synchronized flows of goods, information, people, and, above all, mutually acceptable definitions of that need to be fitted into a globally differentiated matrix.

Notes

1. For an elegant and non-academic statement of the position see Mick Brooks, 'Mick Brooks, Globalisation and Imperialism, In Defence of Marxism', 11 April 2006, http://www.marxist.com/globalisation-imperialism-economy110406-5.htm.
2. Amin, *Capitalism in the Age of Globalization.*
3. Latour, *We Have Never Been Modern.*
4. Pieterse, 'Globalization as Hybridization'.
5. Ross and Trachte, *Global Capitalism.*
6. Majumdar and Bandopadhyay, 'A Sporting Colony for Growing Global Capital', 257–69. V. Krishnaswamy, 'Football and Globalization'. *Frontline*, 19 July 2002, 10–11.
7. Cohn, *An Anthropologist Among The Historians.*
8. Just how violent the Maidan can get, is revealed in an anecdote star striker Chima Okorie narrated to renowned sports journalist Novy Kapadia. It happened in the 1985–86 season, when Chima was playing for Mohammedan Sporting. In spite of Chima scoring three goals, the match still ended in a draw. After the match the 'boys' of the Secretary started jostling the striker, alleging that he had purposely not scored enough goals. One of them suddenly pulled out a pistol and some bullets. He then proceeded to put the bullets into the pistol in full view of the striker before holding it to his head. The giant of Calcutta football by his own admission froze where he stood. Even after the 'boys' had laughed at his fear and left, the mighty Nigerian had remained paralyzed by fear for a long time. Kapadia and Kundu, 'Chima Okorie's "Passage to India"', 267.
9. King, 'Race and Cultural Identity'.
10. Goffman, *The Presentation of Self in Everyday Life.*
11. St Louis, 'Sport and Common-Sense Racial Science', 31–45.
12. Majumdar and Bandopadhyay, *Goalless.*
13. Nag, 'Amaar Dekha Bideshi Footballer-ra'.
14. 'Do We Need Africans to Play Football?' *Times of India*, 12 January 2005.
15. Mallick, 'Kolkata-e Bideshi Football-er Bajar'.
16. Quoted in Majumdar and Bandopadhyay, *Goalless,* 122.
17. Sanjoy Majumdar, 'Rooting for Brazil in Calcutta', *BBC News*, 12 June 2006. website: http://news.bbc.co.uk/1/hi/world/south_asia/5071330.stm.
18. Choudhury, 'Choturtho Sreni-r Bideshi-r Sthan Kolkata-e'.
19. 'Alvito-r Lok Dekhano Shasthi'. *Ananda Bazar Patrika*, 4 January 2007 (in Bengali).
20. Conversations with Sabysachi Mallick, a reporter for *Kick Off*, the Indian Football Association's official magazine.
21. Conversations with Rafique Sattar, Executive Editor of *Kick Off.*
22. Kapadia and Kundu, 'Chima Okorie's "Passage to India"', 266.
23. 'News of the Month', 9 May 1999, www.indianfootball.com website: http://www.indianfootball.com/news/m199905.html
24. 'Alvito-r Lok Dekhano Shasthi'. *Ananda Bazar Patrika*, 4 January 2007 (in Bengali).
25. Conversations with Anirban Ray Sarkar, Rafique Sattar and Sabyasachi Mallick.

26. 'CM Bid to End Funeral Fiasco'. *Times of India*, 20 February 2004; 'Nigerian Footballer Laid to Rest'. *Asia Pulse*, February 2004; 'Lawrence of Nigeria Finally Rests in Peace'. *Times of India*, 22 February 2004.
27. Uddalak Mukherjee, 'Off Side on a Foreign Field'. *The Telegraph*, 13 June 2005.
28. '4,000 Preventive Arrests Made on Holi'. *Times of India*, 19 March 2003.
29. Mukherjee, 'Off Side on a Foreign Field'.
30. P.K. Banerjee, 'Indians Getting Weak in Their Knees'. *The Telegraph*, 4 August 1999.
31. Dasgupta, 'Firey Ashuk Holud Pakhi'.
32. Sarkar, 'Oporadh-er Ondhokar-e Dubchhe Football Math'.
33. Conversations with Sabyasachi Mallick and Rajarshi Chatterji, sports reporter of the Bengali daily *Ek Din*.
34. Facilities at government hospitals in the country are free and are frequently over-stretched. They are as a consequence resorted to only by those who are unable to afford the wide range of private medical facilities.
35. Majumdar and Bandopadhyay, *Indian Football*, 259.
36. Sarkar, 'Oporadh-er Ondhokar-e Dubchhe Football Math'.
37. Majumdar and Bandopadhyay, *Indian Football*, 291.
38. See, for example, Mallick, 'Ek Lakh Dorshok Mughdhoh Korlo Dave-ke'.
39. To appreciate this change, see Kumar, *Arbi Rochito Kolkata Football.*

References

Amin, Samir. *Capitalism in the Age of Globalization*. London: Zed, 1997.

Choudhury, Dibyendu. 'Choturtho Sreni-r Bideshi-r Sthan Kolkata-e' [The Place of Fourth-Grade Foreign Players in Kolkata Football]. *Kick Off,* no.7 (2007): 13.

Cohn, Bernard S. *An Anthropologist among the Historians and other Essays.* New Delhi: Oxford University Press, 2004.

Dasgupta, Kunal. 'Firey Ashuk Holud Pakhi' [Come Back Yellow-Bird]. *Kick Off,* no.5 (2004): 6–7.

Goffman, Erving. *The Presentation of Self in Everyday Life.* New York: Anchor Books, 1959.

Kapadia, Novy and Apurba Kundu. 'Chima Okorie's "Passage to India"'. *Contemporary South Asia* 10 (2001): 265–72.

King, Colin. 'Race and Cultural Identity: Playing the Race Game inside Football'. *Leisure Studies 23,* no.1 (2004): 19–30.

Kumar, Shibram. *Arbi Rochito Kolkata Football* [RB's Calcutta Football]. Calcutta: Probhati Prokashoni, 2002.

Latour, Bruno. *We Have Never Been Modern,* trans. C. Porter. Cambridge, MA: Harvard University Press, 1993.

Majumdar, Boria and Kaushik Bandopadhyay, 'A Sporting Colony for Growing Global Capital: Globalization and Indian Soccer', *Goalless: The Story of a Unique Footballing Nation,* 163–175. India: Penguin, 2006.

——— *Goalless: The Story of a Unique Footballing Nation.* India: Penguin, 2006.

Mallick, Sabyasachi. 'Kolkata-e Bideshi Football-er Bajar' [The Market for Foreign Players in Kolkata]. *Kick Off* 4 (2003): 15.

——— 'Ek Lakh Dorshok Mughdhoh Korlo Dave-ke' [Dave Awed by One Lakh Spectators]. *Kick Off* 6 (2005): 13.

Nag, Anjan. 'Amaar Dekha Bideshi Footballer-ra' [The Best Foreign Players I Saw]. *Kick Off* 3 (2002): 27–8.

Pieterse, J.N. 'Globalization as Hybridization'. In *Global Modernities*, ed. M. Featherstone, S. Lash and R. Robertson. London: Sage, 1995.

Sarkar, Jeet. 'Oporadh-er Ondhokar-e Dubchhe Football Math' [Kolkata Football Sinks in the Mire of Crime] (in Bengali). *Kick Off* 5 (2004): 9.

St Louis, Brett. 'Sport and Common-Sense Racial Science'. *Leisure Studies* 23, no.1 (2004): 31–46.

Ghati-Bangal on the Maidan: subregionalism, club rivalry and fan culture in Indian football

Boria Majumdar

> It was an unimportant match between East Bengal and a local team in the late 1970s. The match was just about to start. A small crowd was chatting near the main entrance of the ground. Suddenly a middle-aged man with messy hair, red eyes and a worn out look appeared at the gate. While entering the ground he anxiously asked the gatekeeper whether the match had begun. The gateman replied in the negative. A few other members who knew the man came to him and asked why he was so late in arriving on that day. The man hesitantly replied: 'My younger son passed away in the morning. I am coming straight from the crematorium.'[1]

> In a League match in the late 1970s, Mohun Bagan won by a big margin. After the match the jubilant crowd rushed towards Esplanade to board buses and trams on the way home. A few bare-bodied young lads were standing on the rod of the tram's wheel, hanging on to the windows with one hand. They were waiving their shirts like Mohun Bagan flags. As the tram suddenly stopped at a road signal, one of the lads got thrown onto the street. His feet appeared to be run over by the wheels of the tram. However, as the tram started to move, the lad ran and jumped onto the rod to catch the tram. After the tram left the place, a severed toe was found amidst a few drops of blood while a thin red line stretched along the tramline. The pain got lost in the euphoria of victory.[2]

The incidents cited above are but a few of the most popular sporting lore that have grown around the eternal rivalry between India's two most glorious football clubs – Mohun Bagan and East Bengal. Even though anecdotes are not always reliable, they convey a simple truth in spirit: rivalry between the two clubs mirrors the oppositional identities, social differences and emotional commonalities inherent in Indian society and culture. This essay seeks to suggest that while the roots of the origin and consolidation of this football rivalry lie in the social and sub-regional differences of contemporary Indian society, its playing out in the last 25 years can only be meaningfully explained in terms of club loyalty, fan culture and commercial transformation.

Contours of social conflict in Indian football

Paul Dimeo, one of the few scholars to have written about this rivalry, in a recent intervention on the history of club-conflict in Calcutta football, has argued that the fascinating rivalry in India's club football between Mohun Bagan and East Bengal can be interpreted in terms of an ethnic conflict between the Hindu settlers of West Bengal and the Hindu immigrants from East Bengal in the aftermath of the Partition of 1947.[3] But this rigid ethnic polarization, probably emanating from the writer's lack of awareness about the fluidity of cultural identities of the two groups of people sharing more or less a broadly common language, religion and cultural past, seems not only over simplistic but also flawed. As Cornell and Hartman have argued: 'Ethnicity, then, is identification in ethnic terms … A population or social collectivity may be simply an ethnic category, assigned an ethnic identity by outsiders. Once that objective becomes subjective – that is, once that population sees itself in ethnic terms, perhaps in response to the identity outsiders assign to it – it becomes an ethnic group.'[4] Even this definition does not justify Dimeo's premise since the *Ghati-Bangal* binary can be meaningfully interpreted in terms of a perceptional cultural clash between sub-regional sentiments. As this essay will demonstrate, an intense club rivalry based on aggressive fan culture gradually replaced the sub-regional tension that lay at the root of the initial configuration of the rivalry.

Under colonialism, Indians employed football to express nationalist, communal or regional identities. The turnover from colonialism to Independence added a further dimension to football. In the aftermath of Partition, large-scale Hindu migration from East Pakistan (now Bangladesh) to West Bengal created serious socio-demographic tension resulting in a distinct cultural conflict in Bengali society. The sub-regional identity of the East Bengali Hindus clashed with the established Hindu settlers of West Bengal, who designated their East Bengali counterparts derisively as *Bangals*. In Calcutta, the *Bangals* started competing with the West Bengali Hindus for the dominance of the city. The *Bangals*, with their common memory of a homeland and everyday culture and a shared experience of suffering and migration, fought hard to earn a living, acquire economic strength, social position and cultural recognition to ensure survival in a hostile environment. They returned the compliment by labelling the locals as *Ghatis*, after a distinctively shaped vessel used commonly in West Bengal. While the *Ghati-Bangal* conflict epitomized an ethnic rivalry in Indian society, the identities seemed more 'instrumentalist', that is, constructed, than 'primordialist', that is, fixed and ascribed.

The *Ghati-Bangal* conflict has sent ripples across the football field. As the immigrants sought to preserve their cultural identity and integrity in a new society, they searched for avenues to assert themselves. Football, in this context, was appropriated by the East Bengali Hindus as a cultural tool to establish their ethnic identity and cultural excellence. Consequently, the Maidan became a cultural space where the opposed identities of the *Ghatis* (settlers) and *Bangals* (immigrants) came to be produced and reproduced through a bitter rivalry between Mohun Bagan, the club of the *Ghatis* and East Bengal, the club of the *Bangals*. While this arch football rivalry struck another blow to Indian footballing nationalism, it, paradoxically, played an important role in assimilating the immigrants into the host community. With time, however, this fluid sub-regional football culture proved ephemeral and a more virulent club rivalry between Mohun Bagan and East Bengal based on intense team loyalty overtook the erstwhile sentiment at national level competitions throughout India.

Ghati-Bangal in Indian society

The terms *Ghati* and *Bangal,* as mentioned earlier, refer to people with their respective original habitats in West and East Bengal. However, while the term *Bangal* has found a place in most standard Bengali lexicons as a meaningful word, *Ghati* is not included in any of them. Reference to the people of East Bengal as *Bangals* is evident in Bengali literature since the twelfth century.[5]… *Bangals* became a butt of ridicule in West Bengal, especially in nineteenth-century Calcutta, as evident from Dinabandhu Mitra's[6] memorable drama *Sadhbar Ekadashi* where he depicted this attitude perfectly.[7] Well-known Indian sports writer Moti Nandy succinctly sums up the essence of this contemptuous attitude of the West Bengalis towards the Bangals since the nineteenth century:

> From the beginning of the nineteenth century, people who came from East Bengal were treated with condescension by the original settlers of Calcutta, who compared them with country bumpkins. On the stage and the screen, East Bengalis appeared invariably as jesters. To express their contempt, the Calcutta Bengalis called them *Bangals*.[8]

It is, however, difficult to determine as to how the word *Ghati* appeared in the Bengali lexicon. Moti Nandy refers to a letter in the *Ananda Bazar Patrika* in the late-1980s, which attempted an explanation:

> In the nineteenth century, when water taps were unknown in every home in Calcutta, each household had its own well. The pots and buckets would often fall into the well. In the afternoon some men would do the rounds of the neighbourhood with a rope and a hook, shouting 'Ghati tulben? Ghati tulben?' 'Want the pots taken out?' Finally, they abbreviated their call to just shouting 'Ghati! Ghati!' in front of the houses. The East Bengalis who lived in these areas at the time heard this daily uproar and assumed that the locals of Calcutta were referred to as 'Ghatis'.[9]

Rupak Saha, a journalist of the *Ananda Bazar Patrika*, offers a different view. According to Saha, the word, unlike *Bangal*, is of recent vintage, and it first came into vogue in the nineteenth century. He is of the opinion that the *Bangal* students of Calcutta, overturning the slur used against them by the West Bengalis, introduced the term to ridicule them. Since the West Bengalis used a 'ghati' for all their household work, the term was purposively taken as synonymous to their identity by the East Bengalis.[10] There is another popular explanation of the origin of the word:

> Once when a person from Gaur went to visit his East Bengali relative, he forgot his 'Ghati'. On arrival, he could not concentrate on anything for not having his essential 'Ghati' with him. Ultimately he attempted to steal one from a neighbour's house, but was subsequently caught. For his heinous act, the image of the people of Gaur, i.e. West Bengal, was permanently tarnished. Henceforth they were labelled 'Ghatis'.[11]

Whether or not these explanations are correct, neither community is apt to lose its temper when identified as *Ghati* and *Bangal* today.

The development of derisive attitudes aside, the difference between *Ghati* and *Bangal* was clearly discernible in terms of dialect, manner, dress, food habits, rites and rituals and even appearance, transcending wider similarities of religion, language and a common cultural past. These mostly *cultural* differences, though not rigid, had the potential to create sharply distinctive *social* identities in times of heightened socio-political tension. The partition of Bengal in 1947, followed by a massive influx of East Bengali Hindu refugees into West Bengal, created the occasion for a sub-regional social conflict to flourish.

In the aftermath of partition, the East Bengali refugees founded in East Bengal a club of their 'own', representing their ethnic 'self' to fight and win against the 'other', that is, the West Bengali Hindus. As the latter mockingly named East Bengal 'the club of the *Bangals*', they, in turn, renamed Mohun Bagan 'the club of the *Ghatis*'. Consequently, the *Ghati-Bangal* rivalry on the Maidan divided Bengali Hindu society into two camps during every football match between East Bengal and Mohun Bagan. Interestingly, as Moti Nandy writes: 'These two communities even divided the aquatic population in a symbolic manner – the prawn for the *Ghatis* and the hilsa for the *Bangals*. In the evening after a football derby, the prices of prawn and hilsa used to rise or fall depending on the result of the match.'[12] Though the rivalry deepened after partition, it had begun when the East Bengal Club was formed in 1920 in an unusual context.

A synoptic history of the East Bengal Club

The East Bengal Club was started originally as one for East Bengali players by East Bengali people to ameliorate sporting grievances born out of continuous discrimination against them by Calcutta's Bengali clubs.[13] The birth of the club can only be meaningfully explained in the context of this ethnic polarization in contemporary Bengali society. In fact, the club was born as a mark of protest against injustice, bias and discrimination meted out to sports organizers and players from East Bengal. At the turn of the century, football had moved to districts of East and North Bengal. In East Bengal, Dacca was the centre of football's growing stature and popularity. Players hailing from Dacca and adjoining regions used to come to Calcutta to gain wider recognition at competitive level. That they performed well and sometimes better than their West Bengali counterparts is borne out by the fact that eight of the eleven players of the victorious Mohun Bagan team in 1911 originally came from East Bengal.[14] Even the legendary Mohun Bagan defender Gostho Paul came from a village in the Faridpur district of East Bengal.[15] Despite this noticeable excellence of East Bengali players, a large number of them frequently became victims of discrimination at the hands of West Bengali club organizers, officials and players.[16] The foundation of the East Bengal Club was a direct outcome of such an incident.

In 1919, Sailesh Basu, a footballer from the Vikrampur pargana of Dacca, distinguished himself as a player of the Jorabagan Club. However, Basu was excluded from the team in the crucial tie of the Coochbehar Cup in the following year.[17] He soon realized that his East Bengali ethnicity had cost him his place in the side. He even complained to the club's Vice-President Suresh Chaudhuri, who, despite his best efforts, failed to remedy the situation. As a result, both severed relations with the club. Chaudhuri, a rich and influential businessman, was originally the zamindar of Nagarpur of Mymensingh district in East Bengal. To combat the insult, he decided to form a club by mobilizing East Bengali players and enthusiasts in and around Calcutta. Sailesh Basu, along with another East Bengali player Nosa Sen, assisted him in founding the East Bengal Club in August 1920. The very name of the club was important as it clearly appealed to the discriminated East Bengalis in West Bengal for support. The club prospered with patronage from people from different walks of life – Taritbhushan Roy, Raibahadur of Bhagyakul, Saradaranjan Roy, Principal of the Metropolitan College (present Vidyasagar College) and Pankaj Gupta, one of the greatest sports administrators India has produced. The organizers of the club formed a modest team of East Bengali players in a few days and emerged champions in a 6-a-side tournament called Hercules Cup held at Shyam Park in north Calcutta. One of its matches was reported in a local newspaper, which noted with surprise the presence of an enthusiastic crowd to cheer the newborn club.[18] Since its inception, the club had a reasonable support base all over Bengal.

A review of the history of the club's next five years points to a complex equation between social power relations and the mechanisms of sports administration in contemporary Bengal. Suresh Chaudhuri and Taritbhushan Roy, (joint secretaries of the club) both being socially influential in Calcutta and having good relations with British officialdom, utilized their power and position to earn the club's affiliation with the IFA. East Bengal was soon allowed to play in the Second Division League[19] and given a ground on the Maidan.[20] The meteoric rise of East Bengal to a position of respectability, however, was not well taken by its sister clubs in Calcutta. The subsequent controversy over East Bengal's promotion to the First Division of the Calcutta Football League in 1925 serves to illustrate this point.

East Bengal earned a much-deserved promotion to the First Division in 1925 amidst debate and controversy within the rank and file of the IFA. Most historians of the East Bengal Club argue that the deadlock was ultimately resolved through the initiative of the Maharaja of Santosh, Manmathanath Raychaudhuri, then President of the club.[21] In October 1924, the members of the League Committee at a special meeting held at the residence of the Maharaja, abolished the rule that restricted the number of Indian teams that could play in the First Division League to two and introduced the standard rule of promotion and relegation. This decision, scholars agree, earned East Bengal a well-deserved promotion. Interestingly, most scholars point out that while the European representatives of the committee strongly supported the motion in East Bengal's favour, the two Indian members representing Mohun Bagan and Aryan strenuously opposed the move.[22]

A look at newspaper reports on the issue in 1924–25, however, points to a different course of events that eventually led to the club's success in earning the promotion. This engaging story clearly shows how the Bengali clubs led by Mohun Bagan and Aryan opposed East Bengal's promotion to the First Division. The League Committee's decision to accord East Bengal the promotion in its Annual General Meeting on 15 April 1924[23] was reversed in its special meeting a week later under strong pressure from other Indian clubs.[24] In protest against this unjust decision, all the European clubs withdrew from the League leaving Mohun Bagan and Aryan as the only two teams to compete for the title.[25] The withdrawal of the European Clubs and their deadline to the League committee in support of East Bengal was strongly condemned by their Indian counterparts.[26] Against such allegations, a representative of one of the European clubs argued in *The Statesman* that the Europeans had in mind the progress of Indian football. He was certain that East Bengal's presence and participation in the First Division of the Calcutta League would substantially enhance the competitive edge and glamour of the tournament.[27] Pankaj Gupta played a major role at this juncture to promote the cause of East Bengal. In his words:

> I was approached by East Bengal Club to help them in their mission to be promoted to the first division.
>
> Late Mr. Thomas Lamb [later became Sir Thomas Lamb] was then the key man of the Calcutta Football Club … I approached Thomas Lamb and he joined hands with me in our fight to delete such restrictions in regard to promotion in the first division … Although I was not a member of the East Bengal Club for the sake of sporting justice I took a lead on this issue, and the late Mr. A.B. Rosser joined hands with us and helped us in a great way. Late Mr. Medlycott of the Customs opposed our move but ultimately we succeeded and restrictions were removed. Late Mr. Medlycott left the meeting in a hurry and subsequently resigned from the Hon. Secretaryship of the IFA.[28]

The Statesman also expressed deep surprise at the Indian teams' (especially Mohun Bagan and Aryan) hostile attitude towards East Bengal. The most probable reason for such hostility, according to the paper, was an anxiety over the potential challenge East Bengal would pose to the two leading Indian clubs' in terms of popularity and player acquisition.[29]

The club, however, by the 1930s, had lost its exclusive sub-regional character and could field no more East Bengali players than Mohun Bagan or other Bengali clubs.[30] But the name and banner of the club continued to inspire an emotional attachment among the East Bengali population in West Bengal. This particular emotional set-up, hardened more by the West Bengalis' discriminatory remarks and attitude, was an extension of the social conflict between *Ghati* and *Bangal*. And it lay, along with the growing communalism in Indian football, at the root of fragmentation of Indian sporting nationalism in the 1940s.

Ghati-Bangal conflict on the football field

Paul Dimeo has argued that: 'Before partition, East Bengal and Mohun Bagan had a friendly relationship … and, until the cataclysmic political changes of 1947, the two clubs saw each other as siblings'.[31] The evidence he provides in support of his view, however, is not substantial. According to him, that the clubs shared a common ground, and that Mohun Bagan hosted a celebratory tea party for their 'younger brothers' at the latter's first ever League triumph in 1942 are sufficient to prove the point.[32] He further suggests:

> The main difference at this time [the 1930s–40s] was that while Mohammadan Sporting's rivalry with several Hindu clubs prompted serious communal violence, the two most successful Hindu clubs were on friendly terms … Hindu clubs [mainly Mohun Bagan and East Bengal] cooperated in opposition to Muslim clubs, and in opposition to the last remnants of competitive British clubs.[33]

Dimeo's chief concern is to situate the *ethnic* footballing rivalry between the two clubs in the context of post-partition immigration. Dimeo, however, confuses his position by furnishing contradictory evidence: 'Yet, an exhibition match in 1942 between the "Bengalees" – a term referring to the West Bengalis – and the Rest, took players' individual ethnicity as relevant: the Rest including Muslims, Europeans and East Bengalis.'[34]

Dimeo's views defy contemporary realities of Indian football. First, sharing of a common ground was not to become a factor precipitating friendship, but a source of discord as the *bhadralok* dominated Mohun Bagan resented this option forced upon them by the police. Mohun Bagan's hosting of a tea party at East Bengal's first League win in 1942 may have been a rare occasion of goodwill. Such gestures were shown to impress the public with the club's versatility rather than to honour rival success. It was, however, the occasions of virulent enmity that proved of relevance in the 1930s. As has been pointed out, Mohun Bagan scrupulously opposed East Bengal's promotion to the First Division in 1925. This resulted in long-term bitterness between the two clubs. Their first meeting in any first class competition saw the infant club beating their more renowned rival 1-0 in the final of the Coochbehar Cup.[35] In their first encounter in the League, East Bengal's 1-0 victory over their opponent was a sweet revenge on all counts.[36] In the same year, East Bengal raised an objection over the legality of one of Mohun Bagan's players, J. Sen.[37] This move led to further hardening of relations. The enmity continued unabated in the 1930s. For example, the League Council was forced to transfer the match between the two clubs in 1932 to the CFC ground to abort possible hooliganism. An unprecedented number of policemen had to be employed to control law and order in and around the ground on that day.[38]

More importantly, Dimeo's conception of Mohun Bagan-East Bengal cooperation in opposition to a Muslim club, that is, Mohammadan Sporting, is a grossly flawed one. Two specific instances prove the point. During the 1939 League competition, Mohammadan Sporting, East Bengal and Kalighat jointly withdrew from the Calcutta Football League in protest against the IFA's cynical attitude towards them.[39] At this juncture, J.C. Moitra, a reputed Bombay-based sports journalist, while expressing his full sympathy with the IFA's decision to suspend the 'recalcitrant clubs' and strong condemnation for the unsporting action of the clubs, maintained:

> The association of East Bengal and Kalighat with Mohammadan Sporting may seem a little strange at first sight. Because they are not Muslims, though they have a sprinkling of them in their composition. Their affinity lies in a different direction ... They are the strongest supporters of importation of players from outside. It is a well-known fact that Mohun Bagan have sternly set their face against this move ... Evidently, club rivalry and jealousy, which are much deeper and stronger than we see on the surface, have made strange bed-fellows.[40]

Mitra's comments and his unwitting reference to Mohun Bagan bring out the realities of club rivalry in Calcutta football. The clubs went on to form a rival football association called the Bengal Football Association on 12 August 1939 and started a new tournament called the Brabourne Cup. Although the crisis was averted through negotiations in early 1940, the episode clearly demonstrates that East Bengal was in no mood to *cooperate* with Mohun Bagan in opposition to Mohammedan Sporting. The joint venture of East Bengal and Mohammedan Sporting to combat the IFA decision, according to Moitra, was 'backed by persons who hold high offices in the Ministry of Bengal'.[41] This again, in direct contradistinction to Dimeo's view, points to a fruitful cooperation between the two clubs against IFA's favouritism of Mohun Bagan.

Even at the height of communal tension in Bengal on the eve of partition, IFA was alarmed at the increasing spectator violence on the occasion of every Mohun Bagan-East Bengal match. For example, the return League match between the two teams that ended in a goalless draw leading to East Bengal's League triumph in 1946 witnessed rampant hooliganism and violence. The supporters not only exchanged words, but also threw bricks, stones and soda bottles at each other.[42] The Mohun Bagan tent was raided and ransacked either by dejected club supporters or rival cohorts. The club lodged a complaint with the IFA against East Bengal for the incident, which the latter strongly denied.[43] The IFA President Major Stanhope even urged the two clubs to move jointly to mitigate such unfortunate happenings in future.[44]

The degree of social sensitivity and divergence evidently visible in the Mohun Bagan-East Bengal rivalry before partition, however, should not be exaggerated. This bitter rivalry between supporters of the two clubs shifted from a fluid to a rigid/exclusive state only after the partition of Bengal in 1947. Hindu refugees started to arrive in droves in West Bengal from East Pakistan after 1947. Moti Nandy captures the tragedy of this refugee exodus brilliantly:

> Searching for a roof over their heads in the city and its surrounds and a fistful of rice twice a day, they began their struggle for survival under conditions of unbearable hardship. Lost and impoverished in an unknown territory and hostile environment, faced with severe adversities, they would sometimes lose the battle and fall back, then return once more to dream of settling down to a secure and normal existence.[45]

A more recent observation may be of more value here:

> The experiences of the refugees after being uprooted and upon their arrival in West Bengal were far from pleasant. They were forced to live in cramped government-run relief camps. There small sums were handed out to them as doles and they were given meagre family rations. In overall terms they were treated no better than beggars. No efforts were made to create employment opportunities to enable them to eke out a living.[46]

In counterpoint to their stressful plight, the Hindu refugees discovered the East Bengal Club, which was waging their battle on the sportsfield and, surprisingly enough, winning! 'For these ravaged and embittered masses', remarks Nandy, 'the one source of hope, pride and victory lay in the triumphs of the Club named after their abandoned homeland'.[47] In fact, a spell of five years (1949–53) in the immediate aftermath of partition and the refugee influx, witnessed dazzling performances from the famous 'Five Pandavas' of the East Bengal forward-line, viz. Vengkatesh, Apparao, Dhanraj, Ahmed Khan and Saleh, leading the club to a series of successes in national level tournaments.[48] These victories, for the uprooted *Bangal* migrants, soon became a cultural weapon to fight discrimination. In other words, the *Ghatis* being identified as antagonists in their subconscious, the Club's victory over Mohun Bagan on each occasion instilled a new confidence in their hearts. Naturally, they began to assemble under East Bengal's red-and-yellow banner.

It has been argued with some justification that if 'Mohammadan Sporting Club had brought with it hatred through its aggressive communalism born of a minority's natural instinct for self-preservation', 'East Bengal brought anger through regional, cultural and language differences in the backdrop of a hostile social, economic and political environment'.[49] Press reports of matches between the two clubs in the 1950s and 1960s, either in the Calcutta League and Shield or in national level tournaments like the Durand Cup in Delhi and Rovers Cup in Bombay confirm the presence of massive crowds. The IFA Shield final between East Bengal and Mohun Bagan in 1947 had to be abandoned on the first day due to spectator violence.[50] In the Shield final between the two clubs in 1950, a huge police force had to be stationed at the ground to avert violence.[51] These skirmishes gradually extended to engulf the whole of the Calcutta Maidan, so much so that the IFA decided to conduct the League with regular assistance from the Calcutta Police in 1951.[52] East Bengal, however, objected to this decision and a bitter rivalry ensued between the club and the police. The matter assumed such a controversial dimension that the Chief Minister had to intervene to settle matters.[53] The Chief Minister also expressed concern over the question of the organization and control of the game in 1955. Disappointed with the IFA's role in the process, he proposed the formation of a central organization to control the game in Calcutta.[54] The very next year East Bengal, along with a few other clubs, filed a petition to the IFA against biased refereeing in the League. The referees' bias, according to the petition, was intended to favour one particular club. They urged IFA to change the scenario within a week.[55] Needless to say, the favoured club was Mohun Bagan.

Throughout the 1950s–60s, the rivalry between Mohun Bagan and East Bengal continued to prosper on sub-regional and cultural lines. While the refugees, backed strongly by the Communists, waged a pitched battle against the Congress-led West Bengal Government on the political plane,[56] East Bengal led the onslaught on the cultural plane, that is, on the football field. The situation became so alarming in the late 1950s that Dr B.C. Roy, then Chief Minister of West Bengal, suggested a change in club names which carried religious, regional or ethnic overtones.[57] Further, Football's politicization in the context of increasing spectator violence in the 1950s was a major source of discord between the IFA on the one hand and clubs like East Bengal, Mohammadan Sporting or Aryan on the other. The *Ghati-Bangal* war on the football field and the political war on the streets of Calcutta merged in the 1950s–60s to produce a strong identification of sport with politics. And the resultant craze and euphoria for this arch rivalry between the two clubs was to dominate Indian football culture in the next decade as well.

From *Ghati-Bangal* conflict to club rivalry

The configuration of Indian football in terms of a social conflict between *Ghati* and *Bangal* on ethnic lines took an aggressive turn in the 1970s. The war of liberation in East Pakistan and the emergence of Bangladesh in 1971 led to fresh immigration of Hindus into West Bengal. This added substantially to East Bengal Club's support base as the club served as a rallying point for the immigrants' hurt sentiments embodying a shared *memory*. Strikingly enough, the first half of the 1970s was a glorious period for the club.[58] More importantly, during the six years from 1970 to 1975, the club conceded only one defeat at the hands of Mohun Bagan.[59] Naturally therefore, the supporters of the club dominated the Maidan in this period.

The immigration of the early 1970s coincided with a period of intensive social tension and political turmoil in West Bengal in the wake of the anti-establishment Naxalite movement that used violence and terror as means to achieve its end. The football field failed to isolate itself from this violence. As a result spectator behaviour began to undergo qualitative changes. As Surojit Sengupta, the footballer-turned-sports journalist, has remarked, 'In the context of the Naxal Movement in the early 1970s, political uncertainty and social depression often turned Calcutta's football ground hot and violent'.[60] Emotional bonding with a club rapidly acquired a violent temper; aggression became more pronounced and a win or loss produced spontaneous euphoria or retaliation. Spectators used to stand in queues for days on end to obtain their cherished tickets to watch matches. Skirmishes and feuds were common during long waits for tickets. People also were injured or fell ill at times. In the 1975 Shield final, East Bengal defeated Mohun Bagan 5-0. After the fourth goal was scored, one East Bengal supporter had a heart attack out of sheer ecstasy and had to be taken to hospital immediately.[61] For a 25-year-old young Mohun Bagan supporter named Umakanto Palodhi, the ignominious defeat aroused so much dejection that he committed suicide that night. The suicide note he left is revealing: 'By becoming a better Mohun Bagan footballer, I wish to take revenge of this defeat in my next birth.'[62] Subrata Bhattacharyya, a player of that Mohun Bagan team recounted later:

> Three hours passed since the match had ended. It was 9 o'clock at night. Noticing that thousands of supporters still surrounded the tent, I fled through the back door along with Prasun Banerjee [another player of the team] and took refuge at a restaurant by the side of the river Ganges. It was only at 2.30 a.m., well past midnight, that Sailen Manna [a veteran and most revered Mohun Bagan footballer] came in a police jeep and rescued us to a mess at Elliot Road.[63]

Again, when East Bengal defeated favourites Mohun Bagan in a 1977 League encounter,[64] a young Mohun Bagan supporter poisoned himself by drinking a bottle of pesticide.[65] The post-match report pointed to the extremely unruly behaviour of the crowd and mentioned that joyous reaction of the East Bengal supporters after the match became uncontrollable.[66] Instances of the crowd going overboard are widespread in contemporary press reports. What these trends of crowd behaviour bring to light is that behind the façade of eternal enmity between the two clubs, inspired by a long-term ethno-cultural conflict, lay a deeper and more intense force of club loyalty.

In modern society, sporting rivalry inflamed by club loyalty breeds social *difference* while social divisions based on affiliations of race, regionalism, ethnicity, community or religion inform and reinforce such rivalries.[67] On this premise, the social polarization of fan culture has the capacity to produce recurrent spectator clashes, which often assume violent forms. Indian football, too, witnessed such a series of clashes around the Mohun Bagan-East Bengal rivalry during the three decades following independence. In the late 1970s, as a columnist of a leading Calcutta based sports magazine noted, the transformation in the character of spectator behaviour during the years 1978–79 was sudden and unprecedented.[68] The matter came to a head in 1980 when, during a rather unimportant League match between the two teams at the Eden Gardens in Calcutta, clashes between supporter groups led to widespread violence in the stadium resulting in a stampede that cost 16 diehard fans their lives.[69] The immediate context that sparked off widespread violence was an ugly tackle by Dilip Palit, a tough East Bengal defender, upon Bidesh Basu, a mercurial Mohun Bagan forward, and the latter's spontaneous retaliation by kicking the former, ten minutes into the second half. The referee gave both their marching orders for their offences. However, the supporters, enraged by the incident, became involved in a free-for-all while the police remained mere spectators. Thirteen fans died while several others were seriously injured. Three more died at the hospital later on. The next day, the leading Bengali daily *Ananda Bazar Patrika* headed its match report on the first page with the by-line: 'Football: the New Killer in Calcutta! Thirteen died, hundreds injured. Pathetic outcome of the derby match.'[70] The incident was severely condemned by all and, in an open letter, Amal Dutta, a renowned football coach of Indian club teams, wrote to Jyoti Basu, the-then Chief Minister of West Bengal:

> You have done the right thing by not coming to see the match. In that case, you would have had to bear the pain of watching the loss of a number of young lives simply due to inaction on the part of your police … This accident surely disproves your worth whatsoever as minister for Home and Sports … You won't be excused even if you immediately appoint an enquiry commission, which will be another eyewash. You must have realized the extent of decline of moral values among the youth during the course of the Federation Cup football played earlier this year. It must be well known to you that football is now more than a game to the Bengali – it is life for many of them. To sustain this intensity for the game, a large section of the unemployed, aimless and reckless take drugs before and during a match like this. This information is well known to the police department and should have been reported to you. Besides, in the last few years, spectators have got used to carrying arms such as blades, razors, knives, brick and iron-rods while watching their favourite clubs play especially in the 60 paise gallery. Whether your police have made any sincere attempt to stop this hooliganism or arrest the culprits is not known. It is really surprising as to how your government could take the responsibility of organizing such an important match without having made any attempts to avert clashes and arranging seating of rival supporters in two different blocs. How can you evade the responsibility for the disaster?[71]

This tragedy was a jolt to the rising fervour of Indian football enthusiasm. It cast a heavy shadow on Indian footballing society and brought about unfortunate changes in Bengal football.

New challenges to club rivalry

While supporters of the two clubs looked upon cultural and temperamental differences extremely seriously, the players never conformed to this perceptional equation of *Ghati-Bangal*. *Ghatis* like Arun Ghosh earned fame playing for East Bengal, while *Bangals,* such as Gautam Sarkar rose to prominence as players of Mohun Bagan. Both admitted that identification of the clubs with *Ghatis* or *Bangals* was entirely the misrepresentation of a section of loyal supporters and sometimes of a few club officials; footballers hardly played any role in it.[72] Since 1980, the supporters' rivalry on sub-regional lines also began to fade away, as memories of Partition and the old homeland itself grew weaker. Dimeo, however, makes this point unwittingly, yet pertinently:

> By the 1980s, though, identity markers were becoming less distinct. The memory of East Bengal as 'home' was the preserve of a fading generation of migrants, their sons and daughters more at home in West Bengal. Inter group relationships became more common, dialects less pronounced, and cultural traditions passed away. There are cases of fans with East Bengali parents supporting Mohun Bagan. Thus, a liminal, in-between space developed that contravened the polarity of previous years.[73]

How should the continuing enmity between the two clubs over the last 25 years be explained? The tradition of long-term rivalry, the consolidation of an oppositional identity, the convention of a supporters' culture and intensification of club loyalty – all of these contributed to sustain the excitement of the 'battle royal' of Indian football in a most critical period, when Indian football experienced recurrent fluctuation in terms of standard, popularity and professionalism. Despite radical changes in the Indian sporting map in the 1980s – the organization of the Asian Games at Delhi (1982), India's World Cup victory in cricket (1983) followed by the Mini World Cup triumph two years later (1985), the live telecast of World Cup football since 1982 and of the European and Latin American league and cup matches (since 1987), the organizational laxity of the All India Football Federation, and most important of all, the utter failure of the national and regional football bodies and the two great Calcutta clubs to adapt to the challenge of globalization, commercialism and professionalism till the mid-1990s – the intensity of rivalry between Mohun Bagan and East Bengal showed no signs of abatement. However, the rivalry faced a real challenge in 1997 when both clubs were sponsored and marginally bought off by the same company, viz. the United Breweries Group. The commercialization of Indian football, however, is a complex story, discussed elsewhere. After the sponsorship deal entered into by Mohun Bagan and East Bengal in 1997, there arose a large-scale apprehension among supporters that the age-old enmity would come to an end, as both clubs were sponsored by the same corporate house. Yet, what continues to dominate Indian football is a desperate rivalry between the two Bengali outfits.[74] In the Federation Cup semi-final of 1997, an unprecedented 131,000 spectators watched the match between the two – a world record at any club level first class match.[75] Their rivalry is rightly compared to the ones between Brazil and Argentina, Flumenitz and Flamengo (Brazil), River Plate and Boca Juniors (Argentina), Barcelona and Real Madrid (Spain), AC Milan and Inter Milan (Italy), Manchester United and Arsenal (England), Bayern Munich and BFC Leverkussen (Germany), and Ajax Amsterdom and PSV Aindhoven (the Netherlands).[76] What still differentiates this rivalry from other Indian club rivalries is the intense emotional attachment of supporters towards *their* club and the vehement opposition to the *others'* club. A recent incident is revealing: In late May 2003, Mohun Bagan Club, bogged down by internal strife and court cases, could not arrange for the money to retain its star players including the club's heart-throb Jose Ramirez Barretto, the mercurial Brazilian forward. Learning this from newspaper reports, one ardent supporter of the club decided to sell off his ancestral house and asked the club authorities to complete the formalities of payment from the sale proceeds.[77] The club officials understandably refused the offer but took pride in it as a reflection of the club's continuing tradition and glory. As East Bengal, the foremost enemy of his club had won all the five tournaments they had participated in the previous season, including the all-important National League title with a nearly all win record against Mohun Bagan, the fan could not bear the thought of a repeat of the same story the following year. Hence, to retain the star forward, who, he believed could ameliorate the plight of the club against its arch-rival; he offered his only asset for the sake of the club. This oppositional perception of *self* and *other* will continue to shape the future of the most fascinating club rivalry in Indian football.

Notes

1. Rupak Saha, 'Bangalir Football'. *Desh*, 28 August 1993, 21–2.
2. Ibid., 22–3.
3. Dimeo, '"Team Loyalty Splits the City into Two'.
4. Cornell and Hartman, *Ethnicity and Race*, 21.
5. *Sadukti Karnamrita*, a twelfth-century text, mentions the word meaningfully. Mukundaram Chakrabarty's *Chandimangal*, a sixteenth-century text, also mentions the word in a derogatory sense. Another contemporary text *Chaitanya Charitamrita* clearly reveals that the *Bangal* of East Bengal became a comic figure in West Bengal for his style of pronunciation.
6. Dinabandhu Mitra was a noted Bengali playwright of the late nineteenth century. His most famous piece, *Neel Darpan*, depicted the story of exploitation and oppression of Indian peasants by the European indigo planters in the middle of the century. The staging of the play created a stir among the Bengali populace in the wake of the Indigo Revolt of 1859.
7. For more layers on this trend, see Musa, 'Ghati-Bangal er Birodh Nispatti', 235–42.
8. Nandy, 'Football and Nationalism', 249–50.
9. Ibid.
10. Saha, *Itihase East Bengal*, 12–13.
11. Ibid.
12. Nandy, 'Football and Nationalism', 249.
13. Historians of the East Bengal Club have noted this aspect of discrimination against the East Bengali players and people and unanimously pointed to the exclusive regional character of the club at its birth and its impressive beginning in Calcutta football. For details, see Bandyopadhyay, *Cluber Naam East Bengal*; Dutta, *Glorious East Bengal*; Nandy, *East Bengal Club, 1920–1970*; Mashai, *East Bengal Cluber Itihas*; Saha, *Itihase East Bengal* (all in Bengali).
14. Among these eight players, goalkeeper Hiralal Mukherjee and right back Rev. Sudhir Chatterjee came from Faridpur district; the famous Bhaduri brothers of the team, Sibdas and Bijoydas, were from Rajshahi; scorer of the final, Abhilash Ghosh, right winger Kanu Roy and half back Rajen Sengupta from Dacca; while another half back Nilmadhab Bhattacharyya hailed from Barisal.
15. Incidentally, Gostho Paul is the only Bengali player to be honoured with a statue in the Calcutta Maidan. Paul's early career, his rise to sporting fame and the legend that grew around his striking personality are well delineated in his two biographies: Saha, *Chinese Wall*; Dutta, *Footbller Mahanayak Gostho Paul.*
16. It was hard for the East Bengali players to get a berth in the well-known Bengali teams of Calcutta in the 1910s, while the few who were fortunate experienced exclusion from the final playing 11 on different pretexts on crucial match days.
17. According to Santipriya Bandyopadhyay and Paresh Nandy, this match between Jorabagan and Mohun Bagan was played on 28 July 1920. For details, see Bandyopadhyay, *Cluber Naam East Bengal*, 28–9; Nandy, *East Bengal Club*, 28–30. Another club historian, Rupak Saha, thinks two East Bengali players, viz. Sailesh Basu and Nosa Sen, faced exclusion in Jorabagan's semi-final match against Calcutta Football Club in the Coochbehar Cup. When Jorabagan made it to the final and faced Mohun Bagan, both players featured in the match at Suresh Chaudhuri's instance. Jorabagan, however, lost the game, and the onus fell on the poor performance of the two *Bangal* players. Insulted and hurt by the incident, Chaudhuri left the club along with them. Saha, *Itihase East Bengal*, 15–16. Yet a few others like Pandit Masai and Shukharanjan Ghosh have argued that Sailesh Basu faced the discrimination of the club management not in a football match but in a cricket match against Calcutta Cricket Club during 1919–20 season. Masai, *East Bengal Cluber Itithas*, 1–2; Ghosh, *Bharatiya Footballe Tin Protidvandi*, 79–80.
18. *Amrita Bazar Patrika*, 13 August 1920.
19. It was quite unusual for a club like East Bengal to earn a berth to play in the second division of the League in the very first year of its existence. It was again due to Suresh Chaudhuri's influential links with the European members of IFA and his personal relations with other East Bengali social magnates that the club achieved this distinction. East Bengal filled the vacuum created by the withdrawal of Tajhat Club from the second division. In this case, too, Chaudhuri reaped the harvest of his friendly relations with the Raja of Tajhat in East Bengal, who owned the club. Moreover, the East Bengali players of the erstwhile Tajhat club joined East Bengal. For details *see* Bandyopadhyay, *Cluber Naam East Bengal*, 33–5; Nandy, *East Bengal Club*, 37–40; Saha, *Itihase East Bengal*, 20–1.
20. According to the existing rule of the Maidan, two clubs used to share one common ground. Taritbhushan Roy came to learn that Mohun Bagan shared its ground with National Association, which by that time hade ceased to exist. He referred this discrepancy to the police authorities and subsequently demanded

the share for East Bengal. It was then that Police Commissioner Charles Tegart ordered Mohun Bagan to share its ground with East Bengal. This sudden decision enraged the Mohun Bagan officials. Saha, *Itihase East Bengal*, 20; Nandy, *East Bengal Club*, 47–8.

21. Bandyopadhyay, *Cluber Naam East Bengal*, p.45; Dutta, *Glorious East Bengal*, pp. 10–11; Pandit Masai, *East Bengal Cluber Itihas*, pp. 17–18; Saha, *Itihase East Bengal*, p. 22–23.
22. Ghosh, *Bharatiya Footballer Tin Protidvandi*, 81.
23. Three leading newspapers of Calcutta – *The Statesman*, *The Englishman* and *Amrita Bazar Patrika* – published detailed reports of the meeting on 16 April 1925.
24. *The Englishman*, 22 April 1925.
25. Ibid., 24 April 1925.
26. *The Statesman*, 22 April 1925.
27. Ibid.
28. Gupta, 'Story on Calcutta Customs Club', 14.
29. *The Statesman*, 22 April 1925.
30. A number of worthy footballers from East Bengal played for Mohun Bagan throughout the first half of the twentieth century. The list includes names such as Nagen Kali, Hemango Basu, Rabi Basu, Bagha Som, Sanmatha Datta and K. Datta. For details see Sen, *Kheladhular Bichitra Kahini*, 21–9.
31. Dimeo, '"Team Loyalty Splits the City into Two"', 100.
32. Ibid.
33. Ibid., 101.
34. Ibid.
35. *The Statesman*, 24 August 1924.
36. *The Statesman* of 29 May 1925 reported that although Mohun Bagan enjoyed larger spectator support, East Bengal too could count on the support of a sizeable section.
37. *The Englishman*, 30 May 1925.
38. *The Statesman*, 6 July 1932.
39. For a fuller view of Mohammadan Sporting's grievances, see *Mohammedan Sporting Club Souvenir*, 66–8. East Bengal Club's rancour towards IFA resulted from the latter's continuous partiality towards Mohun Bagan Club. For an instructive discussion on the course of events, see Nandy, *East Bengal Club*, 84–7; Saha, *Itihase East Bengal*, 39–43.
40. *Bombay Chronicle*, 9 July 1939.
41. Ibid., 20 August 1939.
42. *Amrita Bazar Patrika*, 7 July 1946.
43. Ibid., 10 July 1946.
44. Ibid., 13 July 1946.
45. Nandy, 'Football and Nationalism', 249–50. The experience of suffering, deprivation and impoverishment of the East Bengali refugees in the aftermath of the partition has been vividly delineated in a rich crop of Bengali literature.
46. Kudaisya, 'Divided Landscapes, Fragmented Identities', 118.
47. Nandy, 'Calcutta Soccer', 319.
48. Thanks to this legendary forward-line, during this period East Bengal won both the IFA League and Shield thrice (League – 1949, 1950, 1952 and Shield – 1949, 1950, 1951); Durand Cup and DCM Trophy twice (Durand – 1951–52 and DCM – 1950, 1952); and the Rovers Cup once (1949).
49. Nandy, 'Football and Nationalism', 250.
50. *The Statesman*, 5 October 1947.
51. *Amrita Bazar Patrika*, 17 September 1950.
52. Ibid., 31 May 1951.
53. Ibid., 22 and 23 June 1951.
54. Ibid., 29 June 1955.
55. Ibid., 22 June 1956.
56. For a useful study of the relationship between Communist political ascendancy in West Bengal and refugee politics, see Chakrabarty, *The Marginal Men*.
57. See the *Amrita Bazar Patrika*, 17, 18 and 24 July 1957. The Chief Minister by these terms apparently referred to Mohammadan Sporting, East Bengal and the Rajasthan Clubs respectively.
58. East Bengal won the League title six times in a row from 1970 to 1975 – still a record. It won the IFA Shield in 1970 and then with a gap of a year in 1971 won every year from 1972 to 1976. The club bagged the Durand Cup in 1970 and 1972; Rovers Cup in 1972, 1973 and 1975; DCM Trophy in 1973 and 1974; and Bardoli Trophy in 1972 and 1973.

59. The sole occasion when Mohun Bagan got the better of their archrivals was in the 1974 Durand Cup semi-final. Mohun Bagan won the match by a solitary goal.
60. Surojit Sengupta, interview with author, 25 August 2002. For Sengupta's fuller views on football culture that grew around the East Bengal-Mohun Bagan rivalry in India, see Sengupta, *Back Center*. Incidentally, Sengupta who was a worthy right winger of East Bengal team in the 1970s, has recently left his job to take charge as the sports editor of *Khela*, the foremost sports vernacular magazine of Bengal.
61. *Ananda Bazar Patrika*, 30 September 1975.
62. Ibid., 1 October 1975. Also see Manas Chakrabarty, 'Mohun Bagan-East Bengal Reshareshi'. *Anandamela*, 19 July 2000, 118.
63. Ibid., 1 October 1975.
64. East Bengal won the match 2-0.
65. *Ananda Bazar Patrika*, 10 July 1977. The report said that the person was taken to the PG Hospital in a very critical condition.
66. According to the same newspaper report: 'total chaos resulted in the streets and different quarters of the city as the euphoric supporters ran wild with *mashals* (fire torches) in their hands from one place to another. There were several complaints against the jubilant crowd, which stopped private cars and scooters on the streets. Bricks were thrown into the ground and on another club's tent resulting in the injury of at least two dozens of people, three of them being rushed to Shambhunath Pandit Hospital. According to the police, eight persons were arrested on that evening.' *Ananda Bazar Patrika*, 10 July 1977.
67. For a most recent consideration of these issues, see Mangan and Ritchie (eds), *Ethnicity, Sport, Identity: Struggle for Status*.
68. *Khelar Asar*, 3 July 1979, 38.
69. The pre-match press reports suggested possibilities of chaos and violence on the match day. In fact, the Federation Cup final between the two teams on 8 May 1980 witnessed extremely unruly behaviour of not only the fans but also the players and club officials. See *Ananda Bazar Patrika*, 15 August 1980; *Khelar Asar*, 16 May 1980.
70. *Ananda Bazar Patrika*, 17 August 1980. For a very insightful coverage of the tragedy, see *Khelar Kagoj*, 1 and 16 Sept. 1980; and *Khelar Kotha*, 1 and 16 Sept. 1980.
71. Amal Dutta, 'Open Letter to Jyoti Basu' (Editorial), *Khelar Kotha*, 1 September 1980.
72. Sengupta, 'Nirapade Bhinna Clube', 184–9.
73. Dimeo, '"Team Loyalty Splits the City into Two"', 106.
74. Intense club rivalries are not uncommon in other centres of soccer in India. Dempo vs. Salgaonkar in Goa, Air India and Mahindra United in Bombay, or Punjab Police vs. JCT Mills in Punjab – all these rivalries attracted or still attract a modest support base, but by no means can claim to have the continuity or tradition of intense enmity that exemplifies the relations between Mohun Bagan and East Bengal.
75. East Bengal won the match 4-1. For details, see *The Statesman* and *Ananda Bazar Patrika*, 14 July 1997.
76. East Bengal supporters always seem to be more aggressive in temper and more violent in reaction while Mohun Bagan supporters look sober and moderate. For such comparisons, see Chakrabarty, 'MohunBagan-East Bengal Reshareshi', 114–17; Saha, 'Bangalir Football', 21–34, especially p.25. However, this kind of comparison was offered as early as 1965, if not earlier. For details, see *Ananda Bazar Patrika*, 19 July 1965.
77. *Ananda Bazar Patrika*, 3 July 2003. Rupak Saha narrates a similar incident of 1991 when an East Bengal fan mortgaged his house and took his wife's gold ornaments to rope in a few good players for the club in times of the club's financial crisis. For details, see Saha, 'Bangalir Football', 23–4.

References

Bandyopadhyay, Santipriya. *Cluber Naam East Bengal* [Name of the club is East Bengal]. Calcutta: New Bengal Press, 1979.

Chakrabarty, Prafulla K. *The Marginal Men, The Refugees and the Left Political Syndrome in West Bengal.* Calcutta: Lumiere Publishers, 1990.

Cornell, S. and D. Hartman. *Ethnicity and Race: Making Identities in a Changing World.* London: Pine Forge Press, 1998.

Dimeo, Paul. '"Team Loyalty Splits the City into Two": Football, Ethnicity and Rivalry in Calcutta'. In *Fear and Loathing in World Football*, ed. G. Armstrong and R. Giulianotti. Oxford: Berg, 2001.

Dutta, Jayanta. *Glorious East Bengal.* Calcutta: Sahitya Prakash, 1975.

______ *Footbller Mahanayak Gostho Paul* [The legend of Football-Gostho Paul]. Calcutta: Anima Prakashani, 1986.

Ghosh, Shukharanjan. *Bharatiya Footballe Tin Protidvandi.* Calcutta: Manju Prakashani, 1986.

Gupta, Pankaj. 'Story on Calcutta Customs Club'. In *Platinum Jubilee: Calcutta Customs Club, 1892–1967.*

Kudaisya, Gyanesh. 'Divided Landscapes, Fragmented Identities: East Bengal Refugees and their Rehabilitation in India, 1947–79. In *Freedom, Trauma and Continuities: Northern India and Independence*, ed. D.A. Low and Howard Brasted. New Delhi: Sage, 1998.

Mangan, J.A. and Andrew Ritchie, eds. *Ethnicity, Sport, Identity: Struggle for Status.* London: Frank Cass, 2003.

Mashai, Pandit (Ramesh Chandra Goswami). *East Bengal Cluber Itihas* [History of East Bengal Club]. Calcutta: Book Garden, 1963.

Mohammedan Sporting Club Souvenir. Calcutta: Mohammedan Sporting Club, 1939.

Musa, Mansur. 'Ghati-Bangal er Birodh Nispatti' [Resolution of Ghati Bangal conflict]. In *Banga Sanskritir Sanhatir Oitihya* [Bengali Cultural Harmony Tradition], ed. Nitish Biswas and Mukulesh Biswas, 235–42. Oikotan Gobeshona Samsad, 1995.

Nandy, Moti. 'Calcutta Soccer'. In *Calcutta: The Living City*, Vol.II, ed. Sukanta Chaudhuri. Oxford: Oxford University Press, 1990.

______ 'Football and Nationalism'. In *The Calcutta Psyche*, ed. Geeti Sen. New Delhi: The India International Centre, 1990–91.

Nandy, Paresh. *East Bengal Club, 1920–1970: Ponchas Bochhorer Sangram o Safalya* [50 years of success and struggle]. Calcutta: Bichitra, 1973.

Saha, Rupak. *Chinese Wall.* Calcutta: Hemlata Prakashani, 1979.

______ 'Bangalir Football'. *Desh,* 28 August 1993.

______ *Itihase East Bengal.* Calcutta: Deep, 2000.

Sen, Sachin. *Kheladhular Bichitra Kahin* [Strange sporting stories]. Calcutta: R.M. Gupta/Geetanjali Book Centre, 1983.

Sengupta, Surajit. *Back Center.* Calcutta: Sunny Publishers, 1986.

Sengupta, Tanaji. 'Nirapade Bhinna Clube'. *Desh* (Binodon sankhya) (1988): 184–9.

Globalizing sport: assessing the World Baseball Classic

Alan Klein

Introduction

With each passing year the arrogance associated with the notion of a baseball 'World Series' involving only North America is made more obvious not only to the American public, but to Major League Baseball (MLB) as well. In 2006, over three quarters of a century after association football's (soccer) first World Cup was played, Major League Baseball formally ventured into the era of global sport when the World Baseball Classic began on 7 March with 16 nations competing. I chronicled this tournament to assess baseball's venture outside of North America, as well as to forge ahead on developing a working concept of globalization.

Despite globalization's centrality to modern life and its readily apparent relationship to sport, we have few in-depth case studies of sport and globalization. Scholars began writing about sport and globalization as early as 1990 when Joseph Maguire published an article on American football's attempt to expand to the UK and Europe.[1] Through that decade several sport journals published issues featuring discussions of globalization, yet book length treatments remained relatively few. In sociology and anthropology, we have only the work of Joseph Maguire; John Sugden and Alan Tomlinson; Alan Bairner; and Toby Miller, A. Lawrence, Jim McKay and D. Rowe – four volumes in all.[2]

While there are strong disagreements among sports scholars as to the directions or outcomes that globalization takes; and even as to what it is, consensus exists on the position of soccer as the standard for globalized sport. Football's crowning jewel – the World Cup – outstrips virtually any other public spectacle in terms of worldwide following. By comparison, the American Super Bowl – the most watched television programme in the US history with 95 million viewers – pales next to the 1.3 billion that watched the final game of the 2006 World Cup or the 30 billion who watched the event over the four weeks it was played. Football is played professionally in more countries (204) than any other sport, and can lay claim to more than a quarter of a billion active players. As staggering as these numbers are, more impressive still is the degree to which soccer is integrated both vertically and horizontally on an international scale. With its complex organization of private clubs, national team and international league structures, the sport is continually played at elite levels all over the world. By comparison, baseball is, as we say, 'small potatoes'. Yet the study of small potatoes may still be able to yield some badly needed insights into globalization, and possibly provide valuable lessons for football as well.

The World Baseball Classic (WBC)

Major League Baseball's 30 team owners created and fund the sport's political and economic nerve centre through the Office of Commissioner of Baseball. Its headquarters in New York City oversees every aspect of the game, and there one finds the division that deals with international efforts: Major League Baseball International (MLBI). Made up of marketing gurus, MLBI is charged with generating revenue, which it does through promoting international exhibitions as well as contracting for the sale of licensed products, corporate sponsorships and television rights. In addition to its revenue generating programmes, however, MLBI is also responsible for developing the game where it exists only weakly and/or not at all – that would be most of the world. I will argue that building a revenue base and developing the sport are in many ways mutually exclusive and require different kinds of people and policy. Moreover, I insist that this structural tension is at the heart of which form MLB's globalization will take.

I spent the years between 2000 and 2006 studying MLBI's various efforts, travelling with their personnel to different venues and interviewing its leading figures. This took me through seven different countries on five different continents. To attempt an understanding of the industry's global efforts, I made an effort to study three representative layers of the sport. They were: the Commissioner's Office where policy is set; a large market franchise (which can undertake all manner of international financial efforts); and a small market franchise (representing those organizations that must compete by carefully managing their financial affairs).

In 1993, Tim Brosnan, then MLB's international head, envisioned a world cup-style tournament, when he wondered aloud, 'Why can't there be something that is ours: that we could own, our own stage?'[3] Baseball Commissioner Bud Selig annually offered vague promises of global efforts, but the industry as a whole did little to move this plan forward. What passed for a global programme was limited to the occasional exhibition game played by major league teams in foreign settings.

Talk of the WBC heated up after 2000 as a result of a convergence of several factors. Revenue from international efforts had steadily grown, making it easier to sell franchise owners on the idea of foreign endeavours. Increasing numbers of foreign players were being signed by major league clubs, changing perceptions held by owners and fans concerning the ability and desirability of foreigners in the game. Most importantly, the growing signs of baseball's declining ability to reproduce both its fan and player bases domestically, had become impossible to ignore.[4] The final impetus pushing MLB into the international arena of tournament play was the decision by the International Olympic Committee to drop baseball as an event after the 2008 Beijing Olympics.

From the beginning, it was clear that the WBC tournament would be strikingly different from the world's leading sporting events: the FIFA World Cup and the Olympics. For soccer, a key feature responsible for its worldwide spread (cultural imperialism aside) was its 'presentation of self' as inclusive and democratic, which was an important structural feature of its international competitions. Becoming a member of FIFA meant that each nation, regardless of size or power, had one vote. Even taking into consideration the political and economic differences within FIFA, it remains structurally and ideologically built upon inclusiveness. Despite its structural inequalities, competing in the World Cup is the merit-based outcome of worldwide competition.[5]

In contrast, the design of the World Baseball Classic was by 'invitation' only. The 16 national competitors did not play their way into the WBC: they were 'selected' on the basis of how entrenched the sport is in their country and MLB's revenue projections for those countries On a practical level, the difficulty of choosing which country is deserving of an invitation is moot since there are only a handful of countries (a dozen at best) that can claim legitimate attachment to the game. The rest of the field was filled out by countries with fledgling baseball presences (e.g. South Africa), but with economies that could support future growth. As a result, the WBC would field teams that claim the best players in the world competing against teams made up of amateurs. This obvious disparity would, it was hoped, be overlooked by the novel prospect of nations vying against each other. While soccer fans have long since grown accustomed to the changing configurations of competitions that have them shift allegiance from club players to national teams, for baseball fans this was a new experience.

At a political level, the idea that MLBI (as an embodiment of the USA) would select who they felt was worthy of playing did little to build international solidarity. Therein, lies another difference between soccer and baseball as globalizing forces. The 'invitation' origin of this baseball tournament may not have intentionally sought to slight others, but slight it did. The Japanese and South Koreans, both highly accomplished baseball-playing nations, were incensed by MLB's structuring of the event. They assumed it would be FIFA-style; that the tournament would be planned collectively 'by all represented nations. As one Korean official scoffed: the 'MLB and their Players Association have decided to host an event that they will "invite" us to? We want more than that.'[6] This view perplexed MLB's producers of the event, 'They feel like we're shoving it down their throats ... they don't understand why we're running it', explained an exasperated Jim Small of MLBI. 'We want to grow the game globally, but at this point we are the ones underwriting it at all levels.'[7] MLB decided that because they are the pre-eminent baseball-playing country, and were funding the tournament, they were entitled to set policy and structure. Other nations saw this as arrogant, 'This whole thing smacks of imperialism on the part of MLB. Why didn't they build a consensus on this before announcing their plans', exclaimed one high-ranking Japanese official.[8] While nationalist passion fuels the playing of international tournaments, it can, at the planning stages, threaten to derail it. Such issues twice forced MLBI to push back the date of the tournament.

Just four months before it was set to begin, another round of politics and national sabre-rattling threatened the tournament when the Cuban team was denied a visa to enter the USA where most of the matches were to be played. Because the prize money that Cubans stood to gain from competing would violate the treaty banning any economic relations with Castro's government, the Bush administration balked at granting access to the Cuban team. Two allies came to Cuba's defence: Puerto Rico and Venezuela both indicated that they would either offer their facilities as playing sites or boycott the event altogether. Its back against the wall, MLB pressed President Bush to relent if the Cubans would agree to donate their earnings to charity. Clouded with political bellicosity and cultural arrogance, many predicted the tournament would fail even if it should ever take place.

The event

Most informed observers considered the outcome of the event a foregone conclusion. Filled with stars, it was assumed that the American team would easily capture the championship. The only question remaining was whom they would beat in the finals. Would they face the talent-laden Dominican Republic (a nation of only eight million, but with 87 players on Major League rosters)? Alternatively, would the USA play Venezuela, second only to the Dominican Republic in foreign major leaguers? Someone, however, had forgotten to tell the competitors about this scenario and upsets took place. The most dramatic de-railing involved the American team being beaten twice: once by – of all teams – the Canadians, and then again by Mexico.

The Dominicans and Venezuelans were also eliminated. In the championship round Japan beat Cuba in a hard fought contest.

The element that WBC producers had hoped would save their embattled first effort was the old sports standby: nationalism. 'The players' incredible enthusiasm drove the fans' excitement', concluded MLBI's Vice President Paul Archey.[9] It is not certain just who inspired whom in this tournament, however anyone watching or playing could not help but be caught up in the nationalist spasms for which events like this are notorious. In an unexpected twist, the American television audiences remained tuned in to the games even after it became clear that the Americans were not the best team. They became enamoured with the skill, enthusiasm and joy of the all the nations that played. The semi-final game pitting Japan against Korea had a healthy audience in the USA, as well as becoming the most watched sporting event in the two Asian countries in over thirty years.[10] The other semi-final saw Dominicans and Cubans playing impassioned baseball, conveying to viewers everywhere how exciting these countries could make the game. All four nations showed Americans that the game was not only played abroad, but also produced foreign players whose consummate skills recalled how baseball used to be played in the USA before the commercialized era of bloated egos and contracts. Nationalism saved the WBC, as it does all international sporting venues.

MLB deserved relatively little of the credit for the tournament's emotional spark, but quickly claimed most of it. The omniscient Commissioner's Office suddenly knew all along that teams were capable of surprise finishes; that fans would infuse the proceedings with cultural and national displays; that players would play as if they cared; and that a pervasive generosity of spirit would somehow seep beyond the baseball world. In short, the WBC knew it could promote the globalization of baseball. It was a smug Commissioner Selig who concluded that, 'We were here (WBC) to not only participate and enhance the internationalization of the sport, but to create interest in a lot of places where there hasn't been any. And we've achieved that.'[11]

Did producing a successful international tournament, allow MLB to take what would be effectively a giant step onto the global stage? To attempt an answer, one must look at the relationship between events such as the World Cup and the World Baseball Classic as well as the industries that produce them. Clearly the intent of MLB (or FIFA) is to promote their enterprises as internationally as possible. We need to understand better what terms such as 'international' or 'world' mean if we hope to unravel their inter-relations. For example, do we think of globalization as merely a term that describes the most spatially pervasive and financially lucrative sporting venue? Or do we take the cultural-corporate media productions of sporting events as accurate reflections of their cultural expansiveness? Should we try to examine international sporting labour and its relationship to capital?

Nationalism plays a dominant role in the rise of both capitalism and globalization, yet it remains a vague concept. Nairn's less than flattering, though important, depiction of nationalism likened it to 'a neurotic individual, with much the same essential ambiguity attaching to it',[12] by which he referred to nationalism's ability to assume wildly divergent political positions (e.g. progressive or oppressive). The 1936 German Olympics' agenda to promote fascist Nazi ideology stands at the opposite end of the pole from the way in which cricket in India was used to subvert colonial rule. Yet both are examples of sporting events that centred upon nationalist identity, illustrating the elasticity, or neurosis, of the concept.

The role played by nationalism in sporting events like the World Cup or Olympics is, from a Weberian perspective,[13] also internally ambivalent: simultaneously promoting solidarity and divisiveness. For Swedes or Germans to bedeck themselves in their nation's colours (virtually making themselves into their nations' flags) and feel a powerful solidarity among like-minded pilgrims, is accompanied by derision of the nation that they are opposing. Sometimes it is good-natured and sometimes appallingly xenophobic. In international sporting events, however, a liminal place exists where the tension between the national self and the foreign other can be expressed. This is carried out through sport as a contrivance built around contest and its ability to mimic war – in short, it is playing at fighting.

Sixty years ago, the anthropologist Gluckman argued that tensions between social groups could be controlled by channelling them through a series of rituals in which hostilities are focused upon rather than dismissed or denied.[14] 'Ritualized rebellion', he termed it. By acting out their hostility in a collectively meaningful and approved manner, societies can neutralize potentially harmful hostilities. There is a distinct component of this concept at play in the way in which nationalism is expressed through international sporting competitions.

Since nationalism refuses to adhere to any specific ideology and seems little inclined to promote anything beyond itself, it functions much like a political zero-sum game. As a result, nationalism is often seen as antagonistic to globalization, prompting a widespread view that it is in danger of being rendered obsolete. In fact, the opposite is the case. National self-interest or agency is a vital check on the excesses of globalization. The nation, in fact, has proven itself quite resilient, even creative, in its relationship with globalization. For example, the insistence of third world nations on technology transfers in negotiating with the foreign multinational corporations operating in their countries is an excellent example of how the nation-state continues to have a role in promoting a society's development.

Developing the sport

'Growing the Game' is an MLB euphemism for trying to develop the sport in nations were it is weak. While it is regarded as vital, MLBI has only employed strategies that combine marketing and passive interventions: determining demographics and employing some combination of media exposure, coaching and play. As was often explained to me, 'We can market ourselves into and out of almost any situation'.[15] To achieve its aims, MLBI has fashioned a worldwide baseball geography based upon the dual notion of how entrenched the sport is and whether or not real revenue opportunities can be encouraged. The result is a 'three tier' categorization of baseball around the world. Tier 1 consists of countries in which the sport is most entrenched and where the marketing of the sport is evolved (e.g. Japan or the Dominican Republic). Tier two countries are developed baseball nations that have yet to achieve the level of Tier one nations (e.g. Korea). Countries such as South Africa or Italy are places where the game has been introduced, but need much further development; hence they are on Tier 3. Tier 3, however, includes most of the world and remains baseball's major challenge.

Future possibilities

Overlooked by the marketers at MLB is the fact that when sport enters another culture, like any foreign cultural product, it does so in a crowded field. There it is mulled over, then accepted, modified or rejected based upon how it resonates with local culture. Hence, game development is, at heart, social engineering. This implies some sort of process whereby – in the instance – the sport is allowed to build a constituency before it can successfully hope to compete with other sports for the best athletes. Attracting the best athletes remains the real measure of successful game development. Over the past decade, MLB has spent millions of dollars trying to gain a toehold in Europe in order to begin this process, with under-whelming results. Germany, Italy and England have been on the receiving end of MLBI's grass roots programmes that teach children the sport in school and then organize leagues for them to play in. The goal has been to create a chain of players beginning at age eight, in order to build a player base that leads to the national team and beyond that to successfully groom professionals. Most recently MLBI has organized an elite academy in Italy in which the best players from various countries in the EU are sent to advance their skills. These efforts have failed for a variety of reasons that begin with the grim reality that Europe is highly developed both economically and in sporting terms, with soccer at the helm. Finally, because they have such well developed identities through their sports there is a measure of hostility toward foreign sports that seek entry, and perhaps in particular those emanating from the USA.

To advance most quickly, MLB should adopt a strategy that converts perceptions rooted in the social sciences into its development programmes. MLB should scale back their investment in places like Germany or the Netherlands, going instead into Eastern Europe where the promise of upward mobility through sport would articulate well with local economic conditions. The relatively under-developed economies in places like the Ukraine not only opens the door to the use of sport as upward mobility, but also allows it to enter a field relatively empty of competing sporting institutions. One need go no further than the Caribbean basin to see how sport and upward mobility have been the wellspring of baseball success.

Other interventions involve the use of cultural and historical features. Hobsbawm and Ranger's notion of 'invented traditions',[16] might be altered to enable a sport and its practices to become imbedded in foreign settings. Game-related rituals or practices could become a spring-board to larger subcultural (or even cultural) practices. As such, what is a recently introduced behaviour could be made to appear as culturally older and promote the notion that affinities exist between new-and-established.[17]

A related strategy would build sport rivalries around lines of social conflict. The working off of any existing social tension – positive or negative – can galvanize fan support. The support of Scottish fans (whose national team had failed to qualify) for the Trinidad and Tobago soccer team in the 2006 World Cup, for instance, centred on the Trinidadian player fortuitously named Jason Scotland, but was also based on the fact that T&T were playing England in the first round and Scotland always supports the team opposing England. The presence of a Palestinian football team in the Israeli Premier League is another illustration of this. Bnei Sakhnin, a West Bank club drew large – albeit hostile – crowds wherever it played in Israel, making it one of the league's biggest draws. When it won the league title in 2005 and came to UEFA to represent the country, Bnei Sakhnin was able to reverse the social hostility and garner an impressive share of national support as it played successfully in its contests – all despite its Arab identity.

It is, likewise, possible to use sport to help overcome social conflict if it is introduced at opportune moments by the most efficacious agency. In post-apartheid South Africa the sport of baseball has been able to make inroads against all expectations. Post-apartheid South Africa has generated a policy that integrates all areas of culture. Sport teams are now required to include at least 40% of peoples of colour, a major advance over the white-only teams of the pre-Mandela era. Because baseball has no significant history in the country, it was perceived to be free from racism by the Mandela government in the early 1990s. As a result it was designated as a desirable sport that should receive government funding. Also, because baseball was being championed by several well-known anti-apartheid activists, it was quickly introduced into over 1,000 schools. At the World Baseball Classic, the South African team boasted that it was fully integrated (50/50) purely on merit, further underscoring its progressive orientation.

Globalization

Because it is ubiquitous as a concept, globalization risks losing meaning at the same time as it is gaining currency. We should, therefore, constantly seek to better define the term. Like many others, I see globalization as a process, in existence for centuries, but growing ever more integrated over time.[18] It is currently shaped by a combination of factors, foremost by a revolutionary technology. Globalization encompasses an economically messy form of capitalism that reconfigures the way we have come to conceive of the world; and, because of this reshaping, it can worsen existing conditions, or, as the anthropologist Tsing claims, contain the promise of something new.[19] By 'new', I refer to new relations or configurations among already existing constituencies and institutions.

An examination of globalization theories from an array of disciplines reveals that, despite their differences, most scholars note a set of common features. First of all, everyone points to technological breakthroughs in information processing and dissemination.[20] These technological advancements have resulted in the ability to instantly move information and make decisions around the world. A second, commonly perceived feature of globalization is that time and space compress.[21] Because we have the ability to affect each other so quickly, far-flung regions are more obviously connected to us, which in turn impacts our social relations. There are economic implications, as production, distribution and consumption take place globally in real time. Third, all agree that globalization occurs within a capitalist framework. The fall of the Soviet Union removed the primary political and economic barrier to G8 capitalism. As markets have integrated and opened up dramatically, so has the claim to unparalleled power by developed nations.[22] While the economic and political consequences are overwhelming they remain, however, far from clear-cut; meaning that economic disparity can be exacerbated or reduced depending upon a host of factors.

Moreover globalization is also a cultural phenomenon, and here too there are some commonly shared conclusions.[23] Centres of globalization are positioned to export or spread their cultural products around the world with ease. Corporate giants not only commercially intrude into every nook and cranny of the world, but do so culturally as well. Individuals, too, can now move about the globe as effortlessly as agencies and corporations, hence, accelerating the movement of culture while theoretically privileging the individual. Virtually all culture is modified to fit these new global frameworks with the result that at least some components of culture wind up becoming more global, more commoditized and accessible.

What makes globalization so contentious is that while it appears to have the ability to level differences; it has demonstrated a much greater likelihood of exacerbating those differences. Contentious splits rage between those who argue that globalization is nothing new, it is simply capitalism with the gloves taken off; and those who think of globalization as having the ability to level first world/third world differences.[24] Arguing one way or another will have an effect on how we conceive of, for example, theories of development. Culturally speaking, does globalization result in 'homogenization' in which dominant centres are able to foist their cultural presence and wares worldwide thus eradicating local cultures? Or, is it possible that local cultures anywhere can begin to export their own presence around the world in ways never before possible (also referred to as 'glocalization')? Can a two-way flow of culture begin to emerge in which segments of heretofore-powerless post-colonial cultures begin to have an impact on the West while simultaneously accepting Western influences?

Testicular and Tough Love Globalization

We would be better served to think of globalization as a series of continua. At one end we might see a tendency for globalization to homogenize world cultures, while the other pole would feature the ability of local culture to affect the west. In between, we may be able to gauge the degree to which social entities capitulate to and/or affect others. In political economic terms, however, rather than think of globalization as either turbo-capitalism or altruistically induced economic reform for the developing nations, I have renamed the ends of the continuum: 'Testicular Globalization' (TG) and 'Tough Love Globalization' (TLG).

Testicular Globalization merges established practices and new conditions to exacerbate existing economic differences thus expanding the gulf separating the first and third worlds. Based on the ability to technologically move capital around the globe, and on the increased ability to open markets, testicular globalization simply strives to further the neo-liberal agenda. Corporations operate in an unfettered climate, making record profits and eliminating the remaining impediments to controlling labour and the environment. At this end of the spectrum, first world/third world distinctions continue or increase, nations are eviscerated, and the environment ruined. TG is a more muscular version of twentieth-century capitalism.

Tough Love Globalization is also an outgrowth of contemporary capitalism, but with a structural twist. Unlike Testicular Globalization, TLG can potentially skirt national economic constraints and, as a result, enable traditionally underdeveloped – but aggressive – nations to seize opportunities throughout the world.. This version is not to be confused with utopian notions in which Third World nations are granted economic reprieve by intentional redistributions of wealth. Tough Love Globalization results from the worldwide movement of capital, production and services on the basis of corporate self-interest and profit *irrespective* of existing economic difference. Any industry or agency that has outworked, outmanoeuvred and/or out foxed competitors attracts what Friedman termed 'the electronic herd' (e-investment).[25] India's ability to become a major player in the information technology field – competing with the USA and others – has attracted significant investment capital (indeed, it is projected that within ten years India will have bypassed the UK as the fifth largest economy in the world). In this instance, India has been able to take advantage of the large portion of its population that has been educated abroad in various cutting edge fields, and who have returned to their homeland to build a successful industry. This effort has been aided by the Indian government, hence rather than think of the nation as antithetical to globalization, the role of the state is absolutely critical in assuring that local industry be given the opportunity to compete effectively on the global stage.

Additionally, by not attempting to curb such state-led efforts, progressive global forces can exist in a healthy tension with the nation-state, strengthening their entire industry worldwide, rather than becoming enmeshed in an unceasing tension between foreign corporations and the state. The key here is to prove to them that these global giants are better served if they de-centre.

While TLG offers a narrow range of upward mobility (via nations and companies possessed of speed and generous incentives) to those from underprivileged backgrounds, it will, by the same token, abandon those who were once on top if they flounder. The rise of India, Ireland and China are illustrations of one side of this capacity. The TLG model, however, can help us understand how entire industrial sectors of advanced countries have fallen behind not only within their own nation, but also relative to developing nations (e.g. the steel industry of the USA). Such trajectories are linked in the TLG model.

Major League Baseball: testicular or tough love?

I conclude that Major League Baseball International has remained at the testicular end of the continuum. In an increasingly interconnected world where spectators and fans have more and more options and diversions, each succeeding generation will be more tempted to explore that range of possibilities. To 'grow their game', sport industries will not only have to venture into the remote corners of the world, but where their sport is already enjoying success they will have to constantly defend their turf against other sports. Conventional knowledge has it that in order to succeed entities should seek to retain and expand authority and control; but in a globalized world it makes more sense to gain influence by relinquishing control and spreading the enterprise. It is baseball, the sport, that needs to gain acceptance, not Major League Baseball in its American corporate guise. Certainly within the context of its World Baseball Classic, MLBI showed no inclination to de-centre or to distribute power.

Major League Baseball is currently attempting to both take the sport into areas that have little or no interest in the game, as well as entrench itself further in nations that have embraced the game. Were MLB to boldly embrace a de-centred policy it would be taking a giant step towards building a rosy future; however, convincing someone accustomed to total control that relinquishing that power would be healthy, is difficult.

Judging from the WBC, if the sport is moving toward globalization, it is doing so at a snail's pace; gingerly testing the waters when it should be diving headlong into it. This slow pace is a function of the enormous economic success MLB is currently enjoying and MLB's smug sense that they are actually becoming global. With revenue projections expected to top $5.4 billion in 2007and robust attendance, the Commissioner's Office is convinced that all is rosy, making it easier to ignore the serious crisis at baseball's core. Unable to reproduce in full both its player and fan bases at home, MLB needs to grow abroad. The decline of MLB over the past 20 years has outstripped all other American sport. Even significant gains made among Hispanic-Americans have not been enough to overcome the loss of the youth market and the virtual abandonment of baseball by African-Americans. Moreover, it is an aging and relatively affluent fan base that accounts for the revenue boom.[26]

At present, approximately 27% of all Major Leaguers and almost 50% of all minor leaguers are foreign-born. When conversations turn to globalization and baseball, labour migration is where the discussion begins and ends. Yet, while global labour migration is one part of the globalization process, it actually works to obscure our view of it. In both soccer and baseball much of the labour flow is talent coming from developing nations to the well-healed clubs of Europe and the USA respectively. Following Ghanaian or Brazilian stars heading to UEFA is hardly meeting globalization's promise of levelling the playing fields between first and third world nations. Rather, it continues the conventional labour flow from south to north. This kind of trans-national flow reflects 'internationalization' rather than globalization. The former belongs to the system already in existence, while the latter – built on a two-way flow – is a harbinger of future globalized forms.

For Major League Baseball or FIFA to become globally advanced, two areas need to be developed. MLB needs to foster the creation of top-flight leagues and franchises in areas of the world that have been thus far ignored. MLB has done nothing in this regard, and occasional efforts in the soccer world have aborted because not enough was known of the sporting culture in those areas to avoid financial pitfalls (e.g. the effort to upgrade the Brazilian leagues). Second, furthering the global movement of capital in which foreign ownership of any team becomes the norm needs to take place. Again, while this is futuristic for baseball, it has already begun in football circles. Foreign ownership of English Premier League teams (Chelsea and Manchester United) is already a fact. As this becomes the norm, it will foster a two-way flow of influence.

Virtually every high-ranking official in baseball has dismissed the idea of spreading teams around the world, citing logistics and economics as insurmountable obstacles. One of the game's most knowledgeable and respected administrators is Sandy Alderson, who until 2006 was the MLB's Senior Vice President. Despite favouring the internationalization of the game, Alderson is quick to cite barriers to globalizing baseball:

> I don't think it's that difficult to project the game over the next decade or two to have developed a global structure. When I think of globalization conceptually, using FIFA as an example, I see FIFA as an organization where the game is played well in a lot of places, and the economics in those places can support the opportunities that come their way. That kind of dual strength lends itself to decentralization. Baseball isn't there yet …Until you see more places develop [the game] MLB will continue to have the power it presently has.[27]

While the objections to moving the sport to the next level are pragmatically based, they can be overcome. By re-aligning the existing major league teams and adding foreign teams, four divisions could be created. At least two of these divisions could contain a number of foreign teams

Table 1. Pacific-Rim Major League Baseball Division.

USA RIM	ASIAN RIM
Seattle (Mariners)	Tokyo (existing professional team)
San Francisco (Giants)	Hanshin (existing professional team)
Los Angeles (Dodgers)	Taiwan (existing professional team)
Los Angeles (Angels)	Korea (existing professional team)
San Diego (Padres)	Sydney (game still needs to be developed)

along with their US counterparts that share a geographic affinity. One oft stated objection is that playing in Asia –in a trans-Pacific league, for instance – would pose insurmountable travel problems for teams from the USA. If, however, we add a number of teams from the Asian Pacific Rim, as in the table below, the team making its way across the Pacific could play enough games at the other end to overcome the jet lag involved in crossing so many time zones.

Hence, when a team from Los Angeles California plays Tokyo, scheduling a long swing to play every other team on that side of the Pacific would be in order. Such swings (already in existence in MLB between east and west coast teams) would be lengthened, taking perhaps a month. The foreign cities named above have long established baseball traditions, and the potential for attracting owners with the resources to compete in these leagues is great.

The second part of this globalizing equation would find capital (owners) within the industry able to move as freely as labour already does. Hence, it would not necessarily be a Venezuelan entity (e.g. CITGO Oil Company) that would own the Venezuelan franchise, just as it would not have to be an American that would own a US team. In the tough love globalized baseball world, the New York Yankees could be owned by Toyota, just as Ted Turner's Atlanta-based media empire could own the Mexican team. Here, capital, like labour before it, would shed its national constraints. At present, only one major league franchise is foreign owned – the Seattle Mariners who are owned by Nintendo's chief Hirochi Yamauchi. The purchase of that team by a Japanese national sparked such a protectionist furore that it is a wonder that it took place at all. In the end Mr Yamauchi had to agree to hold minority-voting rights to clear the protectionist blockade in the MLB Commissioner's Office. When labour and capital become highly mobile, the national dimension of Major League Baseball and even FIFA will begin to recede, or at least lose some of its anchoring properties.

Conclusion

Unlike FIFA, which is structurally well developed globally, baseball must struggle to become viable in Europe, Africa and large swaths of Asia. To remain rooted where it has already succeeded is short-sighted (neglecting its internal economic limitations). As noted, the sense of well-being emanating from the Commissioner's Office dampens the perceived need to expand the sport more innovatively and aggressively, a move, which requires a globalized-view of baseball.

Paul Archey (VP of MLBI) must relinquish his testicular approach toward 'growing the game', a posture that he defiantly embraces:

> Look, we're not operating on a FIFA model. We took all of the economic risk – \$45 million – without being certain of making anything back. More than 50% of the players in the tournament are MLB players, and almost every impact player there was on an MLB payroll, so, 'No', we won't be inviting anyone in at present to make decisions. I don't mind getting input from other countries, but we know what we have to do.[28]

Archey's response to my question is as testicular a globalization statement as one will find, but it is not based purely on arrogance. Rather, in the hands of a marketer, and one who has to answer to owners who demand profit from every international encounter (Archey's budget comes from them), he does what he was brought in to do. What he and others fail to see, and hence cannot articulate, is that generating profit is at odds with developing the sport. Survival and growth at the beginning of this century can still be rationalized as a function of the existing baseball world, but by the end of this century it will have been shown to be a colossal failure. What we need are innovative and opportunistic policy makers – not marketers – who understand what makes events resonate with peoples and cultures. MLB is far from realizing any of these positions, but FIFA should take pause as well, for despite its UN orientation, it too is invested in privileging the nation and is not sufficiently de-centred. To assess how global soccer and baseball are we need to understand the relationship between nationalism and globalization, to determine whether the enterprise favours centralization or decentring, and, most importantly, intensively assess the links between sport enterprise, corporation, labour and the consumer. What can make globalization 'new' is its insistence upon new relationships among old partners, as well as a commitment to integration, egalitarianism and merit on a global scale, which is to say, free from colonial restraints and mindsets, naive ideologies, or the denial of the economic impulses that drive sport. The power of Nike or Adidas needs to be hemmed in with a deft combination of organized consumer groups, labour movements and corporate responsibility. Done well, we can domesticate the beast rather than try to slay the dragon.

Notes

1. Maguire, 'More Than a Sporting "Touchdown"'.
2. Book length treatments of global sport include Maguire, *Global Sport*; Bairner, *Sport, Nationalism and Globalization*; Sugden and Tomlinson, *FIFA and the Contest for World Football*; Miller *et al.*, *Globalization and Sport*. Articles began appearing in sport journals beginning in 1990 (e.g. Maguire, 'More Than a Sporting "Touchdown"'). Twice during the 1990s the *Sport Sociology Journal* devoted issues to the subject of globalization (1991, 1994). In 1996, the *Journal of Sport and Social Issues* also published an issue on the subject.
3. Interview by author (March 18, 2005).

3a. Tim Brosnan, interviewed by author, 18 March 2005.

4. Klein, *Growing the Game*.
5. A caveat is in order here. There are some very revealing studies of FIFA that clearly point to the geopolitics that operate at every level (see Sugden and Tomlinson, *FIFA and the Contest for World Football*, and Darby, *Africa, Football and FIFA*). Third World members are disadvantaged in any number of ways. However, I intended to contrast FIFA's ideology with that of Major League Baseball in an effort to show the relatively early development of the latter.
6. A. Chozick, 'Global Pitch', *Wall Street Journal*, 18 October 2004, 1.
7. Jim Small, interviewed by author, 8 July 2004.
8. J. Gallagher, 'Playing World Baseball Classic in Spring or Fall Makes No Sense at All', *Japan Times*, 8 June 2005, 9.
9. Paul Archey, interviewed by author, 6 May 2006.
10. Ibid.
11. P. Gammons, 'World Baseball Classic Succeeds: Here's Why', *Boston Globe*, 21 March 2006, C1.
12. Nairn, *The Break-up of Britain*, 335.
13. Weber, *From Max Weber*.
14. Gluckman, *Custom and Conflict in Africa*.
15. Interview with Jim Small (Senior Vice President of MLBI) by author, 19 March 2003.
16. Hobsbawm and Ranger, *The Invention of Tradition*.
17. Klein, *Growing the Game*.
18. Friedman, *The Lexus and the Olive Tree*.
19. Tsing, 'The Global Situation'.
20. Castells, *The Rise of the Network Society*.

21. Harvey, *The Condition of Postmodernity*, and Giddens, *Runaway World*.
22. Hoogvelt (2001).
23. See the work by the sociologist Robertson, 'Globalization', 25–44; or anthropologists such as Inda and Rosaldo, *The Anthropology of Globalization*; or cultural studies scholars such as Tomlinson, *Globalization and Culture*.
24. See for example, Held *et al.*, *Global Transformations*; Tsing, 'The Global Situation'; and Friedman, *The Lexus and the Olive Tree*.
25. Friedman, *The Lexus and the Olive Tree*, 109–42.
26. Klein, *Growing the Game*, 18–29.
27. Sandy Alderson, interviewed by author, 9 December 2004.
28. Paul Archey, interviewed by author, 14 January 2006.

References

Bairner, A. *Sport, Nationalism and Globalization*. Albany, NY: SUNY Press, 2001.

Castells, M. *The Rise of the Network Society*. Oxford: Blackwell, 1996.

Darby, P. *Africa, Football and FIFA: Politics, Colonialism and Resistance*. London: Frank Cass, 2002.

Friedman, T. *The Lexus and the Olive Tree*. New York: Anchor, 1999.

Giddens, A. *Runaway World: How Globalization is Reshaping our Lives*. New York: Routledge, 2000.

Gluckman, M. *Custom and Conflict in Africa*. New York: Barnes and Noble, 1964.

Harvey, D. *The Condition of Postmodernity*. Oxford: Blackwell, 1989.

Held, D., A. McGrew, D. Goldblatt and J. Perraton. *Global Transformations: Politics, Economics, and Culture*. Palo Alto, CA: Stanford University Press, 1999.

Hobsbawm, E. and T. Ranger, eds. *The Invention of Tradition*. Cambridge: Cambridge University Press, 1983.

Inda, J. and R. Rosaldo, eds. *The Anthropology of Globalization*. London: Blackwell, 2002.

Klein, A. *Growing the Game: The Globalization of Major League Baseball*. New Haven, CT: Yale University Press, 2006.

Maguire, J. 'More Than a Sporting "Touchdown": The Making of American Football in Britain, 1982–1989'. *Sociology of Sport Journal* 7, no.4 (1990): 213–37.

——— *Global Sport: Identities, Societies, Civilizations*. Cambridge: Polity Press, 1999.

Miller, T., A. Lawrence, J. McKay and D. Rowe. *Globalization and Sport: Playing the World*. London: Sage, 2001.

Nairn, T. *The Break-up of Britain*. London: Verso, 1981.

Robertson, R. 'Globalization: Time-Space and Homogeneity-Heterogeneity'. In *Global Modernities*, ed. M. Featherstone, S. Lash and R. Robertson, 25–44. London: Sage, 1995.

Sugden, J. and A. Tomlinson. *FIFA and the Contest for World Football: Who Rules the People's Game?* Oxford: Blackwell, 1998.

Tomlinson, J. *Globalization and Culture*. Chicago, IL: University of Chicago Press, 1999.

Tsing, A. 'The Global Situation'. In *The Anthropology of Globalization: A Reader*, ed. J. Inda and R. Rosaldo, 452–82. London: Blackwell, 2002.

Weber, M. *From Max Weber: Essays in Sociology*. Ed. H. Gerth and C.W. Mills. London: Taylor & Francis, 1948.

Epilogue: Global Football

Dolores P. Martinez

The Prologue to this collection of essays ended rather tongue-in-cheek with the suggestion that being against global capitalism and pro-football were two impossible positions to maintain. If there were any doubts about such a statement before reading the essay in this issue, there can be none afterwards. From the rather prosaic roots of football in the era of British empire (Mangan), when managers did not have to be ex-players, to the 'desire' of the USA to succeed in a sport that never really has been theirs (Klein, Martinez), in football we have a clear example of a global form of mass entertainment.

The growth of football occurred initially because it was so easy to export: a ball and some players were all that was needed. And if a ball was lacking, rags tied into the right shape, as the great Pele once noted, would do, while goalposts could be any two objects marking something like the correct distance – nets were never a must and even a goalkeeper could be done without. Was there ever a simpler game to teach or learn (the offside rule notwithstanding)? To play football, you did not need to be rich, well-educated or even a man (although that came later), you just needed to be someone not afraid to 'think' with their feet. The world seems full of such talented people and while not every amateur player becomes a professional, the experience of playing the game appears to give rise to legions of fans who closely identify with professional players. Even in a class-based society like Britain, football has widespread and seemingly unlikely fandoms: university professors follow the fate of Chelsea or Man United with same passion as the local postman or cab driver. In France, as Eric Cantona taught an astonished British public, you can even philosophize about it,[1] although Monty Python already knew this, doing an 'existential' football interview in 1969.[2]

Jokes aside, the growth of football in the twentieth century has seen local teams evolve into international clubs that rely on the support of their dedicated fans (Majumdar); with players who move between the local and the national, leaving, for example, Real Madrid mid-season, to play in a match for England against Spain. As the nation-state has come to occupy centre stage in global politics, so too has football come to have an international political aspect. How many team players should be 'foreign' at the local level? Should teams be segregated (Darby) at any level? How much is an international but foreign 'star' worth (Mukharji)? And if an old empire like Britain is going to break up into nation-states, what does this mean for its football teams and supporters (Robinson)? The near universal nature of the game has led to the creation of a truly global regulatory body: FIFA. The rules of the game are made internationally by FIFA and it is FIFA that oversees common problems from violent fans, match fixing, to doping in the sport (Malcolm and Waddington). And FIFA's World Cup is now truly a global competition, much to the surprise of the USA (Klein).

None of this is possible without the existence of global financial structures. The growth in footballers' fees, the money paid for transfers, the cost of buying and owning a club may all be done out of non-profit making love for the game, but is all done on the back of television rights, advertising and related product endorsement businesses. There is money to be made from success in the 'beautiful game', in a way that was unimaginable in the nineteenth century, but which has become a version of the old 'streets paved with gold' myth for would-be players from poor nations in the twenty-first century. Clubs may lose money, but a player may well become rich. Short of becoming a Hollywood, Bollywood or Chinese film superstar, football is the one sure way an otherwise ordinary boy might reach global stardom. It may be the subject of hilarity for some, but David Beckham *is* worshiped as a *bodhisattva* in Thailand.[3]

Thus, we could argue, football mirrors the current global political situation, although it often seems to reverse taken-for-granted global hierarchies. Brazil, not a rich nation, nor highly industrialized, remains the footballing nation par excellence, while the global might of the USA is not matched by its success on the football pitch unless, of course, you count the ladies (Martinez). Symbolically, football success or failure can stand in for the battles that cannot be fought between nations: Japan's and Korea's hosting of the 2002 World Cup, for example, was full of political tensions not widely appreciated by many outsiders.[4] While China's desire to succeed at the game, as with Japan's promotion of the sport (Manzenreiter), has had interesting repercussions in unexpected areas, with gender roles reversed – the Chinese women's team is eleventh in the world,[5] while the men's is nowhere near as high, although it did make the 2006 World Cup – and gender relations having to be re-imagined. Victories such as Iraq's win of the Asia Cup in 2007, beating the heavily favoured Saudi Arabia, are seen to symbolize the triumph of team spirit over tragic political, religious and ethnic adversity.

Yet, if football has become a mirror of the global, it can also hide as much as it reveals. It can portray the nation as unified, while covering up internal fractures that might be played out between local clubs such as the rivalry between the largely Catholic supporters of Celtic FC and the Protestant supporters of Rangers FC in Glasgow, Scotland; or the ethnic tension felt between the largely Basque-identified Atletico Bilboa and Real Madrid. Occasionally, giving the lie to the idea that football matches are a replacement for violence, battles between supporters reveal racist and historically felt prejudices, even (or even more so) when played out between fans watching the game in a pub (Weed). And while legend has it that temporary peace broke out in No-Man's Land on Christmas Eve, 1916, football has also led to war as when Honduras and El Salvador fought for six days in 1969. It is precisely these sorts of contradictions, allegiances and symbolic convergences that make the study of football worthy of the academic gaze.

In light of all this, is there one aspect of football that the academic gaze should focus on more than others? This is a difficult question to answer, particularly with a sport that, as Robinson notes in this collection, can appear to mean so many different things to so many people. What does appear to tie together all the examples I have mentioned, as well as many of the essays in this collection, is the concept of identity. We should not, however think of identity as something concrete; rather as Stuart Hall has noted:

> Identity is not as transparent or unproblematic as we think. Perhaps, instead of thinking of identity as an already accomplished historical fact … we should think, instead, of identity as a 'production', which is never complete, always in process and, and always constituted within, not outside, representation.[6]

Through the example of football it becomes clear how the production of identity for its supporters is constant: now they love their local club, then they support their national team, but come the World Cup, if their nation loses early on, there is always another team to cheer on. As I've already noted, you can be 'elite' and still an ordinary football supporter, two identities that, in the UK at least,[7] are seen to be opposed; you can be a woman who understands the offside rule without having to play, or you can give your heart to woman's football, as I once did. Issues of identity arise for footballers as well. A player can bind himself with great affection to one club and then shock with the move to another. The politics of which nation to play for, also becomes interesting to consider: what if you have an American mother and an English father – whose national team do you sign up to?

You also can hate football or clearly prefer another sport: that is another kind of identity-making as well, one that my children make clear to me every week-end! What you cannot not do, it would seem, is to be unaware of the sport,[8] even if you prefer tennis or come from a nation that prefers cricket or rugby. Every four years, the world explodes and everyone has to adopt some stance on the game. The task of academics who love the sport is to understand all the facets that football now allows us to consider: the personal level, the group dynamics, the big business aspect, the cultural product, the ethnic, political and symbolic facets. As a form of mass entertainment, football has it all and we have yet to plumb its depths.

Notes

1. The French Existentialist Albert Camus famously played goalie for Algeria.
2. Episode 11 of their first season: 'Literary Football Discussion' (1969). See also the DVD *Monty Python Live at the Hollywood Bowl* (1982) for their 'International Philosophy Football Match' in which the Germans (with the surprise inclusion of Franz Beckenbauer) play the Greeks and are refereed by Confucius, with St Augustine and St Aquinas as linesmen. As Wikipedia notes: Nietzsche receives a yellow card after claiming that 'Confucius has no free will'; Confucius says 'Name go in book'. Socrates scored the only goal of the match in the 89th minute, a diving header from a cross from Archimedes (who gets the idea of using the football first after shouting out 'Eureka!'). The Germans dispute the call: 'Hegel is arguing that the reality is merely an a priori adjunct of non-naturalistic ethics, Kant via the categorical imperative is holding that ontologically it exists only in the imagination, and Marx [with apt materialism] claiming it was offside.' http://en.wikipedia.org/wiki/The_Philosophers'_Football_Match).
3. Cf. Daniel Taylor, 'At the very foot of Buddha stands His Poshness Beckham'. *The Guardian Unlimited*, 16 May 2000.
4. See Jonathan Watts, 'The Emperor's New Roots'. *The Guardian Unlimited*, 28 December 2001.
5. In the 2007 Women's World Cup, China only made it to the quarter finals, while Germany beat Brazil for first place. The USA beat Norway for third place.
6. Hall, 'Cultural Identity and Cinematic Representation', 210.
7. The UK must be one of the few European nations whose leaders (the Queen and Prime Minister) do not consistently show up at important international matches, but send family members or other government members instead.
8. One interesting example of how truly global the World Cup is was the surprise hit film from Bhutan, *Phörpa* (The Cup, Norbu 1999), about some Buddhist monks and their attempts to get a satellite dish in the monastery in order to watch the 1998 World Cup.

References

Hall, Stuart. 'Cultural Identity and Cinematic Representation'. In *Black British Cultural Studies, a Reader*, ed. Houston A. Baker, Jr., Diawara, Manthia and Lindeborg, Ruth, H., 210–22. Chicago, IL: University of Chicago Press, 1996 [1989].

Hughes, Terry and Ian MacNoughton (directors). 'International Philosophy Football Match'. In *Monty Python at the Hollywood Bowl*. Columbia Pictures Corporation, 1982.

MacNoughton, Ian (director). 'Literary Football Discussion'. In *Monty Python's Flying Circus,* Season 1, Episode 11. BBC: 1969.

Norbu, Kyentse. *Phörpa* (The Cup). Coffee Stain Productions (1999).

INDEX

Page numbers in **bold** and 'n.' or 'nn.' plus note number indicate tables and notes respectively.